L.A. EXILES

A Guide to Los Angeles Writing 1932–1998

Edited and Introduced by Paul Vangelisti
with Evan Calbi

Photographs by Jen Calbi

MARSILIO PUBLISHERS
New York · 1999

P.O. Box 1039, Cooper Station,
New York, NY 10003

Design and typesetting by Guy Bennett
Cover photograph, *Century Freeway (I-105) Los Angeles,* by John Humble

Special thanks to Toby Oshiro for his invaluable help in researching this project.

Contents

Being Elsewhere

for Marek Stabrowski

According to Samuel Butler, gazing at larger mammals like elephants or hippopotami may offer a cure for emotional disturbances. Though maybe not quite the organic experience, the Los Angeles Basin has proven to be over much of this century the source of a similar, unlikely comfort for the many writers who found themselves here – with their origins, psychic, cultural and otherwise – entirely elsewhere.

Trying to take in this vast metropolitan expanse (the term "city" needs to be surrendered), a great many writers have noted how remarkably non-urban, in any traditional or historical sense, the place actually is. "Only a retired Iowan farmer," J.B. Priestly wrote in "Midnight on the Desert," "would think of Los Angeles as a metropolis. It's a kind of boomtown that has gone mushrooming itself for scores of miles." From James Elroy's polemical "The Big Nowhere," to Mike Davis' problematic "City of Quartz," to the more ideological emphasis of Thomas McGrath's "Lost Angels" or Carey McWilliams' "Island on the Land," Los Angeles has remained, at least in written lore, one of those places poets and fiction writers have avoided or at least never expected to end up in.

What is it that is unexpected here? Once past the distaste or infatuation with the blatant facades, the dream factories, the "theatrical impermanence," in Christopher Isherwood's term, why do we find L.A. not only amenable to work, but an unexpectedly fertile climate for writing? What is it in the seemingly endless sprawl, from the San Gabriel and Santa Monica Mountains westward and southward, that makes for what Igor Stravinsky called "splendid isolation"?

Besides the notorious thermal inversion – what the indigenous inhabitants of the area had noticed centuries before the advent of the car and had named "the Valley of Smokes" – the natural environment of the Los Angeles Basin is most remarkable for its light. The result of extraordinarily stable air trapped between ocean, high mountains and desert (which also in part contributes to the smog), the light here is perhaps the single most distinguishing characteristic for those who have grown accustomed to practicing whatever sedentary or not so sedentary art. Recently, in his exhaustive and excellent, "L.A. Glows" (*The New Yorker*, 2/23/98), Lawrence Weschler explored this phenomenon, with the help of scientists, artists, historians, cinematographers, film directors, architects, novelists, composers and even poets. Weschler concludes that Angelenos, in their various raptures, are actually reacting to a type of light whose quality is principally isolate and meditative, rather than dramatic. "Broad daylight – and, in fact, lots and lots of light – and no shadows," notes artist Robert Irwin, "Really peculiar, almost dreamlike." Or, as Weschler cites architect Coy Howard: "There's something about the environment here – the air, the atmosphere, the light – that makes *everything* shimmer. There's a kind of glowing thickness to the world – the diaphanous soup I was talking about, which, in turn, grounds a magic-meditative sense of presence."

Within this singular environment is another massive force as grand and relentless, and perhaps more disturbing: those unknown men and women who have been slipping in and out of L.A for over a century. Although there is an unstable makeup to the populations of most modern cities, particularly on the West Coast, Angelenos have remained particularly remarkable in their transience. Whether from other parts of the U.S. earlier in the century, or from Latin America and the Pacific Rim more recently, the settlement and growth of Los Angeles has never enhanced cultural stability. In this respect, the first half of the 1900s is certainly no different than the latter half, regardless of the languages the settlers brought here.

Certainly in the 19th, and for a good part of this century, Los Angeles remained in the shadow of San Francisco. As early as 1868, as Mike Davis points out, "A syndicate of San Francisco investors led by Alfred Robinson and Sam Brannan (the famous Mormon vigilante of the 1850s) subdivided the great domain stretching from San Pedro to San Bernardino." The sale of the ranchos "set the pattern for all future California real-estate promotions."[1] In 1880, Los Angeles' population was 11,183; ten years later, after the railroad-promoted real estate boom of 1886–89, the city had grown to over 60,000 – still in marked contrast to San Francisco's 298,997. As late as 1900, Los Angeles numbered 100,000 inhabitants to San Francisco's 343,000. Even by 1930, when Los Angeles had grown tenfold to a population of one million, San Francisco, with its 635,000 inhabitants was still the political, financial and cultural center of the state.

The cultural chip on L.A.'s shoulder is no better exposed than when having to regard its northern neighbor. One has only to browse the daily pages of the *L.A. Times*, that bastion of boomerism and platitude, to notice the Angeleno's stereotypical irritation with San Francisco politics, manners, food and drink. Almost a hundred years later, those arbiters of the group mind, the local columnist, are still portraying San Franciscans as "snobs" (more recently, read "elitists"), "spoiled," "extremists," "eccentric," "effete" and, the most unkindest of all, "liberals."

Besides the obvious struggles for political and economic dominance (not to mention the state's most precious commodity, water), what is in the North-South polarity that irks Angelenos most about residents of The City? To a transplanted San Franciscan now having spent more than thirty years here, the impermanence or transience mentioned earlier seems to be a most significant factor. It is their instability or, if you will, fluidity that causes Angelenos to view lifestyles to the North as essentially unreal, precious and stifling. Unlike San Francisco or New York, where even recent arrivals try to act like San Franciscans or New Yorkers in their daily habits and general demeanor, such is not the case in L.A. People here, even after a good deal of time, still act like Texans or Iowans, Guadalajarans or Salvadorians, Cantonese, Tokyoites or Taiwanese.

With the advent of the railroad, and the city's rapid transformation from a dusty, rather squalid pueblo to a still dusty and, in many ways, more squalid though booming railhead, Los Angeles in the final decades of the 1800s was to establish a migration pattern that would remain through the first three decades of this century. As Carey McWilliams states in his seminal, *Southern California Country: an Island on the Land:*

> In 1890 native-born Californians constituted 25% of the residents of Los Angeles; in 1900, 27%; in 1910, 25%; in 1920, 20%; and in 1930, 20%. Visiting Los Angeles in 1930, Garet Garrett noted that "you have to begin with the singular fact that in a population of a million and a quarter, every other person you see has been there less than five years. More than nine in every ten you see have been there less than fifteen years. Practically, therefore, the whole population is immigrant, with the slowly changing sense of home peculiar to non-indigenous life. The mind is first adjusted, then the conscious feelings; but for a long time – for the rest of the immigrant's life perhaps – there will be in the cells a memory of home that was elsewhere."[2]

McWilliams defines the unique settlement of Southern California by emphasizing that somewhere in the vast, unfocused expanse that is the L.A. Basin, the new arrival seeks someone to share a feeling, a nostalgia for some other place. Inner or emotional life, as well as introspection, must reside elsewhere. "While retaining a 'memory of home,'" McWilliams concludes, "the newcomer in Southern California is not really an exile for he and his kind have always constituted a dominant majority of the population."[3]

As the state societies ("refugees," as they called themselves, from other states of the Union[4]), dominated the broader civic and cultural life in the first several decades of the century, the area's highbrow culture also very early on tried to establish a local identity with a displaced, if not downright mythical history. The Arroyo Set, and its founder Charles Fletcher Lummis, were the cultural mouthpieces for the *L.A. Times'* ruthless boss, Harrison Grey Otis, and his development schemes. Kevin Starr describes Lummis and the Arroyo circle in his *Inventing the Dream,* an important account of the Southern California Booster Era (1885–1925):

> Through the talents of such men, Otis promoted an image of Southern California that dominated the popular imagination at the turn of the century and is alive to this day: a melange of mission myth (originating in Helen Hunt Jackson's *Ramona*), obsession with climate, political conservatism (symbolized in the open shop), and a thinly veiled racialism, all put to the service of boosterism and oligarchy.

Raymond Chandler, in *The Little Sister*, has Phillip Marlowe somewhat more wistfully treat the cultural aspirations of the Arroyo group, with their relentless mix of Italian and Mediterranean, Mission and Southwest revival, physical culture and racial mysticism. Life was easy, privileged, already fading and intrinsically nostalgic (that is, nostalgic in conception), like a permanent summer resort:

> Los Angeles was just a big dry sunny place with ugly homes and no style, but goodhearted and peaceful. It had the climate they just yap about now.... Little groups who

> thought they were intellectual used to call it the Athens of America. It wasn't that, but it wasn't a neon-lighted slum.[5]

In the 1920s the *Times'* subsidy to Lummis' magazine *Out West (The Land of Sunshine)* was cut and the movie industry replaced the Mission Romantics as the cultural front for immigration. The houses of the upper-middle class began swelling from the more sensible and "genuine" Craftsman to Spanish Colonial, fed by the fast money of oil speculation and Hollywood.[6] But even in the glitzy urbanized and car-glutted culture which was to be glamorized in movies for the next forty years, the Arroyo persisted in its single most important cultural legacy – the creation of ersatz history. Today, as film schools fill the ranks of the dream factories, somehow the value of a liberal arts education, particularly the study of literature and history, seem to have as little or, perhaps, even less effect than the Louis B. Mayers or the Harry Cohens on the practice of making movies. The MGM lion roars as dreadfully as ever, with its *ars gratia artis* scrolled beneath. As in Phillip Marlowe's bittersweet, unsparing reminder:

> Real cities have something else, some individual bony structure under the muck. Los Angeles has Hollywood – and hates it. It ought to consider itself damn lucky. Without Hollywood it would be a mail-order city. Everything in the catalogue you could get better somewhere else.[7]

In San Francisco or New York, literary generations tend to judge one another on how they react for or against, interpret and develop a common code of cultural behavior. In Los Angeles this commonality is absent or perhaps present only in so far as each generation develops manners to cope with and ritualize this absence. Company town that it is, cultural history serves as apology for the film and entertainment industry and is invariably made into a yet another fetish and yet another myth. Every decade, perhaps now every four or five years, some cultural boss or entrepreneur heralds the rebirth of the New Hollywood, the New Downtown, the New Venice, the New Culver City, etc., without any significant mention of what came before. One could change the person's name in the article or press release from five or ten or twenty years previous, and the statement would almost word for word remain the same. Not unlike other suburbs and decentralized urban sprawls in contemporary America, the City of Angels thus retains its cultural, social and political amnesia.

Growing yearly more immemorious, Los Angeles now declares itself the Entertainment Capital of the World, and so the circle is complete: from the turn-of-the-twentieth-century New Rome of the Arroyo Set to the turn-of-the-twenty-first-century New Fascist Rome, with its own millennial version of a kindlier, gentler, ever more permissive and accessible Duce. Red-faced and bullfrog-throated as his Mediterranean predecessor, our Commander-in-Chief divides his political capital between Washington and Hollywood, demonstrating that, according to L.A.'s conventional wisdom, it doesn't matter what they write about you, as long as they get the name right. It is not difficult to see why the writer, when not involved in or at least trying to keep his or her distance from Hollywood, finds some form of cultural exile accommodating, if not, in fact, comforting and hospitable.

Where or what, then, is the *elsewhere* writers here find themselves at home in? Why does exile become, in Los Angeles, an habitual condition, even for those born only four or five hundred miles to the north? Given the instability of Los Angeles' cultural models, there is no major American city where the force of an exotic, often bewildering nature has continued to play such a complex role. In some ways, L.A. remains a frontier city where less than an hour from downtown one can be in a national forest where people still get lost and die of exposure. It is also a city where emergency provisions are kept in cars and houses against the threat of earthquake, though the odds are significantly less of being injured by a quake than of being struck by lightning. Because of our belief in, and anticipation of the temporary, L.A. may be the ultimate American city, in every meaning of the word.

The sense of "the last place," spatially as well as culturally, is at the heart of many writers' reactions to finding themselves here. It is as if, in this "Asia Minor of the intellect," as poet Thomas McGrath called it, one is hard up against a dislocation so profound that absolute invention, of the self and its relationship to language, is indispensable to artistic survival. There really never have been literary schools or movements to follow, at least not for long, and any writer who stays for any time and engages the spirit of the L.A. Basin, realizes that after a while the epithets "eclectic" and "maverick" come with the territory. And then, of course, there is Hollywood, where the writer is "the necessary evil," and such questions don't seem important.

The disposition to complete abandon and confrontation with oneself as a writer is nowhere more in evidence than in the conclusion to Tennessee Williams' "The Mattress by the Tomato Patch" – part fiction and part reverie about his time at The Palisades, a Santa Monica apartment building, later demolished and replaced by the crouching intelligence of the Rand Corporation. Williams was fascinated by the manager of The Palisades, "a fantastic woman, half gypsy," as he described her in his *Memoirs*, who becomes a muse for the young writer in the story:

> The perishability of the package she comes in has cast on Olga no shadow she can't laugh off. I look at her now, before the return of Tiger from Muscle Beach and if no thought, no knowledge has yet taken form in the protean jelly-world of brain and nerves, if I am patient enough to

> wait a few moments longer, this landlady by Picasso may spring up from her mattress and come running into this room with a milky-blue china bowl full of reasons and explanations for all that exists.[8]

Even in the notorious hard-boiled and *noir* writers, such as Chandler, James M. Cain, and Nathanael West, not to mention the rather atypical, almost naturalistic William Faulkner of "Golden Land," the landscape and light of the Basin, in contrast to the pretentious and often tawdry goings on, may function as chorus, antagonist and sometimes principal character in a story. The European exiles, predominantly English and German, could never stop making the place more exotic than it was. But even the least susceptible of these, Theodor W. Adorno and Bertolt Brecht, could not help but comment on the singularity of the landscape. Adorno considers the unsettling, ever-changing nature of the country:

> The shortcomings of the American landscape is not so much, as romantic illusion would have it, the absence of historical memories, as that it bears no traces of the human hand.... For what the human eye has seen merely from the car it cannot retain, and the vanishing landscape leaves no more traces behind than it bears upon itself.

Or as Brecht, like Adorno, exiled from what he passionately had come to know as history, mused upon the vegetation and the curious seasonal changes in "Californian Autumn":

> In my garden
> Are nothing but evergreens. If I want to see autumn
> I drive to my friend's country house in the hills. There
> I can stand for five minutes and see a tree
> Stripped of its foliage, and foliage stripped of its trunk.

So, with the writers in this collection, though each differing in emphasis and context, there is a kind of posture against any prior tradition or even personal expectation of art, as if what is most fugitive in writing comes to rest here. Much has been written about the debilitating, sometimes embittering isolation that may easily become the writer's life. On the other hand, too little, I think, has been reported about the adventure of living in the Southland, rather sparingly equipped, as a writer of fiction or poetry.

In Los Angeles, we write as necessarily absent and present: present in the fundamental passion for the craft perhaps felt no more intimately and immediately than in such "splendid isolation"; absent from the fake history, the boosterism, the ever-more insidious banality of what most familiarly, in this town, is called the Business. In the "Foreward" to the 1972 *Anthology of L.A. Poets*, edited by Charles Bukowski, Neeli Cherkovski and myself, Bukowski introduces his own version of Stravinsky's "splendid isolation":

> I think it is important to know that a man or woman, writer or not, can find more isolation in Los Angeles than in Boise, Idaho. Or, all things being fair, he can with a telephone (if he has a telephone) have 19 people over drinking and talking with him within an hour and a half. I have bummed the cities and I know this – the great facility of Los Angeles is that one can be alone if one wishes or he can be in a crowd if he wishes. No other city seems to allow this easy double choice as well. This is a fairly wonderful miracle, especially if one is a writer.[9]

Or, put more tersely and scathingly by S.J. Perlman: "I have always felt that the statement attributed to Irving Thalberg, the patron saint at Metro-Goldwyn-Mayer, beautifully summed up the situation: 'The writer is a necessary evil.' As a sometime employee of his, I consider this a misquotation. I suspect he said 'weevil.'"[10]

Thus, what makes for isolation and instability – the demand the surroundings put on the writer to be both here and elsewhere – is an essential fact of existence. And, in contrast to the transitory quality of social relationships, it is once again nature – and the peculiar amalgam of landscape, air and light – that most properly define the conditions of daily life. To return to Weschler's *New Yorker* piece, he quotes director Peter Bogdanovich on the displeasures of living here, where, even after thirty years, one doesn't get used to the eerie duality and deceptiveness of the light: "I hate the way the light of the place throws you into such a trance that you fail to realize how time is passing. It's like what Orson Welles once told me. 'The terrible thing about L.A.,' he said, 'is that you sit down, you're twenty-five, and when you get up you're sixty-two.'"

What Bogdanovich is perturbed by is what for many writers makes L.A. exile so alluring and, if you wish, "natural," intrinsic to the environment. It is precisely the extreme presence and absence, the simultaneous up close and far away of things the light yields, drawing the writer to lose oneself inward in a most tangible way, not in the least nostalgic or metaphysical. Talking recently with Polish composer Jan A. P. Kaczmarek about his growing sense of wanting to live a good part of the year in Europe, Kaczmarek interrupted himself by stressing that he wanted not to be misunderstood. This place would be always important for him: "Los Angeles brought light to my work." Robert Craft writes about Stravinsky's reaction to music, after a month-long, almost fatal illness, framing the anecdote with the clear presence of mountains some sixty miles away:

> It is a marvelous day, brilliantly sunny and warm although the San Bernardino Mountains glitter like Kilimanjaro with new snow. But my leave-taking is the hardest I have

ever had to go through. It will only be a few days, I tell I.S., and I blame his music as the reason for the trip in the first place. To which he says, '*Je crache sur ma musique.*'"[11]

Behind both composers' remarks, there appears to be a self-critical disposition induced by a sense of location. It is as if music, like writing, must admit its deficiencies before essential, daily phenomena, and draw a certain strength from the acceptance of these vital limitations. Exile, then, does not seem to be so much a condition as a basic form or, perhaps, situation to be explored. Whether in fictive definition or poetic contradiction, the urge to be elsewhere – both here and there – is where life and work, however tenuously, come together. This unfinished world, this adventure in which a writer habitually risks his or her sense of place and self, is where many have finally come to dwell. At the moment, there is no place else to go.

– PAUL VANGELISTI
Los Angeles, 1999

NOTES

1 *City of Quartz* (London: Verso, 1990), 108.
2 *Southern California Country* (Santa Barbara: Pergrine Smith, 1973), 165.
3 Ibid, 166.
4 "By the late twenties," McWilliams notes, the state society federation "boasted a membership of 500,000, representing every state in the union and every province in Canada," in a city of less than a million. In the middle of the same decade, at the Iowa Society picnic, "150,000 Iowans answered the roll call." [Ibid, 169–170]
5 *The Little Sister* (New York: Random House, 1988), 183.
6 *City of Quartz*, 30.
7 *The Little Sister*, 184.
8 *Collected Stories*, 161.
9 *Anthology of L.A. Poets* (Los Angeles/San Francisco: Laugh Literary/Red Hill Press, 1972), 6.
10 *Writers at Work: the Paris Review Interviews* (New York: Viking, 1965), 253.
11 *Stravinsky* (New York: Knopf, 1972), 338.

L.A. EXILE

316 S. Kentor (Brentwood)

Theodor W. Adorno (1903–1969)

Theodor W. Adorno entered the United States in 1938. By all accounts, Adorno rejected modern America – its political order, its economic system and particularly its culture. He never felt at home in America and remained throughout his stay an exile. Since he spent most of his time in Los Angeles, a fragmented view of his temporary home seemed inevitable. He was not, however, too haughty to take aim at even the most blase of American adornments, such as the rules of the cocktail party: "the taboo on talking shop and the inability to talk to each other are in reality the same thing. Because everything is business, the latter is unmentionable like rope in a hanged man's home. Behind the pseudo-democratic dismantling of ceremony, of old-fashioned courtesy, of the useless conversation suspected, not even unjustly, of being idle gossip, behind the seeming clarification and transparency of human relations that no longer admit anything undefined, naked brutality is ushered in."

Adorno was as capable of perceiving the beauty of the land: "Beauty of the American landscape: that even the smallest of its segments is inscribed, as its expression, with the immensity of the whole country."

As certain as his sense of alienation while in America, Adorno's time in exile proved to be productive. In Los Angeles he collaborated with Max Horkheimer on *Dialectic Of Enlightenment*. He used the breaks from this collaboration, as he described in his introduction, to compose *Minima Moralia*. Adorno returned to Germany in 1948 with Horkheimer and reopened their Frankfurt Institute for Social Research.

from *Dialectic of Enlightenment* (1944)

(written with Max Horkheimer)

TWO WORLDS

Here in America there is no difference between a man and his economic fate. A man is made by his assets, income, position, and prospects. The economic mask coincides completely with a man's inner character. Everyone is worth what he earns and earns what he is worth. He learns what he is through the vicissitudes of his economic existence. He knows nothing else. The materialistic critique of society once objected against idealism that existence determined consciousness and not vice versa, and that the truth about society did not lie in its idealistic conception of itself but in its economy; contemporary men have rejected such idealism. They judge themselves by their own market value and learn what they are from what happens to them in the capitalistic economy. Their fate, however sad it may be, is not something outside them; they recognize its validity. A dying man in China might say, in a lowered voice:

> Fortune did not smile on me in this world.
> Where am I going now? Up into the mountains
> to seek peace for my lonely heart.

I am a failure, the American says – and that is that.

from *Minima Moralia* (1951)

Back to culture. – The claim that Hitler has destroyed German culture is no more than an advertising stunt of those who want to rebuild it from their telephone desks. Such art and thought as were exterminated by Hitler had long been leading a severed and apocryphal existence, whose last hideouts Fascism swept out. Anyone who did not play the game was forced into inner emigration years before the Third Reich broke out: at the latest with the stabilization of the German currency, coinciding with the end of Expressionism, German culture stabilized itself in the spirit of the Berlin illustrated magazines, which yielded little to that of the Nazis' "Strength through Joy," Reich autobahns, and jaunty exhibition-hall Classicism. The whole span of German culture was languishing, precisely where it was most liberal, for its Hitler, and it is an injustice to the editors of Mosse and Ullstein or to the reorganizers of the *Frankfurter Zeitung*, to reproach them with time-serving under Nazism. They were always like that, and their line of least resistance to the intellectual wares they produced was continued undeflected in the line of least resistance to a political regime among whose ideological methods, as the Führer himself declared, comprehensibility to the most stupid ranked highest. This has led to fatal confusion. Hitler eradicated culture, Hitler drove Mr x into exile, therefore

Mr x is culture. He is indeed. A glance at the literary output of those emigres who, by discipline and a sharp separation of spheres of influence, performed the feat of representing the German mind, shows what is to be expected of a happy reconstruction: the introduction of Broadway methods on the Kurfürstendamm, which differed from the former in the Twenties only through its lesser means, not its better intentions. Those who oppose cultural Fascism should start with Weimar, the "Bombs on Monte Carlo" and the Press Ball, if they do not wish to finish by discovering that equivocal figures like Fallada spoke more truth under Hitler than the unambiguous celebrities who successfully transplanted their prestige.

Ego is Id. – A connection is commonly drawn between the development of psychology and the rise of the bourgeois individual, both in Antiquity and since the Renaissance. This ought not to obscure the contrary tendency also common to psychology and the bourgeois class, and which today has developed to the point of excluding all others: the suppression and dissolution of the very individual in whose service knowledge was related back to its subject. If all psychology since that of Protagoras has elevated man by conceiving him as the measure of all things, it has thereby also treated him from the first as an object, as material for analysis, and transferred to him, once he was included among them, the nullity of things. The denial of objective truth by recourse to the subject implies the negation of the latter: no measure remains for the measure of all things; lapsing into contingency, he becomes untruth. But this points back to the real life-process of society. The principle of human domination, in becoming absolute, has turned its point against man as the absolute object, and psychology has collaborated in sharpening that point. The self, its guiding idea and its *a priori* object, has always, under its scrutiny, been rendered at the same time non-existent. In appealing to the fact that in an exchange society the subject was not one, but in fact a social object, psychology provided society with weapons for ensuring that this was and remained the case. The dissection of man into his faculties is a projection of the division of labor onto its pretended subjects, inseparable from the interest in deploying and manipulating them to greater advantage. Psycho-technics is not merely a form of psychology's decay, but is inherent in its principle. Hume, whose work bears witness in every sentence to his real humanism, yet who dismisses the self as a prejudice, expresses in this contradiction the nature of psychology as such. In this he even has truth on his side, for that which posits itself as "I" is indeed mere prejudice, an ideological hypostasization of the abstract centers of domination, criticism of which demands the removal of the ideology of "personality." But its removal also makes the residue all the easier to dominate. This is flagrantly apparent in psycho-analysis. It incorporates personality as a lie needed for living, as the supreme rationalization holding together the innumerable rationalizations by which the individual achieves his instinctual renunciation, and accommodates himself to the reality principle. But precisely in demonstrating this, it confirms man's non-being. Alienating him from himself, denouncing his autonomy with this unity, psycho-analysis subjugates him totally to the mechanism of rationalization, of adaptation. The ego's unflinching self-criticism gives way to the demand that the ego of the other capitulate. The psychoanalyst's wisdom finally becomes what the Fascist unconscious of the horror magazines takes it for: a technique by which one particular racket among others binds suffering and helpless people irrevocably to itself, in order to command and exploit them. Suggestion and hypnosis, rejected by psycho-analysis as apocryphal, the charlatan magician masquerading before a fairground booth, reappear within its grandiose system as the silent film does in the Hollywood epic. What was formerly help through greater knowledge has become the humiliation of others by dogmatic privilege. All that remains of the criticism of bourgeois consciousness is the shrug with which doctors have always signaled their secret complicity with death. – In psychology, in the bottomless fraud of mere inwardness, which is not by accident concerned with the properties of men, is reflected what bourgeois society has practiced for all time with outward property. The latter, as a result of social exchange, has been increased, but with a proviso dimly present to every bourgeois. The individual has been, as it were, merely invested with property by the class, and those in control are ready to take it back as soon as universalization of property seems likely to endanger its principle, which is precisely that of withholding. Psychology repeats in the case of properties what was done to property. It expropriates the individual by allocating him its happiness.

Palace of Janus. – If one gave way to a need to place the system of the culture industry in a wide, world-historical perspective, it would have to be defined as the systematic exploitation of the ancient fissure between men and their culture. The dual nature of progress, which always developed the potential of freedom simultaneously with the reality of oppression, gave rise to a situation where peoples were more and more inducted into the control of nature and social organization, but grew at the same time, owing to the compulsion under which culture placed them, incapable of understanding in what way culture went beyond such integration. What has become alien to men is the human component of culture, its closest part, which upholds them against the world. They make common cause with the world against themselves, and the most alienated condition of all, the omnipresence of commodities, their own conversion into appendages of machinery, is for them a mirage of closeness. The great works of art and philosophical constructions have remained uncomprehended not through their too great distance from the heart of human experience, but the opposite; and this incomprehension could itself be accounted for easily enough by too great comprehension: shame at involvement in universal injustice that would become overwhelming as soon as one allowed oneself to understand. Instead, people cling to what mocks them in confirming the mutilation of their essence by the smoothness of its own appearance. On such inevitable delusions lackeys of the existing order have in all phases of urban civilization parasitically dwelt: later Attic comedy, Hellenistic arts and crafts, are already kitsch, even though they have not yet at their disposal the technique of mechanical reproduction and that industrial apparatus whose archetype the ruins of Pompeii readily conjure up. Reading popular novels a hundred years old like those of Cooper, one finds in rudimentary form the whole pattern of Hollywood. The stagnation of the culture industry is probably not the result of monopolization, but was a property of so-called entertainment from the first. Kitsch is composed of that structure of invariables which the philosophical lie ascribes to its solemn designs. On principle, nothing in them must change, since the whole mischief is intended to hammer into men that nothing must change. But as long as civilization followed its course randomly and anonymously, the objective spirit was not aware of this barbaric element as a necessary part of itself. Under the illusion of directly helping freedom, when it was mediating domination, it at least disdained to assist in directly reproducing the latter. It proscribed kitsch, that followed it like a shadow, with a fervor certainly itself expressive of the bad conscience of high culture, half aware that under domination it ceases to be culture, and reminded by kitsch of its own degradation. Today, when the consciousness of rulers is beginning to coincide with the overall tendency of society, the tension between culture and kitsch is breaking down. Culture no longer impotently drags its despised opponent behind it, but is taking it under its direction. In administering the whole of mankind, it administers also the breach between man and culture. Even the coarseness, insensitivity and narrowness objectively imposed on the oppressed, are manipulated with subjective mastery in humor. Nothing more exactly characterizes the condition of being at once integral and antagonistic than this incorporation of barbarity. Here, however, the will of the controllers can invoke that of the world. Their mass society did not first produce the trash for the customers, but the customers themselves. It is they who hungered for films, radio and magazines; whatever remained unsatisfied in them through the order which takes from them without giving in exchange what it promises, only burned with impatience for their jailer to remember them, and at last offer them stones in his left hand for the hunger from which he withholds bread in his right. Unresistingly, for a quarter of a century, elderly citizens, who should have known of something different, have been falling into the arms of the culture industry which so accurately calculates their famished hearts. They have no cause to take umbrage at a youth corrupted to the marrow by Fascism. This subjectless, culturally disinherited generation are the true heirs of culture.

Wolf as grandmother. – The strongest argument in the arsenal of apologists for the cinema is the crudest, its mass-consumption. They declare it, this drastic medium of the culture industry, popular art. Their independence of the norms of the autonomous work is supposed to relieve films of aesthetic responsibility, such standards proving in their case reactionary, just as all intentions to ennoble films artistically do indeed look awry, falsely elevated, out of keeping with the form – imports for the connoisseur. The more pretensions a film has to art, the more bogus it becomes. The protagonists of the cinema can point to this and, moreover, as critics of an inwardness now become kitsch, can picture themselves, with their coarse outward kitsch, as the *avant-garde.* If one is once drawn onto this ground, such arguments, fortified with technical experience and professional fluency, become almost irresistible. The film is not a mass art, but merely manipulated to deceive the masses? But through the market the wishes of the public are ceaselessly asserted; collective production by itself guarantees the film's collective nature; only someone out of touch with reality could suspect its producers of being sly string-pullers; most lack talent, to be sure, but where the necessary gifts do come together, then, despite all the limitations of the system, success is possible. The mass taste with which the film complies is not that of the masses themselves but foisted on them? But to talk of a different mass taste than that which the masses actually display is absurd, and everything that has ever been called folk art has always reflected domination. Only in the competent adaptation of production to given needs, not in orientation to an utopian audience, can the unformulated general will, by this logic, be given form. The film is full of lying stereotypes? But the stereotype is of the essence of folk art; fairy-tales are as familiar with the rescuing prince and the devil as the film with the hero and the villain, and even the barbaric cruelty that divides the world into good and evil the film has in common with the greatest fairy-tales, which have the stepmother dance to death in red-hot iron shoes.

All this could be answered only by reflecting on the basic concepts presupposed by the apologists. Bad films cannot be put down to incompetence; the most gifted are broken by the business set-up, and that the untalented flock to it is due to the affinity between lying, and the swindler. The mindlessness is objective; improved personnel could not found a folk art. Its concept arose out of agrarian relationships or an economy of simple commodity production. Such relations and the characters expressing them are those of masters and servants, gainers and losers, but in an immediate, not wholly objectified form. Of course they are no less seamed with class distinctions that late industrial society, but their members are not yet encompassed by the total structure, which first reduces the individual subjects to mere moments, in order then to unite them, impotent and discrete, in the collective. That there is no longer a folk does not mean, however, as the Romantics propagated, that the masses are worse. Rather, it is precisely in the new, radically alienated form of society that the untruth of the old is first being revealed. The very traits which the culture industry claims as the heritage of folk art, become, through the industry itself, suspect. The film has a retroactive effect: its optimistic horror brings to light in the fairy-tale what always served injustice, and shows dimly in the reprimanded miscreants the faces of those whom integral society condemns, and to condemn whom has from the first been the dream of socialization. For this reason the demise of individualist art is no justification for one that deports itself as if its subject and its archaic reactions were natural, whereas its real subject is the syndicate, unconscious certainly, of a few big firms. Even if the masses have, as customers, an influence on the cinema, it remains as abstract as the box-office returns which have replaced discriminating applause: the mere choice between Yes and No to what is offered, an integral part of the disproportion between concentrated power and dispersed impotence. The fact, finally, that in the making of a film numerous experts, and also simple technicians, have a say, no more guarantees its humanity than decisions by qualified scientific advisory boards ensure that of bombs and poison gas.

The rarified talk about the film as an art doubtless befits hacks wishing to recommend themselves; but the conscious appeal to naivety, to the servants' obtuseness that has long since permeated the thoughts of the masters, is equally worthless. The film, which today attaches itself inescapably to men as if it were a part of them, is at the same time remotest of all from their human destiny, which might be realized from one day to the next; and apologetics for it are sustained by resistence to thinking this antinomy. That the people who make films are in no way schemers is no counter-argument. The objective spirit of manipulation asserts itself in experiential rules, appraisals of the situation, technical criteria, economically inevitable calculations, the whole specific weight of the industrial apparatus, without any special censorship being needed, and even if the masses were asked they would reflect back the ubiquity of the system. The producers no more function as subjects than do their workers and consumers, but merely as components in a self-regulating machinery. The Hegelian-sounding precept, however, that mass-art should reflect the real taste of the masses and not that of carping intellectuals, is usurpation. The film's opposition, as an all-encompassing ideology, to the objective interests of mankind, its interlacement with the status quo of profit-motivation, bad conscience and deceit can be conclusively demonstrated. No appeal to an actually existent state of consciousness could ever have the right to veto insight which transcended this state of consciousness by discerning its contradiction to itself and to objective conditions. It is possible that the German Fascist professor was right and that real folk-songs already lived on cultural values that had sunk down from the upper stratum. Not for nothing is all folk art fissured and, like the film, not "organic." But between the old injustice, in whose voice a lament is audible even where it glorifies itself, and alienation proclaiming itself togetherness, insidiously creating an appearance of human closeness with loudspeakers and advertising psychology, is a difference equal to that between the mother telling her child, to allay its terror of demons, the fairy-tale in which the good are rewarded and the bad punished, and the cinema product which forces the justice of each and every world order, in every country, stridently and threateningly into the audience's eyes and ears, in order to teach them anew, and more thoroughly, the old fear. The fairy-tale dreams, appealing so eagerly to the child in the man, are nothing other than regression organized by total enlightenment, and where they pat the onlooker most confidentially on the shoulder, they most thoroughly betray him. Immediacy, the popular community concocted by films, amounts to mediation without residue, reducing men and everything human so perfectly to things, that their contrast to things, indeed the spell of reification itself, becomes imperceptible. The film has succeeded in transforming subjects so indistinguishably into social functions, that those wholly encompassed, no longer aware of any conflict, enjoy their own dehumanization as something human, as the joy of warmth. The total interconnectedness of the culture industry, omitting nothing, is one with total social delusion. Which is why it makes such light work of counter-arguments.

1001 Third St., Santa Monica

Terry Allen (1943–)

Born in Wichita, Kansas, Allen was raised in Lubbock, Texas. He came to Los Angeles to study at Chouinard Art Institute, where he received his BFA in 1966. Since then he has worked in a wide variety of media, including musical and theatrical performances, sculpture, painting, video and installation incorporating any and all of these. His work has been shown at Metropolitan Museum, the National Museum of Modern Art at the Smithsonian, LACMA, the Museum of Modern Art in Paris, as well as Documenta 8 in Kassel, the Sao Paulo, Sydney and Whitney Biennials. His numerous awards include National Endowment and Guggenheim Fellowships, and in 1997 he was inducted into Lubbock's Buddy Holly Walk of Fame. "Truckload of Art" is from *Lubbock (on everything)*, first appearing on disk in 1977, reissued on CD in 1992 from Special Delivery/Topic Records in London.

TRUCKLOAD OF ART (1977)

Recitation: Once upon a time, sometime ago back on the East Coast, in New York City to be exact, a bunch of artists and painters and sculptors and musicians and poets and writers and dancers and architects started feeling real superior to their ego-counterparts out on the West Coast. So they all got together and decided they would show those snotty surfer upstarts a thing or two about the Big Apple, and they hired themselves a truck. It was a big, spanking new white-shiny chrome-plated cab-over Peterbilt, with mudflaps, stereo, tv, am & fm radio, leather seats and a naugahide sleeper. All fresh with new American flag decals and ART ARK printed on the side of the door with solid 24 karat gold leaf type. And they filled up this truck with the most significant piles and influential heaps of Art Work to ever be assembled in Modern Times. And sent it West, to chide, cajole, humble and humiliate the Golden Bear. And this is the true story of that truck.

A Truckload of Art
From New York City
Came rollin down the road
Yeah the driver was singing
and the sunset was pretty
But the truck rolled over
And she rolled off the road

Yeah a Truckload of Art
is burning near the highway
Precious objects are scattered
All over the ground
And it's a terrible sight
If a person were to see it
But there weren't nobody around
(*Yodel*)

Yeah the driver went sailing
High in the sky
Landing in the gold lap of the Lord
Who smiled and then said,
"Son, you're better off dead
Than haulin a truckload
full of hot avant-garde"

Yeah a Truckload of Art
is burning near the highway
Precious objects are scattered
All over the ground
And it's a terrible sight
If a person were to see it
But there weren't nobody around
(*Yodel*)

Yes... an important artwork
Was thrown burning to the ground
Tragically landing in the weeds
And the smoke could be seen
Ahhh for miles all around
Yeah but nobody knows what it means

Yes... a Truckload of Art
Is burning near the highway
And it's a tough job for the highway patrol
Ahhh they'll soon see the smoke
An come a'runnin to poke
The dig a deep ditch
And throw the arts in a hole
(*Yodel*)

L.A. EXILE

Yeah a Truckload of Art
Is burning near the highway
And it's raging far-out of control
And what the critics have cheered
Is now shattered and queered
And their noble reviews
Have been stewed on the road

Yeah a Truckload of Art
is burning near the highway
Precious objects are scattered
All over the ground
And it's a terrible sight
If a person were to see it
But there weren't nobody around

1063 26th St., Santa Monica

Bertolt Brecht (1898–1956)

Brecht lived in Los Angeles from 1941–1947, a time he called his "exile in paradise." He had fled his native Germany and Hitler's advancing troops, and then bounced around Europe for several years in Danish, Swedish and Finnish exile before coming to America.

On July 21, 1941, Brecht and his family arrived in San Pedro aboard a small Swedish ship, the SS Annie Johnson. Almost from the day he landed, Brecht made it no secret that he did not intend to stay in the United States. He always felt himself an exile. He wrote of Los Angeles,"Scratch a bit, and the desert comes through."

Two weeks after arriving, he noted in his journal: "I get the impression of having been removed from my age. This is Tahiti in metropolitan form." In a letter to H.R. Hays, he later said,

"I'm here as if in Tahiti, among palm trees and artists. It makes me nervous." He classified Hollywood films as part of "the world narcotics trade."

A family that lived a few houses away from the Brecht's in Santa Monica in 1941 were convinced that their German neighbors were enemy agents. Brecht's FBI file cited his poem "On the Designation *Emigrants*." The file reads: "It is believed that the substitution of the word 'exile' for 'emigration' is an indication that persons connected with Brecht do not consider themselves immigrants here, but look upon themselves rather as exiles who wait to return to Europe."

In Los Angeles he wrote *Visions of Simone Machard, Schweyk, The Caucasian Chalk Circle* among others. With British actor Charles Laughton (who was Christopher Isherwood's neighbor), he finished the first English version of his play *Galileo* which premiered at the Coronet Theater in July 1947.

Brecht completed his "theatre of exile" in the United States with a final appearance before the House Un-American Acitivites Committee (HUAC) in 1947, as the only foreigner of the "unfriendly nineteen" that opposed the proceedings. After numerous hostile encounters with the "unfriendly ninteen" which deteriorated into a shouting match until the witnesses drew contempt citations, Brecht's appearance (the 11th of the proposed 19) before the committee was a brilliant exercise in duplicity and ambiguity that lead the investigators in circles. A sampling of Brecht's merry dance with HUAC's chief investigator Robert E. Stripling:

Stripling: "Are you familiar with the magazine *New Masses?*"
Brecht: "No."
Stripling: "You never heard of it?"
Brecht: "Yes, of course."
Stripling: "Did you ever contribute anything to it?"
Brecht: "No."(Which, of course, he hadn't technically, hav-

ing assisted Eva Goldbeck in writing an article for the journal about his ideas of theater which appeared in December 1935.)

The trip to Washington was only a small detour on his way to New York from Los Angeles. The day after his hearing, he was on a flight back to Europe. As he told Don Ogden Stewart after arriving in France, "When they accused me of wanting to steal the Empire State Building, I thought it was high time to leave."

LANDSCAPE OF EXILE

But even I, on the last boat
Saw the gaiety of the dawn in the rigging
And the grayish bodies of dolphins emerge
From the Japanese Sea.

The little horsecarts with gilt decorations
And the pink sleeves of the matrons
In the alleys of doomed Manila
The fugitive beheld with joy.

The oil derricks and the thirsty gardens of Los Angeles
And the ravines of California at evening and the fruit market
Did not leave the messenger of misfortune unmoved.

ON THINKING ABOUT HELL

On thinking about Hell, I gather
My brother Shelley found it was a place
Much like the city of London. I
Who live in Los Angeles and not in London

L.A. EXILE

Find, on thinking about Hell, that it must be
Still more like Los Angeles.

In Hell too
There are, I've no doubt, these luxuriant gardens
With flowers as big as trees, which of course wither
Unhesitantly if not nourished with very expensive water. And
fruit markets
With great heaps of fruit, albeit having
Neither smell nor taste. And endless processions of cars
Lighter than their own shadows, faster than
Mad thoughts, gleaming vehicles in which
Jolly-looking people come from nowhere and are nowhere bound.
And houses, built for happy people, therefore standing empty
Even when lived in.

The houses in Hell, too, are not all ugly.
But the fear of being thrown on the street
Wears down the inhabitants of the villas no less than
The inhabitants of the shanty towns.

HOLLYWOOD ELEGIES

I

The village of Hollywood was planned according to the notion
People in these parts have of heaven. In these parts
They have come to the conclusion that God
Requiring a heaven and a hell, didn't need to
Plan two establishments but
Just the one: heaven. It
Serves the unprosperous, unsuccessful
As hell.

II

By the sea stand the oil derricks. Up the canyons
The gold prospectors' bones lie bleaching. Their sons
Built the dream factories of Hollywood.
The four cities
Are filled with the oily smell
Of films.

III

The city is named after the angels
And you meet angels on every hand.
They smell of oil and wear golden pessaries
And, with blue rings round their eyes
Feed the writers in their swimming pools every morning.

IV

Beneath the green pepper trees
The musicians play the whore, two by two
With the writers. Bach
Has written a Strumpet Voluntary. Dante wriggles
His shrivelled bottom.

V

The angels of Los Angeles
Are tired out with smiling. Desperately
Behind the fruit stalls of an evening
They buy little bottles
Containing sex odors.

VI

Above the four cities the fighter planes
Of the Defense Department circle at a great height
So that the stink of greed and poverty
Shall not reach them.

CALIFORNIAN AUTUMN

I

In my garden
Are nothing but evergreens. If I want to see autumn
I drive to my friend's country house in the hills. There
I can stand for five minutes and see a tree
Stripped of its foliage, and foliage stripped of its trunk.

II

I saw a big autumn leaf which the wind
Was driving along the road, and I thought: tricky
To reckon that leaf's future course.

THE DEMOCRATIC JUDGE

In Los Angeles, before the judge who examines people
Trying to become citizens of the United States
Came an Italian restaurant keeper. After grave preparations
Hindered, though, by his ignorance of the new language
In the test he replied to the question:
What is the 8th Amendment? falteringly:
1492. Since the law demands that applicants know the language
He was refused. Returning
After three months spent on further studies
Yet hindered still by ignorance of the new language
He was confronted this time with the question: Who was
The victorious general in the Civil War? His answer was:
1492. (Given amiably, in a loud voice). Sent away again
And returning a third time, he answered
A third question: For how long a term are our Presidents elected ?
Once more with: 1492. Now
The judge, who liked the man, realized that he could not

Learn the new language, asked him
How he earned his living and was told: by hard work. And so
At his fourth appearance the judge gave him the question:
When
Was America discovered? And on the strength of his correctly
answering
1492, he was granted his citizenship.

LETTERS ABOUT THINGS READ

(Horace, *Epistles II, i*)

1

Take care, you
Who hymn Hitler! I
Who have seen the May and October processions
On the Red Square and the inscriptions
On their banners, and on the Pacific coast
On the Roosevelt Highway the thundering
Gasoline convoys and carriers laden
With five automobiles, one on top of the other, know

That soon he will die and dying
Will have outlived his fame, but even
If he were to succeed in making this earth
Uninhabitable, by
Conquering it, no song
In his honor could last. Too soon, admittedly
The scream of agony, a whole continent's even
Dies away to be able to stifle
The torturer's eulogy. True
Even those who hymn misdeeds may possess
Mellifluous voices. And yet

L.A. EXILE

The dying swan's voice is counted the loveliest: he
Sings without fear.

In the little garden at Santa Monica
I read in the pepper tree's shade
I read in Horace of a certain Varius
Who hymned Augustus (that is, what good luck, his generals
And the Romans' corruption did for him). Only small fragments
Preserved in another man's work attest
Great poetic skill. It was not worth
The labor to copy more.

II

With pleasure I read
How Horace traced the Saturnian art of verse
Back to those peasant burlesques
Which did not spare great families, till
The police forbade lampoons, compelling
Those with a grudge to develop
An art more noble and air it
In lines more subtle. At least that is how
I construe that passage.

LETTER TO THE ACTOR CHARLES LAUGHTON CONCERNING THE WORK ON THE PLAY 'THE LIFE OF GALILEO'

Still your people and mine were tearing each other to pieces when we
Pored over those tattered exercise books, looking
Up words in dictionaries, and time after time
Crossed out our texts and then
Under the crossings-out excavated
The original turns of phrase. Bit by bit –
While the housefronts crashed down in our capitals –

Bertholt Brecht

The facades of language gave way. Between us
We began following what characters and actions dictated:
New text.

Again and again I turned actor, demonstrating
A character's gestures and tone of voice, and you
Turned writer. Yet neither I nor you
Stepped outside his profession.

(*trans. Ralph Manheim*)

2966 Belden Dr. (Beachwood Canyon)

James M. Cain (1892–1977)

The Cains moved to Hollywood in 1931, when James left his position as managing editor at the *New Yorker* for a $400 a week (twice what he was making at the magazine), six-month contract as a screenwriter for Paramount. His wife, Elina, was excited to move to Southern California, having lived most of her life in Finland. Leo, her son and an ardent sports fan, looked forward to living in the city hosting the 1932 Olympics. Daughter Henrietta was convinced she would become a movie star. Soon after arriving, Cain wrote to a friend, "I didn't see one dead dog, banana peel, coat hanger, old shoe, basket of rotten fruit, or any of the things that would have been commonplace in New York. I began noticing the wide, beautifully paved streets, the parking lots, many more than eastern cities would have, and the movie theaters."

Cain explained his decision to work, and his failure to be successful, as a screenwriter: "I wanted the picture money. I worked like a dog to get it, I parked my pride, my aesthetic convictions, my mind outside on the street, and did everything to be a success at this highly paid trade. I studied the "Technique" of moving pictures, I did everything to become adept at them. The one thing I could not park was my nose. My dislike of pictures went down to my guts, and that's why I couldn't write them."

Double Indemnity was serialized in *Liberty* in 1935. Cain, in a letter to his agent, realized that writing *Double Indemnity* was rewriting his novel, *The Postman Always Rings Twice*, in serialized form: "I have no interest in murder stories per se, but as long as they don't come out in book form, it doesn't count." Cain once wrote Alfred Knopf that *Double Indemnity* was "a piece of tripe and will never go between covers while I live."

Raymond Chandler despised Cain's novels. He once described Cain as "a Proust in greasy overalls, a dirty little boy with a piece of chalk and a board fence and nobody looking," adding that "everything he touches smells like a billy goat." Oddly enough, Chandler agreed to co-write the screenplay of *Double Indemnity* with director Billy Wilder. Chandler made changes to the book's dialogue and, surprisingly, Cain concurred. The film was released in 1944 and the two ended up becoming friends.

from *Double Indemnity* (1936)

I drove out to Glendale to put three new truck drivers on a brewery company bond, and then I remembered this renewal over in Hollywoodland. I decided to run over there. That was how I came to this House of Death, that you've been reading about in the papers. It didn't look like a House of Death when I saw it. It was just a Spanish house, like all the rest of them in California, with white walls, red tile roof, and a patio out to one side. It was built cock-eyed. The garage was under the house, the first floor was over that and the rest of it was spilled up the hill any way they could get it in. You climbed some stone steps to the front door, so I parked the car and went up there. A servant poked her head out. "Is Mr. Nirdlinger in?"

"I don't know, sir. Who wants to see hirn?"

"Mr. Huff."

"And what's the business?"

"Personal."

Getting in is the tough part of my job, and you don't tip what you came for till you get where it counts. "I'm sorry, sir, but they won't let me ask anybody in unless they say what they want."

It was one of those spots you get in. If I said some more about "personal" I would be making a mystery of it, and that's bad. If I said what I really wanted, I would be laying myself open for what every insurance agent dreads, that she would come back and say, "Not in." If I said I'd wait, I would be making myself look small, and that never helped a sale yet. To move this stuff, you've got to get in. Once you're in, they've got to listen to you, and you can pretty near rate an agent by how quick he gets to the family sofa, with his hat on one side of him and his dope sheets on the other.

"I see. I told Mr. Nirdlinger I would drop in, but – never mind. I'll see if I can make it some other time."

It was true, in a way. On this automobile stuff, you always make it a point that you'll give a reminder on renewal, but I hadn't seen him for a year. I made it sound like an old friend, though, and an old friend that wasn't any too pleased at the welcome he got. It worked. She got a worried look on her face. "Well – come in, please."

If I had used that juice trying to keep out, that might have got me somewhere.

I pitched my hat on the sofa. They've made a lot of that living room, especially those "blood-red drapes." All I saw was a living room like every other living room in California, maybe a little more expensive than some, but nothing that any department store wouldn't deliver on one truck, lay out in the morning, and have the credit OK ready the same afternoon. The furniture was Spanish, the kind that looks pretty and sits stiff. The rug was one of those 12 × 15s that would have been Mexican except it was made in Oakland, California. The blood-red drapes were there, but they didn't mean anything. All these Spanish houses have red velvet drapes that run on iron spears, and generally some red velvet wall tapestries to go with them. This was right out of the same can, with a coat-of-arms tapestry over the fireplace and a castle tapestry over the sofa. The other two sides of the room were windows and the entrance to the hall.

"Yes?"

A woman was standing there. I had never seen her before. She was maybe thirty-one or -two, with a sweet face, light blue eyes, and dusty blonde hair. She was small, and had on a suit of blue house pajamas. She had a washed-out look.

"I wanted to see Mr. Nirdlinger."

"Mr. Nirdlinger isn't in just now, but I am Mrs. Nirdlinger. Is there something I could do?"

There was nothing to do but spill it. "Why no, I think not, Mrs. Nirdlinger, thanks just the same. Huff is my name, Walter Huff, of the General Fidelity of California. Mr. Nirdlinger's automobile coverage runs out in a week or two, and I promised to give him a reminder on it, so I thought I'd drop by. But I certainly didn't mean to bother you about it."

"Coverage?"

"Insurance. I just took a chance, coming up here in the daytime, but I happened to be in the neighborhood, so I thought it wouldn't hurt. When do you think would be a good time to see Mr. Nirdlinger? Could he give me a few minutes right after dinner, do you think, so I wouldn't cut into his evening?"

"What kind of insurance has he been carrying? I ought to know, but I don't keep track."

"I guess none of us keep track until something happens. Just the usual line. Collision, fire, and theft, and public liability."

"Oh yes, of course."

"It's only a routine matter, but he ought to attend to it in time, so he'll be protected."

"It really isn't up to me, but I know he's been thinking about the Automobile Club. Their insurance, I mean."

"Is he a member?"

"No, he's not. He's always intended to join, but somehow he's never got around to it. But the club representative was here, and he mentioned insurance."

"You can't do better than the Automobile Club. They're prompt, liberal in their view of claims, and courteous straight down the line. I've not got a word to say against them."

That's one thing you learn. Never knock the other guy's stuff.

"And then it's cheaper."

"For members."

"I thought only members could get it."

"What I mean is this. If a man's going to join the Automobile Club anyway, for service in time of trouble, taking care of tickets, things like that, then if he takes their insurance too, he gets it cheaper. He certainly does. But if he's going to join the club just to get the insurance, by the time he adds that $16 membership fee to the premium rate, he's paying more. Figure that in, I can still save Mr. Nirdlinger quite a little money."

She talked along, and there was nothing I could do but go along with it. But you sell as many people as I do, you don't go by what they say. You feel it, how the deal is going. And after a while I knew this woman didn't care anything about the Automobile Club. Maybe the husband did, but she didn't. There was something else, and this was nothing but a stall. I figured it would be some kind of a proposition to split the commission, maybe so she could get a ten-spot out of it without the husband knowing. There's plenty of that going on. And I was just wondering what I would say to her. A reputable agent don't get mixed up in stuff like that, but she was walking around the room, and I saw something I hadn't noticed before. Under those blue pajamas was a shape to set a man nuts, and how good I was going to sound when I started explaining the high ethics of the insurance business I didn't exactly know.

But all of a sudden she looked at me, and I felt a chill creep straight up my back and into the roots of my hair. "Do you handle accident insurance?"

Maybe that don't mean to you what it meant to me. Well, in the first place, accident insurance is sold, not bought. You get calls for other kinds, for fire, for burglary, even for life, but never for accident. That stuff moves when agents move it, and it sounds funny to be asked about it. In the second place, when there's dirty work going on, accident is the first thing they think of. Dollar for dollar paid down, there's a bigger face coverage on accident than any other kind. And it's the one kind of insurance that can be taken out without the insured knowing a thing about it. No physical examination for accident. On that, all they want is the money, and there's many a man walking around today that's worth more to his loved ones dead than alive, only he don't know it yet.

6520 Drexel Ave. (Fairfax district)

Raymond Chandler (1888–1959)

Chandler first arrived in Los Angeles in 1913, working odd jobs – on an apricot ranch for 20¢ an hour, and in a sporting goods store, stringing tennis rackets for $12.50 a week. In August 1917, he enlisted in the Canadian Army (born with dual British-American citizenship), and went off to fight in World War I. He returned to Los Angeles in 1919, and worked his way up from accountant to an executive at Dabney Oil Syndicate, until he was fired in 1932. He soon began writing, and his first published story, "Blackmailer's Don't Shoot, " appeared in the notorious pulp *Black Mask* in 1933. Chandler continued to write for *Black Mask*, and later *Dime Detective*, until the 1939 publication of his first novel, *The Big Sleep*.

Of Hollywood, Chandler once wrote that "the pretentiousness, the bogus enthusiasm, the constant drinking and drabbing, the incessant squabbling over money, the all-pervasive agent, the strutting of the big shots (and their usually utter incompetence to achieve anything they start out to do), the constant fear of losing all this fairy gold and being the nothing they have really never ceased to be, the snide tricks, the whole damn mess is out of this world. It's like one of these South American palace revolutions conducted by officers in comic-opera uniforms – only when the thing is over and the ragged dead men lie in rows against the wall, you suddenly know that this is not funny, this is the Roman circus, and damned near the end of a civilization."

From La Jolla, in a 1951 letter to British publisher Hamish Hamilton, Chandler wrote that Los Angeles had become "a grotesque and impossible place for a human being to live in." In a 1956 letter to Jessica Tyndale, Chandler sounded more uncertain: "I know now what is the matter with my writing or not writing. I've lost any affinity for my background. Los Angeles is no longer my city, and La Jolla is nothing but a climate and a lot of meaningless chi-chi...There's nothing for me to write about. To write about a place you have to love it or hate it or do both by turns, which is usually the way you love a woman."

from *The Little Sister* (1949)

CHAPTER 13

I drove east on Sunset but I didn't go home. At La Brea I turned north and swung over to Highland, out over Cahuenga Pass and down on to Ventura Boulevard, past Studio City and Sherman Oaks and Encino. There was nothing lonely about the trip. There never is on that road. Fast boys in stripped-down Fords shot in and out of the traffic streams, missing fenders by a sixteenth of an inch, but somehow always missing them. Tired men in dusty coupes and sedans winced and tightened their grip on the wheel and ploughed on north and west towards home and dinner, an evening with the sports page, the blatting of the radio, the whining of their spoiled children and the gabble of their silly wives. I drove on past the gaudy neons and the false fronts behind them, the sleazy hamburger joints that look like palaces under the colors, the circular drive-ins as gay as circuses with the chipper hard-eyed carhops, the brilliant counters, and the sweaty greasy kitchens that would have poisoned a toad. Great double trucks rumbled down over Sepulveda from Wilmington and San Pedro and crossed towards the Ridge Route, starting up in low-low from the traffic lights with a growl of lions in the zoo.

Behind Encino an occasional light winked from the hills through thick trees. The homes of screen stars. Screen stars, phooey. The veterans of a thousand beds. Hold it, Marlowe, you're not human tonight.

The air got cooler. The highway narrowed. The cars were so few now that the headlights hurt. The grade rose against chalk walls and at the top a breeze, unbroken from the ocean, danced casually across the night.

I ate dinner at a place near Thousand Oaks. Bad but quick. Feed 'em and throw 'em out. Lots of business. We can't bother with you sitting over your second cup of coffee, mister. You're using money space. See those people over there behind the rope? They want to eat. Anyway they think they have to. God knows why they want to eat here. They could do better home out of a can. They're just restless. Like you. They have to get the car out and go somewhere. Sucker-bait for the racketeers that have taken over the restaurants. Here we go again. You're not human tonight, Marlowe.

I paid off and stopped in a bar to drop a brandy on top of the New York cut. Why New York, I thought. It was Detroit where they made machine tools. I stepped out into the night air that nobody had yet found out how to option. But a lot of people were probably trying. They'd get around to it.

I drove on to the Oxnard cut-off and turned back along the ocean. The big eight-wheelers and sixteen-wheelers were streaming north, all hung over with orange lights. On the right the great fat solid Pacific trudging into shore like a scrubwoman going home. No moon, no fuss, hardly a sound of the surf. No smell. None of the harsh wild smell of the sea. A California ocean. California, the department-store state. The most of everything and the best of nothing. Here we go again. You're not human tonight, Marlowe.

All right. Why would I be? I'm sitting in that office, playing with a dead fly and in pops this dowdy little item from Manhattan, Kansas, and chisels me down to a shopworn twenty to find her brother. He sounds like a creep but she wants to find him. So with this fortune clasped to my chest, I trundle down to Bay City and the routine I go through is so tired I'm half asleep on my feet. I meet nice people, with and without ice picks in their necks. I leave, and I leave myself wide-open too. Then she comes in and takes the twenty away from me and gives me a kiss and gives it back to me because I didn't do a full day's work.

So I go see Dr. Hambleton, retired (and how) optometrist from El Centro, and meet again the new style in neckwear. And I don't tell the cops. I just frisk the customer's toupee and put on an act. Why? Who am I cutting my throat for this time? A blonde with sexy eyes and too many door keys? A girl from Manhattan, Kansas? I don't know. All I know is that something isn't what it seems and the old tired but always reliable hunch tells me that if the hand is played the way it is dealt the wrong person is going to lose the pot. Is that my business? Well, what is my business? Do I know? Did I ever know? Let's not go into that. You're not human tonight, Marlowe. Maybe I never was or ever will be. Maybe I'm an ectoplasm with a private license. Maybe we all get like this in the cold half-lit world where always the wrong thing happens and never the right.

Malibu. More movie stars. More pink and blue bathtubs. More tufted beds. More Chanel No. 5. More Lincoln Continentals and Cadillacs. More wind-blown hair and sunglasses and attitudes and pseudo-refined voices and waterfront morals. Now, wait a minute. Lots of nice people work in pictures. You've got the wrong attitude, Marlowe. You're not human tonight.

I smelled Los Angeles before I got to it. It smelled stale and old like a living room that had been closed too long. But the colored lights fooled you. The lights were wonderful. There ought to be a monument to the man who invented neon lights. Fifteen stories high, solid marble. There's a boy who really made something out of nothing.

So I went to a picture show and it had to have Mavis Weld in it. One of those glass-and-chromium deals where everybody smiled too much and talked too much and knew it. The women were always going up a long curving staircase to change their clothes. The men were always taking monogrammed cigarettes out of expensive cases and snapping expensive lighters at each other. And the help was round-shouldered from carrying trays with drinks across the terrace to a swimming pool about the size of Lake Huron but a lot neater.

The leading man was an amiable ham with a lot of charm, some of it turning a little yellow at the edges. The star was a bad-tempered brunette with contemptuous eyes and a couple of bad close-ups that showed her pushing forty-five backwards almost hard enough to break a wrist. Mavis Weld played second lead and she played it with wraps on. She was good, but she could have been ten times better. But if she had been ten times better half her scenes would have been yanked out to protect the star. It was as neat a bit of tightrope walking as I ever saw. Well it wouldn't be a tightrope she'd be walking from now on. It would be a piano wire. It would be very high. And there wouldn't be any net under it.

CHAPTER 19

The studio cop at the semicircular glassed-in desk put down his telephone and scribbled on a pad. He tore off the sheet and pushed in through the narrow slit not more than three quarters of an inch wide where the glass did not quite meet the top of his desk. His voice coming through the speaking device set into the glass panel had a metallic ring.

"Straight through to the end of the corridor," he said, "you'll find a drinking fountain in the middle of the patio. George Wilson will pick up there."

I said: "Thanks. Is this bullet-proof glass?"

"Sure. Why?"

"I just wondered," I said. "I never heard of anybody shooting his way into the picture business."

Behind me somebody snickered. I turned to look at a girl in slacks with a red carnation behind her ear. She was grinning.

"Oh brother, if a gun was all it took."

I went over to an olive-green door that didn't have any handle. It made a buzzing sound and let me push it open. Beyond was an olive-green corridor with bare walls and a door at the far end. A rat trap. If you got into that and something was wrong, they could still stop you. The far door made the same buzz and click. I wondered how the cop knew I was at it. So I looked up and found his eyes staring at me in a tilted mirror. As I touched the door the mirror went blank. They thought of everything.

Outside in the hot midday sun flowers rioted in a small patio with tiled walks and a pool in the middle and a marble seat. The drinking fountain was beside the marble seat. An elderly and beautifully dressed man was lounging on the marble seat watching three tan-colored boxers root up some tea-rose begonias. There was an expression of intense but quiet satisfaction on his face. He didn't glance at me as I came up. One of the boxers, the biggest one, came over and made a wet on the marble seat beside his pants leg. He leaned down and patted the dog's hard short-haired head.

"You Mr. Wilson?" I asked.

He looked up at me vaguely. The middle-sized boxer trotted up and sniffed and wet after the first one.

"Wilson?" He had a lazy voice with a touch of drawl to it. "Oh, no. My name's not Wilson. Should it be?"

"Sorry." I went over to the drinking fountain and hit myself in the face with a stream of water. While I was wiping it off with a handkerchief the smallest boxer did his duty on the marble bench.

The man whose name was not Wilson said lovingly, "Always do it in the exact same order. Fascinates me."

"Do what?" I asked.

"Pee," he said. "Question of seniority it seems. Very orderly. First Maisie. She's the mother. Then Mac. Year older than Jock, the baby. Always the same. Even in my office."

"In your office?" I said, and nobody ever looked stupider saying anything.

He lifted his whitish eyebrows at me, took a plain brown cigar out of his mouth, bit the end off and spit it into the pool.

"That won't do the fish any good," I said.

He gave me an up-from-under look. "I raise boxers. The hell with fish."

I figured it was just Hollywood. I lit a cigarette and sat down on the bench. "In your office," I said. "Well, every day has its new idea, hasn't it."

"Up against the corner of the desk. Do it all the time. Drives my secretaries crazy. Gets into the carpet, they say. What's the matter with women nowadays? Never bothers me. Rather like it. You get fond of dogs, you even like to watch them pee."

One of the dogs heaved a full-blown begonia plant into the middle of the tiled walk at his feet. He picked it up and threw it into the pool.

"Bothers the gardeners, I suppose," he remarked as he sat down again. "Oh well, if they're not satisfied, they can always –" He stopped dead and watched a slim mail girl in yellow slacks deliberately detour in order to pass through the patio. She gave him a quick side glance and went off making music with her hips.

"You know what's the matter with this business?" he asked me.

"Nobody does," I said.

"Too much sex," he said. "All right in its proper time and place. But we get it in carload lots. Wade through it. Stand up to our necks in it. Gets to be like flypaper." He stood up. "We have too many flies too. Nice to have met you, Mister –"

"Marlowe," I said. "I'm afraid you don't know me."

"Don't know anybody," he said. "Memory's going. Meet too many people. Name's Oppenheimer."

"Jules Oppenheimer?"

He nodded. "Right. Have a cigar" He held one out to me. I showed my cigarette. He threw the cigar into the pool, then frowned. "Memory's going," he said sadly. "Wasted fifty cents. Oughtn't to do that."

"You run this studio," I said.

He nodded absently. "Ought to have saved that cigar. Save fifty cents and what have you got?"

"Fifty cents," I said, wondering what the hell he was talking about.

"Not in this business. Save fifty cents in this business and all you have is five dollars worth of bookkeeping." He paused and made a motion to the three boxers. They stopped whatever they were rooting at and watched him. "Just run the financial end," he said. "That's easy. Come on children, back to the brothel." He sighed. "Fifteen hundred theaters," he added.

I must have been wearing my stupid expression again. He waved a hand around the patio. "Fifteen hundred theaters is all you need. A damn sight easier than raising purebred boxers. The motion-picture business is the only business in the world in which you can make all the mistakes there are and still make money.

"Must be the only business in the world where you can have three dogs pee up against your office desk," I said.

"You have to have the fifteen hundred theaters."

"That makes it a little harder to get a start," I said.

He looked pleased. "Yes. That *is* the hard part." He looked across the green clipped lawn at a four-story building which made one side of the open square. "All offices over there," he said. "I never go there. Always redecorating. Makes me sick to look at the stuff some of these people put in their suites. Most expensive talent in the world. Give them anything they like, all the money they want. Why? No reason at all. Just habit. Doesn't matter a damn what they do or how they do it. Just give me fifteen hundred theaters."

"You wouldn't want to be quoted on that, Mr. Oppenheimer?"

"You a newspaper man?"

"No."

"Too bad. Just for the hell of it I'd like to see somebody try to get that simple elementary fact of life into the papers." He paused and snorted. "Nobody'd print it. Afraid to. Come on, children!"

The big one, Maisie, came over and stood beside him. The middle-sized one paused to ruin another begonia and then trotted up beside Maisie. The little one, Jock, lined up in order, then with a sudden inspiration, lifted a hind leg at the cuff of Oppenheimer's pants. Maisie blocked him off casually.

"See that?" Oppenheimer beamed. "Jock tried to get out of turn. Maisie wouldn't stand for it." He leaned down and patted Maisie's head. She looked up at him adoringly.

"The eyes of your dog," Oppenheimer mused. "The most unforgettable thing in the world."

He strolled off down the tiled path towards the executive building, the three boxers trotting sedately beside him.

"Mr. Marlowe?"

I turned to find that a tall sandy-haired man with a nose like a straphanger's elbow had sneaked up on me.

"I'm George Wilson. Glad to know you. I see you know Mr. Oppenheimer. "

"Been talking to him. He told me how to run the picture business. Seems all it takes is fifteen hundred theaters."

"I've been working here five years. I've never even spoken to him."

"You just don't get pee'd on by the right dogs."

"You could be right. Just what can I do for you, Mr. Marlowe?"

2106 Lemoyne (Echo Park)

Frank Chin (1940–)

Born in San Francisco, Frank Chin is the son of a Chinese immigrant father and a fourth generation Chinatown mother, whose father had worked in the steward service of the Southern Pacific Railroad. From 1962–1965 he worked clerk jobs around the Western Pacific Railways Oakland yard and left to attend the University of California at Santa Barbara. As Chin himself recalls, "I left the Western Pacific for the University of California at Santa Barbara, where I got my AB in English in February of 1966, then hired on the Southern Pacific Railroad out of Oakland Terminal as a brakeman. I was the first Chinese American brakeman on the Southern Pacific since Chinese built the Central Pacific over the Sierras."

Fiction writer, playwright, essayist and script writer, Chin was the principal editor of the seminal Asian-American anthology, *Aiiieeeee!*, in 1975. Chin has published a collection of stories, *The Chinaman Pacific & Frisco R.R. Co.* (1988), and two novels, *Donald Duk* (1991) and *Gunga Din Highway* (1994). Chin's theatrical experience has been extensive, with the American Conservatory Theatre in San Francisco encouraging him to start the Asian American Theatre Workshop there in 1973. As Chin notes, "I founded the Workshop as the only Asian American theater that was conceived as a playwright's lab and not a showcase for yellows yearning to sell out to Hollywood. I failed." His plays, *The Chickencoop Chinaman*, *The Year of the Dragon* and *Gee, Pop!* have been produced in New York, Los Angeles and San Francisco, while a television production of *The Year of the Dragon* aired on PBS as part of its "Theater in America" series.

A collection of his essays from the 1960s to the present, *Bulletproof Buddhists*, was published in 1998. "I am a writer,"Chin insists, "I have written short fiction, plays, non-fiction, reviews, essays, opinion and research pieces on Chinese and Japanese America. I have also written the backs of bubble gum cards, radio contests, documentary films on fishing and boxing, and hacked."

from *Gunga Din Highway* (1994)

Imogene tells me Aloha went through college and came out a nutritionist but couldn't stand to see people dying after all her menu planning and avoided patients and taught nutrition awhile then became a Satanist and is now a born again Christian carrying a paper shopping bag with string handles full of fundamentalist tracts to pass out at the funeral.

Aloha doesn't put her bag down to hug me. She keeps hold of the bag, swings it up with her arms closing around me and the bag full of pulp born again Christianity bumps me in the small of my back. "God loves you," she says. Terrific. I'm thrilled.

The tong men, pa's longtime friends begin arriving. The last of the first generation of old time Chinatown bigshots. Pa was a big man in the Chinatown orgs. His village association. His family association. The Alliance of Four Families. The Canton City Wooey Goon. The City Wooey Goon's "young men's club," the tong within a tong.

The young men's club is to the City Wooey Goon what the Shriners are to the Masons. Pa was also a past president and advisor to the all powerful tong of the tongs, the Big Alliance. He was famous in Chinatown as an immigrant who made it in Hollywood playing Charlie Chan's American-born Number Four Son, and a Chinatown legendary snappy dresser, womanizer and spendthrift. In the tongs these very same rotten qualities made him a skillful and popular arbitrator and soother of trouble between tongs between brothers between Chinatowns.

The old men climb out of their son's or son-in-law's cars. Some are helped out. As they pass me, they hand me the white envelope of bok gum, white gold, a sign of respect and pledge of brotherly protection from pa's brothers of the tong within a tong. These are the old old men, the ones I have not seen before, the ones who come out only for the funerals of their own kind. One old man in a five year old suit asks me who is going to speak for the three big tongs pa was big in. "I don't know" I say in basic bad manners Cantonese, "All I know is a Catholic priest is going to speak."

That shocks the old man. He recovers and says "Funerals are for the children, the family, and the friends. Why is this stranger speaking, and none of your father's friends?"

"Please wait a minute," I say, "I'll get my older brother." I go into the chapel after China Brother and a few of the old men follow me in. They stand at the back of the chapel with a view of the whole chapel with the high vaulted ceilings in front of them, and woof at him. China Brother whines and yaps. The clashing voices form an off-chord that hovers saxxing on an endless breath high over the funeral. I ask them to step outside with China Brother. They all step outside. China Brother's wife peeks out of the door and wants us to go back inside and talk. She doesn't want the TV news to see. I say, "No! No dickering and niggling bullshit over the old man's dead body. His funeral is enough of a humiliation already. "

Ah-Joe Joes put his hands in his pockets, shifts his weight from foot to foot, looks down at his toes and whines and peeves. He insults everyone and is too stupid to see he's embarrassing himself. "No, no one speaks," China brother says. "It's too complicated. I don't want complications."

The old men are pissed. They got up early to ready themselves for the drive across the bay. "No matter what you think of your father, you can't humiliate him this way. You can't let a Catholic priest speak, when your father was no Catholic, and then not let his friends speak. You want to insult your father's friends too? That's not what funerals are for. Think of your funeral, and what you're showing your children with this business, Ah-Joe Joe."

They come to a compromise. A friend of pa's who like pa is big in the big three associations will speak for all three and that will be that. Fine. I think. It's settled.

Inside Aloha insists on sitting in the front row and next to me. Pa looks awful. His toupee is still on his forehead. No one has touched him. The tong men are confused by Polly Jade's presence and will not go up to pa's casket because they will have to pass her. Still, a few brave the walk up and breaking all tradition and forced to commit an insult they do not acknowledge any of pa's kin as being close. They shake no one's hand, offer condolences to no one. I'm thinking China Brother has in his anger and self-pity not failed to fuck everything up, just everything about pa's funeral, when he asks me to say a few words about pa. I refuse, "It's too late. Let the tongman speak and that will be that."

"The tongman is not going to speak," China Brother says. There's no one to make the announcement about the time and place of the gah way fon, the banquet after the funeral. He wants me to do it. No. No. No. "Go tell them Jade Village. Four o'clock," Joe Joe growls and gags.

"You write a note and I'll take it back to the Catholic muk see," I say.

"You write a note," China Brother says.

"This is your party, your word, China Brother. You write the note. Or no note, period," I say. It takes him ten minutes to control himself enough to write the name and address of his restaurant on the back of his business card that has the name and address of his restaurant. He adds the time, on the note.

On my way up the aisle to the back I see all my mother's sisters are here. Longman, Jr's daughters and grandchildren by his first wife, and his son and daughter by his second wife are here. Uncle Mort is here with his radiant redhead. The priests look like I'm catching them doing nasty things with each other. I ask them to make the announcement please. Jade Village. Four o'clock.

Polly Jade is fattened up, bawling. The boys are bored. Polly Jade's white friend, Charlie Chan and Ben Mo and Pandora are not immune to the mean hostile vibes aimed their way. The tall bald headed Chink in glasses grins stupidly and catches my eye. You wanta connect with me, fuckhead? How about a crowbar up your ass, sugarlips? He hides behind Polly Jade's bulk.

Aloha opens her Bible and points a verse out to me, and reads it out loud. "Idolatry!" she says.

I take out my felt tip and write, "Cool it!" over the verse and close her Bible. The shuffle of the priests' skirts scratches and echoes around the chapel. Aloha sits on her heels by Polly Jade reading the Bible to her. I have had enough.

I stand and turn and see my mother's Big Aunt Willy and her drones, my mother's sisters, the four living reminders of the legendary five beauties. Big Aunt Poppy, her fine black and hennaed hair thin as prairie grass after a fire, puts her glasses on to see me. Her eyes bulge and swell up in the lenses into fish-shaped smears. My brother's children and their children wear clothes as light and bright as paper and look like lanterns. Imogene pouts and Ira wears no makeup. They're looking at me as if I'm on stage.

And to my right is Hollywood, my father's dream come true, with my father's real father in the front row. Two white men. The old Charlie Chan seems to be trying to look down between Aloha's legs as she crouches in front of Polly Jade. The new Charlie Chan. The new authors. The new numbered son. And none of my old friends.

I'm in the center aisle playing chicken with an elderly Catholic priest and his Chinese servant. Everyone seems to be wearing noisy paper clothes. Yes, no one wants to wear what they're wearing here, ever again. In the name of Charlie Chan the Father, Charlie Chan the Son, Charlie Chan the Ghostly Host. I look into the Catholic priest's eyes through his glasses and see frothy whites with two winking dark holes in their centers, like the foam of two cups of cappuccino jiggling around holes made by two quarters.

I walk out. Fuck it.

I go to see Longman, Jr. the Hero. He's back in the hospital. The pain is worse. More of his liver is so much more enemy meat eating him out of the picture. He floats on the bed. Virginia is with him. I want to thank her for not being at the funeral, but don't.

He smells like death and maggots covered in baby lotion. I'm right about the baby lotion. His skin is as dry as paper matches and hurts. The rest of the smell is Junior. The TV is on above the bed. It's an old black and white. George Steven's *Gunga Din*, with Cary Grant, Victor McLaglen, and Douglas Fairbanks Jr. in pith helmets as three British soldiers in Colonial India and Sam Jaffe in a turban as Gunga Din their water boy who helps the British make war against his people. This is not the Movie About Me. Pa is neither Number Four Son nor the Chinaman Who Dies in this movie. Pa is not in this movie. Or is he? He might be. I don't change the channel.

Virginia sits by the bed .The window lays light over her shoulder and she uses it to knit by. I haven't seen a woman knit in years.

"I wondered how much you'd take before you came down here," Virginia says.

I give the Hero and the loyal Virginia the spectacle and dreariness of pa's funeral. Charlie Chan. Polly Jade. The Jekyll and Hyde boys. Pandora Toy and my blood brother Ben Mo. Two white limousines. The news. The rickety old bones of the tongs. China Brother's art of negotiation. Aloha and her Christian shopping bag. The skirts of the Catholic priest sounding like someone chewing corn flakes.

Longman, Jr. is somewhere in 1944. How did he get there? Virginia says it's the morphine. He's taken a little at seven this morning but because his liver's not cleaning his blood the way it should the morphine stays in his blood and sends him on this tall one. We joke about him becoming hooked. Virginia says Imogene doesn't approve of drugs for fear of Longman, Jr. becoming an addict.

"What're you doing, huh, Ulysses?" the words pain out of the Hero's withered face. His face is too far gone. It hurts too much for him to wear his glasses. He can't see me. I know he's trying. I can't look at him. Instead I look up at the TV.

It's the night funeral scene at the end of *Gunga Din.* I say "Oh, look, Pa's favorite movie. What am I doing?" The campfires burn. Rudyard Kipling stands by the officer reciting the poem Gunga Din over the coffin, as Cary Grant and Douglas Fairbanks, Jr., and Victor McLaglen look on, wounded, rescued, heroic. By flickering firelight the officer reads:

'E carried me away
To where a dooli lay
An' bullet come an' drilled the beggar clean,
'E put me safe inside,
An' just before 'e died,
"I 'ope you liked your drink," sez Gunga Din.
So I'll meet 'im later on
At the place where 'e is gone –
Where it's always double drill and no canteen.
'E'll be squattin' on the coals
Given' drink to poor damned souls,
An' I'll get a swig in hell from Gunga Din!
    Yes, Din! Din! Din!
You Lazarushian-leather Gunga Din!
    Though I've belted you and flayed you,
    By the livin' Gawd that made you,
You're a better man than I am, Gunga Din!

The pipes and drums squeal and thud Auld Lang Syne and march off into the darkness and Sam Jaffe in darkie makeup and a full dress uniform emerges superimposed ghostly over the scene. Not my father in darkie makeup. Not my uncle Mort. Not Spencer Tracy. Nothing but the real old movie. The ghost of Gunga Din smartly salutes and breaks into a grin. The End.

"I'm writing zombie movies, and novels, Junior. I write the movies for this company of four guys. I write the novels for myself. The first movie I scripted for them *The Night of the Living Hollywood Dead* made them lots of money. It made them so much money they bought me a stadium bigscreen TV that covers a whole wall of my place in L.A. and pay all my electric bills for the next ten years. They're all ancients of TV Hollywood producers, harkening back to the days of Studio One, and Playhouse 90 . Last week they called me for a script conference on the new zombie movie, and they tell me, Ulysses, we want to open this with a pastel dream sequence. Pastel? You mean colors? You want to crap up the script with descriptions of colors and decor? No, no no, they say, Pastel. You know what we mean. Pastel! Oh, pastel. What is that some new Hollywood code word? What do you mean pastel? You know, Ulysses, they tell me, Pastel! The birds are singing, the bees are buzzing, the sun is shining, the grass is green… Pastoral! I say, Pastoral! Yeah! the Four Horsemen say, Pastel!"

I shake my head. It's too much to expect the hero to laugh. I don't want to hear him laugh. I laugh. "After all this time and making all this money for them and writing this new zombie movie for them I realize the English we are speaking to each other is not the same language at all. English is not a common language."

"You going to Cal, Ulysses?" Junior asks me. His breathing sounds like crumpling cellophane. I look at him. He's carved out of a carrot and the carrot's dried up and rotting. If he were meat, he would have been thrown out weeks ago. Where is he now? Nineteen fifty what? I nod.

I say, "Yeah, Junior I'm going to Cal. It seems to be a good school."

"Go down to the yard office and get a job for the summer, like I told you," he says, answering true to the way it is back then. Junior dozes in and out of who knows when and where, Virginia knits and I watch TV till it's time for me to leave for the gah way fon, the banquet after pa's funeral where China Brother still shakes his head and publicly tries to refuse the white envelopes of bok gum. The third tallest tongman there, in a wool suit the color of Rita Hayworth's hair in *Pal Joey*, shoots me a look of anger and weariness and gently influences China Brother to a table on the other side of the lacquered screen partitioning the room. China Brother gets up from the table speaking too loudly and sounding offensive, petty and stupid all the way, accepts the influence. A few soft pats. Heavy sighs. A show of restrained irritation and uncomfortable feet.

"Go with them," Auntie Orchid says. I stand and walk away from our island of seven occupied tables through an orchard of empty tables and white linen table cloths to the table behind the lacquered screen. I sit down without being asked across from the tall old tongman and next to China Brother.

"I thought you ask the Catholic mook see to make announce where and when is the gah way fon?" he leans back and says putting me in my place in front of the humiliated tongmen.

"You mean he didn't make the announcement?"

"No, he didn't. What're you say about that?" China Brother asks as if it's my fault.

"It's your problem. You trust that Catholic priest, not me, I'm a Chinaman, I know Christians never keep their word. Lying to each other and breaking promises is called faith in God, ask the Aztec, ask the Mayan, ask the Modoc, ask the..."

"Ask me," the tall tongman says and slightly leans over the table.

The tall tongman gingers in on his pinching shoes and asks China Brother to start serving the food. He is angry. "Everyone is here. No one else is coming. It is not right to keep them sitting and waiting. Why not start serving now?"

"Not till I pay first," Ah-Joe Joe says. As he waits for the daylight manager to return with the bill, he opens the white envelope of bok gum from the restaurant employees, counts it, one hundred dollars in bills and adds the bills to the piles of bills then makes one more count of the piles, notes the totals and shoves the addition to me. "You want to count it? See for yourself! Go ahead."

"No, you're the first son. What you do is right," I say.

"I want you to count it!"

"Ah-Joe Joe. Don't be this way," the tongman soothes. "Accept things for the gesture of respect to your father they are, and don't be this way. No one is giving this bok gum to offend you."

China Brother doesn't flip a glance the old man's way and before the old man has all his words out, says to me, "Here I want you to add it up for yourself. Count the money for yourself. I want everything on the up what's up! That's the kind of guy I am. I want everybody to know that about me. I don't want any questions about my honesty!"

"It's not your honesty that's in question," I say.

"You don't count, nobody eats," China Brother says.

I laugh. I have him. "I don't want to touch that money, after you've shit on it. I don't care to eat here myself, so I don't care if anybody eats. No matter what. You are the first son. Eat or no eat. You are in charge. It's your word that counts. Not mine," I say. "But Pa's friends don't deserve this. I'll count the money. And you and I never have to speak to each other again. Don't call. Don't write. Don't drop by. Ever."

The tongman looks down at the floor. I count the money.

1260 N. Wetherly Dr. (Sunset Strip)

Robert Craft (1924–)

Having already spent part of the summer of 1948, and most of the summer of 1949 with the Stravinskys, Robert Craft arrived in Los Angeles on a bus from New York in December of 1949 and entered the role in the Stravinsky household he would maintain for the next twenty-two years. According to Craft, Vera Stravinsky "recalls that in their first years in Hollywood they would return from movie stars' parties and read Dostoevsky together, 'to remind ourselves about human beings.'"

An associate and musical assistant to Stravinsky, Craft has been referred to by some as an adopted son, but himself writes that "the Stravinskys and I were more like companions than parents and son." Despite their respect for each other, the feud between Stravinksy and Schoenberg was substantial enough for mutual friends of the composers to avoid mentioning one to the other. Schoenberg's name was not spoken around Stravinsky, and Stravinsky's was not spoken around Schoenberg. Craft, though part of the Stravinsky household, visited Schoenberg frequently. As Craft later wrote, "I think that I alone was aware that neither composer knew anything about the other's music, having realized that each of them had been unwilling to examine his own prejudice – Schoenberg's being that Stravinsky depended on formulas and a bag of tricks, Stravinsky's that Schoenberg was a slave to a rigid, abstract system." After Schoenberg's death, Craft (who had become a friend of Schoenberg's daughter, Nuria) was able to convince the Stravinskys to have dinner with Schoenberg's widow and daughter.

Craft was also responsible for guiding Stravinsky past his resentment, nudging him in the direction of the Schoenberg school and exposing him to the twelve-tone system. As Craft describes the change of heart: "A week later, he [Stravinsky] asked to go for a drive to Palmdale, at that time a small Mojave Desert town, where the Stravinskys liked to eat spareribs and drink Bordeaux from thermos bottles in a cowboy style restaurant. On the way home, he startled us, saying that he was afraid that he could no longer compose and he did not know what to do. For a moment he broke down and actually wept, whereupon Mrs. Stravinsky convinced him that these were feelings and the musical problems, whatever they were, would pass. He referred obliquely to the powerful impression that the Schoenberg piece had made on him, and when he said that he wanted to learn more, I knew that the crisis was over; so far from being defeated, Stravinsky would emerge a new composer."

Robert Craft

from *Stravinsky: Chronicle of a Friendship, 1948–1971* (1973)

AUGUST 10, 1949

Lunch at the Farmers' Market with the I.S.'s, Christopher Isherwood, and the Huxleys, the latter cooing at each other today like newlyweds, or oldlyweds making up after a spat. Owing to its extensive variety of salads, seeds (Aldous eats quantities of sunflower seeds, for his eyes), nuts, health foods, exotic fruit (Milton: "The savoury pulp they chew, and in the rind"), the restaurant is a Huxleyan haunt. Most of the other tables are held down by drugstore cowboys, movie stars, Central European refugees, and – to judge by the awed glances in our direction – Aldine and Igorian disciples. All are vegetarians, for the nonce, and all nibble at their greens like pasturing cows.

Virginia Woolf likened Isherwood to a jockey, and it is easy to see what she meant. Nothing in his clothes suggests that profession, of course, and I might add that they are less conspicuously suited to Hollywood than those of Aldous or I.S. (both of them sporting much too resonant neckwear, as if their sense of the dapper had run to seed at such a remove from the more discriminating centers of haberdashery). It is a question rather of the stature, bantam weight, somewhat too short legs, and disproportionately, even simianly, long arms, a comparison forced on the attention because of their frequent employment for metrical purposes. In short, it is in the build of the man that one sees how Mrs. Woolf saw him, whether at the pari-mutuel window or the furlong post: as an ornament of the track and the turf.

His manner is casual, vagabondish, lovelorn. One does not readily imagine him in a fit of anger or behaving precipitately or enduring extended states of great commotion. At moments he might be thinking of things beyond and remote, from which the conversation brusquely summons him back to earth. But he is a listener and an observer – he has the observer's habit of staring – rather than a propounder and expatiator, and his trancelike eyes will see more deeply through, and record more essential matter about, us than this verbosity of mine is doing about him. At the same time, his sense of humor is very ready. He maintains a chronic or semi-permanent smile (a network of small creases about the mouth), supplementing it with giggles and an occasional full-throttle laugh, during which the tongue lolls. (This happens as he tells a story of why he is no longer invited to Charlie Chaplin's: "Someone told him I had peed on his sofa one night while I was plastered.") But he is not at ease in spite of the drollery. Underneath – for he is as multi-layered as a *mille* (which in practice is rarely more than a *huit* or a *dix*) *feuilles* – are fears, the uppermost of which might well be of a musical conversation or high general conversation about The Arts. But I could be miles off. Perhaps he is merely suffering from the prohibition rule of the Farmers' Market, and in this case the contents of I.S.'s thermos bottles will come as an agreeable surprise.

Isherwood brings greetings to All-deuce (as he pronounces it) from a Swami. The voice, both in pitch and volume, is somewhat too high, and the words are too deliberated. Aldous, replying, digresses to make room for a ribald story, which Isherwood follows like an eager schoolboy, exclaiming, "Oh boy!" once, and rubbing his knees in anticipation of the outcome. He also says "heck!" "swell" "by golly!" "gosh!" and "gee-whiz!"

How do the two men regard each other apart from their evident mutual affection? Isherwood cannot match the softly orating Huxleyan delivery or the Huxleyan intellectual ammunition (a stunning aside on the "haeccities of the later Persian mystics," an apt quote from the *Biathanatos*, and the most recent information about amino acids and cellular differentiation). But then, the younger man has made his name partly because of his wariness of fluency at supernal intellectual altitudes. Is he mildly baiting the sage, perhaps, gently tweaking his nose a bit by that overly credulous way of asking those further questions about the marvelous, the horrendous, and the barely believable that loom so large in the older man's talk? Or does he regard him as ever so slightly unbalanced from too much book learning? Not really deranged, of course, like Don Quixote, but a bit "off" nevertheless?

And am I wrong in sensing just the faintest tinge of doubt on the Huxley side as to the hundred per cent impregnability of his younger colleague's spiritual dedication and final severance from The World? And in detecting just the hint of a suspicion that one last unburned boat may still be hidden somewhere in the reeds? We suppose, in any case it is the I.S.'s impression as well as my own – that the younger man is obliged to apply himself to those spiritual exercises which the older man masters merely by turning his mind to them. But while the Huxley universe is the larger of the two, the author does not sit more securely in the center of it than the author of the Isherwood books does in the center of the Isherwood universe. Partly for this reason, it is more of an encounter to meet Isherwood than to meet Aldous, though another reason is simply that most of us are little more than enchanted audiences to Aldous, not because he wills it that way, but because we have no choice. Finally, whatever the truth of these speculations, how improbable a team the two of them make to represent Vedanta in the Wild West!

I.S., as I know him, is even less comfortable than Isherwood. He dislikes being outnumbered by Englishmen speaking their language, and these particular Englishmen probably seem to him too freely, richly verbal, for in I.S.'s book the important things must never be, cannot be, said. But I.S. presents an almost exaggerated contrast in other ways as well: in, for instance, his deep diapason (versus their duet of flute-stops); in his love of concreteness (the Englishmen's talk about religion must seem abstract to him, for he believes in the physical existence of the Devil and his Infernal Regions, as at one time people believed in centaurs and mermaids); and in the autocracy and absoluteness of his views, though these can seem more extreme than they are because of his imperfect command of the flutey language's syntactic qualifying paraphernalia.

I would exchange some, if less than half, of my kingdom for a peek at the picture these two observers draw of I.S. Will they discover that the barricade of epigrams, paradoxes, *bons mots*, conceals nothing at all in their line, the line of "intellect"? Or will they conclude that the treasures are being kept to the deeps out of reticence, to be surfaced again on other, more favored days? Whatever the answer, and both conclusions would be wrong, the polite side of I.S., that Bellona's armor of will in the man and of style in the music ("Music may symbolize, but it cannot express"), is the only side anyone except V. ever sees.

Why, then, have so many people mistaken I.S. for an "intellectual"? Primarily, I think, because it was his own preferred image of himself. He is vain of his "factual knowledge," and would actually like to be regarded as a mere *summa* of erudition, the wielder of the ultimate gavel of sophisticated judgment. Nor will he tolerate such terms as "instinct" and "genius" in regard to himself, pretending instead that "brains" and "technique," meaning the mastery of means and the perfection of the ear, constitute the composer's full equipment. "Emotions," I hardly need to add, are scarcely allowed to be an ingredient. Moreover, he seems to think of the affective functions as physiologically zoned, like the separation of emotion and intelligence in Comte's *tableau cérébral*.

Little as it matters, I.S.'s intellectual world apart from music has been formed to an unusual extent by his intimates. He is in fact radically susceptible to personal influence, which I say because I can see the reactive effects that I myself have had on him. (V. has said that I am the only friend in his adult life who has disagreed with him and survived, which is a dubious distinction both as to conduct and as to consequence.) For my own part, and though it hardly requires saying, I entertain few if any fixed views capable of withstanding "rigorous intellectual investigation" (I am a "feeler" rather than a "thinker," myself), and I certainly want no responsibility for any of them, musical or otherwise, settling on such a man. But the point is I.S.'s susceptibility, not *whose* view.

NOVEMBER 14, 1967

Finally, a criminal eight weeks late, I.S. is given an arterial injection of radioactive phosphorus, by a doctor in a rubber suit and what might be a welder's helmet. Three nurses, like the three queens accompanying Arthur to Avalon, wheel the patient to a lead-lined room in the basement, and immediately afterwards a thrice-daily series of abdominal and subcutaneous heparin injections is begun.

The mental wanderings are even worse than yesterday. Before the trip to the x-ray room, he asks us to look after his wallet, which he has not had on his person since long before the hospital. (This may be no more than a habit of concern about his pocket valuables when disrobing for x-rays in the past.) But on the return to the room, he asks if we have "enough *Frantzuski Geld* to tip the porters." When dinner comes, moreover, he insists on eating from his own tray, thinking himself in his room at home, and when V. says that it isn't there, he points to where she can find it. Then as we leave for dinner ourselves, he asks to come to the restaurant with us. He will be able to do that very soon, I tell him. But after considering this for a moment he replies, heartbreakingly, "Oh, I realize I am not able to eat with you, but I could watch." He also begs to be taken for a "promenade" in the car. And no doubt troubled by his mistake in thinking he was home, he asks how it is there now. Very bad, I say, for we miss him all the time. "You remember how you used to describe us as a '*trio con brio*'? Well, please hurry and get well so we can be one again."

He has a period of hallucinations – a heparin side effect, the doctors say – apprehending people who are not present but failing to see us and his nurses when we are only inches away. Once he asks why there are two watches on his right wrist from which even the one has now been removed. His comments, in Russian, V. says, are "nonsensical" and "delirious," which greatly upsets her; nor is she impressed by my argument that this unreality is better for him now than the truth. Then suddenly, in the midst of the rambling, he drops a remark showing such a perfect sense of reality that we know that underneath it all his mind is holding on tight. Overhearing us mention a music critic whose name has not come up in years, he wants to know whether the said critic is dead or alive. "Dead," V. says, but I.S. is suspicious. "No, he is probably alive and in Argentina."

His mind seems to be divided into two parts, of which only the part dealing with the outer world and the present is confused. But this, too, is natural, given the disruption of his time sense by medicine schedules and drugs, and the dislocation as a consequence of staring at hospital walls, not, after all, so unlike the walls of his bedroom at home.

The other, the creative part of the mind, appears to be unaffected. In the evening, during one of his lucid spells, I tell him that the BBC would like him to compose from six to ten seconds of music which, together with a multicolored eye by Picasso, would form the signature of a new color-television channel. The creative mind instantly seizes the idea and moves ahead with it like a prow. "The limitation to six seconds rules out chords, as well as rhythms in any conventional sense, though many notes can be used at once. But an eye means transparency, which means in turn that the sound should be produced by very high instruments, possibly flutes, compared with which oboes are greasy and clarinets oily."

I leaf through a book of Watteau drawings with him, but he complains that the reproductions do not show scale. And he is annoyed by a phrase in the commentary about the new sophistication in the appreciation of Watteau at present. "Whatever comes later is more sophisticated," he says "which later-comers should remember as they look forward, as well as back."

NOVEMBER 20

"Where are you?" he asks, hearing me enter the room this morning, and as I approach the bed, he puts his good hand to my face as if he were totally blind. He is so heavily drugged, too, that he speaks only at great intervals. "How long will it last?" he says at one point, and again, "How much longer?" Then for the first time in all these months: "I don't want to live this way." I try to make him believe that he will soon be home and composing, but he nods his head weakly toward his left hand, saying: "I need my hand; I am maimed in my hand." I am more worried about his eyes, however, and most worried of all about the amount of fight left in him. Already, as the Duke of Albany says in *Lear,* "The oldest hath borne most."

NOVEMBER 23

It is Thanksgiving Day in the most wonderful way possible, for the long-prayed-for miracle has happened. The finger color has returned to normal, and I.S. has not complained of pain or taken painkiller in seventy-two hours. His sight is not restored, and he is unable to distinguish faces in what, as he describes it, seems to be a dioramic blur; but his eyes turn rapidly toward and focus quickly on us. He sits in a chair for a while, too, which makes him look much thinner than in the bed. And while he is up, his daughter reads to him, and is quickly pounced on for mistakes in Russian pronunciation. Incredible man! Only three days ago he was in a semi-coma, his left hand a half-silted estuary of gangrene, his body worn out by months of sickness and pain, through which, however, and as Suvchinsky said, he himself was a torch. And now he has come out of it, actually recrossing the Styx. "How much is it costing?" he asks me suddenly, and in all these weeks no words have sounded so good. I.S. is back in decimal-system reality. Thank God.

He is pepped up – from glucose – jumpy, brittle, anxious, ready to fly off the handle at any and everything. "I have had enough medical philosophy," he informs his most discursive physician, and to a nurse who advises him to "Relax," his retort is: "What? And leave the driving to *you*?" He is suffering drug withdrawal, of course, and a mountain of after-effects. But I like the friction.

V. is ill and in bed today. Her own diagnosis is 'flu, but I think "battle fatigue" would be more accurate. The crisis last weekend was too much for her, and she has kept her fear too long inside.

NOVEMBER 28

I bring I.S. home at noon, his departure having been delayed by requests for autographs from every nurse on the floor, which he gives, of course, embellishing some of them with musical notations. Outdoors, out at last from that stultifying hospital, he looks as pale as junket and, dressed in a suit, terribly thin, shrunken, and frail.

As I help him from the car into the house, he says that it must seem to me as if I am "towing a wreck." But weak as he is, he props himself on the couch and will not go to bed. Contemptuous of medicines now, he balks at his quarter-hourly doses of milk. "Milk is the Jesus Christ of the affair," he says, to which profanity V. responds with: "Now at least we see how much better you are." But he is not having any of that. "Not better, bitter," he corrects. Then, to divert him, V. plays patience and asks him to keep the tally for her in his head. His scores, she says – not meaning any pun – are perfect.

He asks for today's newspaper (which says that Zadkine, another coeval, has died) and the post. The latter contains Malraux's *Anti-Mémoires*, with the author's dedication: "*Pour* Igor Stravinsky, *avec mon admiration fidèle.* " But I.S. jumps on this. "When was he ever *'fidèle'*? He said once that music is a minor art." And so I.S. is still I.S.

Later in the day, when the doctors call to congratulate themselves, he flummoxes them, too, as he has done at every stage, telling them that "The finger and the eyes are from the same cause." The chief neurosurgeon corroborates this to me privately, in fact, saying that not one but three thromboses occurred just before that tardy radioactive phosphorus, and that some peripheral vision in the left eye is permanently lost. At the moment, however, I.S. is distressed less by the damage to his eye than by a gas pain; and when the doctors seek to remind him that he has not suffered alone, he snaps at them with "Maybe, but you don't have this gas pain." (Apostrophizing them later, he remarks that "It was very well-paid suffering for them.") But he is beginning to talk like a doctor himself. "Is the pain merely spasmodic," he asks, "or could it be organic?" One of the medics, in parting, tells him that "Healing takes longer at eighty-five, Mr. Stravinsky," but I.S. turns on this with "Damn eighty-five."

He watches *Daktari* in V.'s room tonight, but tosses and turns in his bed afterward, tormented, he says, about the state of his mind. At eleven o'clock I go to V. to see if she is all right, and find her in her dark room, quietly crying, tears streaming down her face. Not once during the whole ordeal did she ever lose control, and only now is it clear that she had begun to lose belief and was only continuing to pray that he would ever be home again. After an hour of trying to talk her into some "peace of mind," I am summoned by the night nurse to help with I.S., who is not asleep in spite of his pills. I try to fake some more good cheer with him, but he says he is "in a bad way psychologically." When I leave him he answers my last inane "Please stop worrying" with "I am not worrying any more, only waiting," which wrenching remark kills the possibility of any sleep of my own. "Old people are attached to life," Sophocles says, condemning it as a fault.

DECEMBER 1

Hallelujah! The platelets have fallen to 900,000, and the white count – "my blood policemen," as I.S. tells it, though he is also using such nonmetaphorical terms as oenosyllophyl – is down to 17,000, from 37,000 only a few days ago. His diet is less strict now, too, and henceforth the taste of milk can be cut with larger swigs of scotch. This news raises I.S. out of the apathy – black melancholy, rather – into which he had fallen the day after his homecoming, when he had apparently expected to be able to skip rope. After dinner we listen to Opus 131 and the *Dichterliebe*, the first music heard in the house since he entered the hospital. And with the music he comes to life, grunting agreement with Beethoven at numerous moments in the quartet and beating time with his left hand, which is protected by an outsized mitten, like the claw of a fiddler crab. Whereas he has been unable to read words, his eyes travel easily with the score (being guided by a quite exceptional "ear").

DECEMBER 6

It is a marvelous day, brilliantly sunny and warm although the San Bernardino Mountains glitter like Kilimanjaro with new snow. But my leave-taking is the hardest I have ever had to go through. It will only be a few days, I tell I.S., and I blame his music as the reason for the trip in the first place. To which he says, "*Je crache sur ma musique.*"

8021 Jovenita Canyon Rd. (Laurel Canyon)

Robert Crosson (1929–)

Born in Canonsburg, Pennsylvania in 1929, he came to Pomona, California as a teenager. He graduated from Pomona High School in 1947, and received his BA in English from UCLA in 1951. For several years he was a professional actor in radio, television and films. As Crosson later described his odyssey to writing: "In 1956 I made my first and only trip to Europe where, lacking funds to pay my return fare, I was employed (in Mallorca) as a piano player, black marketeer and pimp for eight (international) prostitutes. In 1960 returned to UCLA to do postgraduate work in Library Science but dropped out: to take a job as a dishwasher at a local café, and write my first novel (unpublished)."

His first book was the long poem *Geographies* (Red Hill Press, 1981), followed by *Abandoned Latitudes* (with John Thomas & Paul Vangelisti, Red Hill, 1983), *Calliope* (Illumi-nati Press, 1988),

The Blue Soprano (a bilingual edition with artist William Xerra, ML&NLF, Milano, 1994) and, most recently, a poetry chapbook *In the Aethers of the Amazon* (Seeing Eye Books, 1998). In 1980 his radio play, *The Party: a Reunion* was produced by the Los Angeles Theater of the Ear (LATE) for KPFK Radio.

Crosson's work was included in the Los Angeles anthology *Poetry Loves Poetry* (ed. Bill Mohr, Momentum Press, 1985) and, in 1989, he was awarded a poetry fellowship by the California Arts Council.

THE DAY SAM GOLDWYN STEPPED OFF THE TRAIN

inside wot? he thot, incorruptible?
no films that long anyway except gone with the wind
best known as a martha raye song when she sung jazz
or the wizard of oz & we all know where that went.
boxoffice gold brick roads did vast service to.

put moons in skies where there ws none
& turned stanford's pig's-ear into a goldmine
a fool a minute dont give a sucker an even break
them bad years people wanted ginger rogers to believe in
flying down to anyplace without an airticket
free for a dime with taps and dancing girls
on the wings.

class my ass,
try canoeing the colorado rapids without an oar
up at dawn to get the sun right (inside wot? he thot
incorruptible) coming back to the tent at night
too tired to get dressed for dinner.

Robert Crosson

Chapter One

The letters come to me by accident.
A friend needed cash & sold them at a bargain.
This was history, I told myself (money maybe,
but you don't kiss nobody's ass for nothing):
how the hell to make a story of it? Who the
Sam Goldwyn, which the Muybridge? Letters lied.
Maybe a movie. Pictures made sense, I sez to myself,
who needs to read? That horse-trotting ws Stanford,
governor of California: you can't prove horses race
all fours off the ground, you don't get yr paycheck.
Was the railroad made it happen.
Houdini cdnt done better.
    To hell with the chinamen.

as the man sez: talk straight
straight man or chorus line stand on that rock
Of a morning, out there waiting no chink would crow to
one picture is worth ten-thousand crackups fly
upsidedown

try barreling off niagra on a sled sometime
once across the border they want to see yr emigration
papers.

hortense powdermaker you needed, let's face it
all you have to do is look at neveda city
dickens over from england and read mark twain
embellishing the frog, likewise left happy wife
& family (in a photograph

stood on that damned mountain half the morning
& had to work with glass

the 49th parallel is a high rock with a guy standing
in leggings and boots
a young uncle hanged with his shoes tied

all you have to do is look at nevada city
first concession of course is to discount literacy
carnegie did it with steel mills
inside wot? he thot
(cantering

Chapter Two
One has to be careful here.
The 49th parallel is a high rock with a guy in leggings and boots. This photograph was shot at 6/30 am without breakfast.

twelve fools a minute saddled up that boardwalk
incorruptible? big bucks is where the country goes
a man needs vision.

dickens read mark twain with a high rock standing
you riding across them plains in a smoker
never once bothered to look out the window

first-class letters posted sentence & paragraph
them guys knew where the buck is
they built the railroad

mud and mosquitoes
four-mile trestles with ties and trackbed
read up & down

all chinamen.

Scene Three

Died.
Day after the war, Willie-Rose-Bud Hearst
opens east wing of his Roman swimming pool.
A man is shot, boat capsizes: Esther Williams
opens another restaurant, helicopters can't get in.
Giraffes rampage the lumberyard.

hortense powdermaker reads mark twain
embellishing the frog left happy wife
and family in a photograph
his granddaughter wound up
at arms hotel on highland avenue.

Synopsis

Sam runs for mayor: Muybridge supports. Chinese restaurants become unfashionable. Health-food stores proliferate... Eastman Kodak turns its back. Sam wins by a narrow margin... Police on horse-back run down whores on Sunset Boulevard... Sam is shot. The pope rallies. Iranians take over Beverly Hills. The City Council disbands streetcars; in-cinerators become a bond issue. Sam writes a musical. People are ransomed at airports. Burbank housewives

are flown to Rochester. Political candidates support
harpsichord concerts. Theater owners host barbeques
in back yards. Kodak wins. Sam, run out as an entertainer,
retires to the Valley. His rock opera is a success.

nina gabrilowitsch is found dead on somebody's
front steps in laguna.

kennedy dies, Weyerhauser plants trees.
everybody jogs

P.O. Box 138, Santa Monica

Edward Dahlberg (1900–1977)

"I was born," wrote Dahlberg, "in the Barren Grounds, where love is stunted as a lichen. What passes for erudition, but is void of affection, is hemlock. Therefore, I live in exile among the frigid swarm. Long ago I would have perished had I not pined for absolutes, though they do not exist. (It is told by Eunapius, the ancient biographer, that Plotinus saw the Absolute four times.)"

Edward Dahlberg was born in Boston in 1900 to a single mother, who struggled to support him as a child, eventually sending him to the Jewish Orphan Asylum in Cleveland, where he spent most of his adolescence. "I have been true to my past in that I have always been an orphan," he noted years later.

Dahlberg worked as a messenger for Western Union in Cleveland and in Kansas City, hoboed around the West (settling in Los Angeles for a time), and endured a brief stint in the Army before enrolling at the University of California at Berkeley. He transferred to Columbia University where he graduated in 1925 with a BS in Philosophy.

He lived in New York, Paris, Monte Carlo, and Brussels before his first book, *Bottom Dogs*, was published in 1930. *The Sorrows of Priapus* was published in 1957. About the book, Dahlberg observed: "I had been shackled to the *Sorrows* since 1951, beginning to study for it in New York; I continued it at Topanga Canyon and Santa Monica, again taking up the *Sorrows* in Berkeley, where it rained for eight months. (I recommend horrid weather for the writer, for then he has nothing else to do but meditate.) By the time I had finished it, I fainted and fell on the floor, which reminds me of the fabled pelican, who nourishes fledglings with her own blood."

from *The Sorrows of Priapus* (1957)

Man must be classed among the brutes, for he is still a very awkward and salacious biped. What shape he will assume in the future is vague. There are many traits of early man he has lost, and it is plain that he is much more given to falsehood, robbery and lawsuits than the primitive. The first two-legged man scratched himself because he had an itch. Men now lie and steal for pleasure. Primeval natures wallowed without thought, but soon as men began thinking how pleasant it was to rub themselves and to have deliriums from mud, they employed their minds to achieve what paleolithic mankind did without being lascivious.

Men lie, not alone for profit, but to root in Circe's mire. No pigmy or cave-dweller wears more bizarre or dirty raiment than present-day man. He is often as offensive as the gland on the back of the Brazil peccary. He would rather tell a lie than the truth because his sole purpose is to be a grub.

He is the most ridiculous beast on the earth, and the reason for this is his mind and his pudendum. He sacks nations, or throws away his reason to see the petticoat of Aspasia or Helen empurpled by murex or the lichen at Madeira. The procreative organ in the camel is behind, but in man it is in front, and unless he is too fat to look over his belly, he pays more attention to this gibbous organ than to his arms, his talus, or anything else. He frequently forgets how his arms look, and is surprised to find a wen on his jaw, and he rarely knows whether his pupils are brown or ochreous, but he is always mindful of his testes hanging between his legs like folly.

In the Book of Enoch the scribe says that the first two-legged creatures had the private parts of great studs, and it may well be that Methuselah and Jared and Mahalalel were mountains and that from their middle hung hills which were their organs of generation. Otherwise, it is impossible for one to imagine how they could live for nine hundred years without wearing out their genitals. It is known that Og, King of Bashan, had an iron bedstead seven cubits long, and that the giants of Anak had six fingers.

Adam bare stones long before he begat Seth. Human life began as procreative mud, and later man was a shark with a human face. There was a human species with a lion's mouth and the legs of a giraffe, for anterior to the neolithic period diverse animals mingled. Many of our traits are found in the countenance of the bear and in the lip of the pard. The story that the pigmies were chased from the River Strymon by cranes is also a fable of our bird origin.

The old gods were ocean, rivers, animals, fish, birds; Noah was a fish, and Plato supposed that Oceanus was the father of Saturn, and there is as much natural history in this as mythology. Men and rivers are demigods and beasts; the Scamander is the river's mortal name; Zeus called the fierce water Xanthus; in the *Iliad* it is reported that the bird, said to be named *chalcis* by the gods, was Cymindis among men. This is the heroic conception of human fate.

Pleasure brings about the most violent transport in men, and of all the animals in the earth none is so brutish as man when he seeks the delirium of coition. Democritus of Abdera, unable to bear being stung by any female foot in sandals, or round skirt, was said to have plucked out his eyes. He was as mad as a boar for the shape of Venus; when the testicles of the boar are swollen he is at times so beside himself that he rubs them against a tree until he is castrated. The female deer hates copulation because the penis of the stag is as tough and spinous as a palm leaf; the pain the stag gives her is considerable but she cannot overcome her passion for him.

One marvels what man will do to have his skin scraped. Antony lay with Cleopatra at Daphne for this foolishness, and though he gave all his force to her, his delights were not as long as those of the ordinary fly. One cannot submit a little to sexual excitement without hankering after more such raptures. When birds are continent their testes are internal, but after sexual intercourse the penis is very conspicuous.

Whether man is more lecherous than the partridge is doubtful, but he is not as chaste as the raven, who bleeds from the eyes during coition. The man of sensibility is not satisfied with ordinary coupling; all the arts of Lais of Corinth cannot furnish his skin and veins with the infinite sensations he demands. Pain affords him infatuate happiness unknown to four-legged creatures. He is almost the only animal that cohabits at all times. With the exception of the pigeon, a bird which abstains only a few days in the year, man has the most lickerish tail of all beasts. This has made him very unruly, and double in his words and deeds. Unlike the elephant he has no seasons for his venery. This pachyderm, after impregnating the female, avoids this excitement for two years.

The elephant is an exemplary teacher. It is in many respects a rational animal, and repents of its anger, which is rare among men; when it kills its master, it grieves and sometimes starves to death. The dam suckles her young six years, and many elephants live as long as people. When an elephant is sick he is given wine to drink, and when he has an eye disease, these warm, friendly orbs are bathed in cow's milk. His wounds are healed by butter. These are the simples that the Homeric heroes gave to each other at Troy, and the poet of the *Iliad*, as well as Plato, would have paid the tenderest regard to this superior beast whose diet, medicines and habits are far better than those of the vast multitudes in the earth. The elephant, doubtless, was no less a monitor than the heifer which is so often seen beside the seated Buddha.

Countless adulteries are committed without lust, and with no thought to the peril which attends this folly. Animals do not give each other the pox; when men attempt to lie with a beast it rejects the malady that is said to be the companion of human genius. The adulterer is more sense less than the earthworm who keeps part of his tail in the hole he inhabits when copulating so he can disappear at once should he see an adversary. The tibulae hide in the hedges all day, and seek the delights of the female at dusk.

Most people are furtive, but very few are ashamed; the elephant prefers to copulate near an obscure river bank, and the camel retires to the desert to rut. Modesty has been undermined because it is not generally known that the camel, more continent in his thoughts than a modern vestal, requires a whole day to complete such exercises.

Few labor for anything else but to exchange their sexual properties with blowsy dowds, or to rival the fox which has a bony penis: even the impotent are like the aged boar who waits for the tired female to lie down before he will risk his feeble appendage.

When the camel opens its mouth it looks like the greatest ass, though the ancients made the strongest bowstrings out of its pudendum. The egg of the *sepia* pretends to be black myrtle seeds; the vine the polypus deposits is its ovum.

The rhyades remain quiet until the equinox, and the grasshopper is said to sit upon the olive and reeds when it casts its skin, but man now stays in one place only long enough to void or feed. His irregular habits and haste make him the inferior of the polypi which unite only in winter, and these creatures conceal themselves for this reason for two months.

The tortoise gives a month to coition. The moose cannot have commerce with a red deer that is too short, but men and women of sundry sizes are suitable to each other. Andromache had too long a body, but not for Hector. Nubian dwarfs were ravishing morsels in Egypt. The pigmies who rode on the backs of partridges, which was a way of saying they were concupiscent, satisfied the giantesses of the Thermodon.

The puma never utters a cry when he mingles with the female. Bucks and does herd separately after the rutting season; man is incontinent whenever he has the occasion.

Men are more obscure to themselves than the elm or marine shells. The *solens* perish after they have been taken away from their borning place; the fir is comely in the sun, and the cedar is a Saul in the mountains. Man does not know when he should plant, or from whom he can glean, or what town is his stony Medusa. The *sepia* deposit their ova near the river Thermodon, for its waters are warm and potable; the eels seek reedy ponds, and the pregnant red mullet lies among the rockweed. Paul the Fourth was an ascetic until his eightieth year, but when he became pope, he sported for hours at table as any mare in heat.

Men are too unstable to be just; they are crabbed because they have not passed water at the usual time, or testy because they have not been stroked or praised. The habits of animals can be ascertained better than the mien of a philosopher. When stags are bitten by the *phalangius* they eat crabs and are healed, but if a man has had a poor or dour sleep, he is waspish the whole day, and is likely to curse his parents.

There are certain fish that only breed in the Pontus, and many of the tunnies run to the Pillars to spawn. The *halcyon* appears only at the setting of the Pleiades and during the solstice. The crocodile is a modest brute whose penis and testicles are internal, and he could be regarded the peer of saints did he keep these members there. The polypus hides its ova in holes which is a lesson for modern women who, when they are with child, go through the streets showing the results of their shame. When the mare wants to sport with the stallion she makes water. But this lubricous mammal is continent compared with man, and he eats herbs, barley and oats which is a diet similar to the sacred table of Pythagoras. One has to travel to India to find a savant as herbivorous and savory as this extraordinary brute.

We scoff at Alexander for burying his horse Bucephalus, but the stone of that stallion shows that he had the separate toes of a human being, and this monument stands in front of the temple of Venus Genetrix. Bucephalus was so named because of the breadth of its head. Plato means wide forehead, and it is interesting to add that the philosopher came of the family of Hippias who were horsemen. The horse is so marvelous to behold that Semiramis was seized with the wildest passions when looking upon this carnal beast.

The horse goes mad pasturing by himself; separated from the human flock man loses his reason. Nietzsche, the wildest intellect of his century, lived in solitude, a Dionysiac disease which in crazy horses was known as the hippomania. In his last Bacchic throes he flung his insane arms about a horse standing in the gutters of Turin.

No one but a perverse person takes exception to horse manure. Droppings of many animals are more healthful than those of people. Human dung, except that of primitive races, is unclean. When the stag's horns are most perfect he has a very offensive odor; unlike man, who wears the same skin all his life, the stag casts his horns, the bird moults, and the despised python sloughs off his vile coat; man's despair is that he smells; he is garbed in the same skin until he rots in the tomb.

The Aztecs sold pots of human excrement for working their leather. Civilized nations regarded primitive man as a savory beast. The ancients, having the highest esteem for the offal of kine, said the oxen of the Sun were stalled near the Ocean where the seascum resembled dung.

Man imagines that because he stands on his legs he is intellectual, but the penguin is a biped who feeds until he can scarcely move; the bear too can stand up. Man's passion for disorder, upheaval and bedlam explains his greed. He attempts to prove that whatever man does is for his advantage. This is not true of him, and sometimes quadrupeds, generally reasonable, are demented or perverse. It is fabled that the mongoose breaks the eggs which the crocodile hatches in the mud though it does not eat them nor derive profit from this act. Man's neck is as long as Plutus: Solomon said, his eyes cannot be filled with seeing nor his ears with hearing. He is so bored that he seeks the naive existence of the sow. Having devoured all the experiences possible to the biped, he now wants to be primitive which he thinks is the same as being chaotic, torpid, or supine the whole day. Baudelaire asserted that he had the wildest desire to be aboriginal, because standing on two legs was too trivial and average for him. Man imagines that could he crawl again as an infant or as any brute in the field, he could recapture a primeval existence. Others are only content with the testicles of animals. Could man moult his skin as the bird its feathers, and have new flesh, he would be innocent. The stag casts his horns every year, and the horse may lose his hoof, but each acquires what he has shed. When the teeth or the hair of men decay, they do not grow the tusks they show whenever they desire sexual frenzies, or the hair that makes them prance and sport and neigh. Were it possible for man to shed his feet or his hands he could have a naive heart.

Man pines to live but cannot endure the days of his life. The learned, crouched over their inkspots, covet the customs of the savage who cohabits with a Lais or Aspasia of the Amazons whenever he pleases, or envy the panther. The poet want to be an animal. "Submit, my heart, sleep the sleep of the brute," said Charles Baudelaire.

Men have more sorrow from their entrails than animals; except backward people or ancient races they have fewer rites pertaining to their ordure. They excrete when they are bored or want a savage pleasure. The father of Beatrice Cenci drew the close-stool over to the fireplace and voided in the presence of his wife and daughter.

The Mohammedan of the old order wipes his buttocks with his left hand since he uses the right one to handle food, plant vines, or to greet people. A Moslem woman can divorce a man with a reeking breath, a fault unknown among the natives of Otaheite. Modern man rushes to the water closet, and after the most summary ablutions, extends his hand to the first person he meets. The ancient Essenes had strict tenets regarding defecation and its burial in secret places. Man at present dungs in his own house and considers himself a delicate creature.

The anthropoid is arrogant, and when he finds a remedy for a malady that is the consequence of a cormorant throat he is elated. Tantalus can never eat or drink enough countries, rivers, or carcasses, and this gluttony is the cause of nearly all human woes.

When the sow has a certain disease, it goes to the mulberry for relief, and when the horse falls into a declining melancholy, the sound of the flute will assuage this fever for which men have found no nostrum. The river horse, after overeating, comes ashore and presses its hide against the sharp rushes until blood flows from a vein in the leg. When ill the stork sups upon marjoram; and stags also, in failing health, graze upon wild artichoke. The pigeon has exquisite revulsions, and at times disrelishes his table as much as men, and then turns to bay leaves for food.

Despite all the spital houses in the world, if a man suffers from strangury, can he do much more than the Sudanese who entreat their idols to let them urinate without difficulty? If it please Zeus may we pass water; to prevent chafing, if Cato be true, put a small branch of Pontic wormwood under the anus.

Socrates described love as the sting of a tarantula. We see that desire dominates the old as well as youth; the senile forget to button their clothes, and leave the door of their trousers ajar, showing what is no more than a relic of a quondam tower. Men lose their goatish powers long before their minds; Montaigne complained that when he was somewhere in his fifties he could not raise that sleepy animal more than three times a week.

The anthropoid is more luckless and unintelligent than animals, and the remedy for his ills is not progress, going forward, which is always to his grave, but turning backwards. He has extirpated most of the beasts which he no longer has as tutors. As a result he does not know whether to cohabit with woman, with man, or with sheep, and there are some who are enormously aroused by the sight of a mare. There is a breed of dog that will copulate with a wolf, and it is believed that a species of dog is derived from the tiger, and there is the Babylonian cameleopard; but, for the most part, the stallion seeks the female of its kind, and the elephant hankers after the same sort of animal that bore him.

Man is more incoherent than any beast in the earth. Schopenhauer has said that pleasure is the absence of pain, but it is not true. Man is not content with negative delights or even with positive transports. Some of his immoral deeds lacerate him, and he finds much satisfaction in being wounded. Man hates what he does, and that is what is moral in him, but he continues to do it, which is why he is Euripides, a spider, or the *Dryophis fulgida*. Man lies in ambush for all creatures, for he is the hunter; the Psalmist cries out that he is the turtledove about to be devoured by the multitude.

The whelp is most greedy for the soul that has fallen down to the ground. In the Psalms the soul flees to a hiding place in the mountains. The prophet rides upon a Cherub who is one of the fowls of the air. Man who is the master of the sheep and the oxen has the tender feet of the hind. He crouches before the bulls of Bashan and dreads man continually. But a little while he is a tree planted by the rivers of water, for all lurk in lairs to harm his branches.

Man is either too stupid or vain to know himself, and too self-loving to understand anyone. He cannot endure his own vices in others, and he is least just when he is railing at the faults of people.

Man is the tragic brute because he can never be as sure of others as the ass or the bull who knows that he is the booty of the wolf. A strong foe is better than a weak friend; the heron is always on guard against the eagle; the *anthus* is a reliable opponent of the horse since both covet the pasture. The deer when it has produced the fawn hides, for she knows what beast will hurt it. The wolf is the enemy of the ass, bull and fox; a mountain cat will embowel a porcupine; in a narrow defile the panther will leap upon a small dog instead of a human being. Men have no such certainties, and the more erudite they are the fewer companions they have. Aristotle in his old age said, "O my friends, there is no friend."

Everything in man is double because he has testes. The old Nile god had the form of a man with a woman's breast wearing a cluster of water plants. The Egyptians extracted from the meanest worm the paint to design jars and the sacred, funeral amphorae. In the time of the Pharaohs dense thickets were said to be the resort of malefactors. This was a proverb, and yet among the Quiché Mayans the gods were seated in the ravines, the forests and among the mosses. Not everyone that goes into the wilderness is Elijah or John.

If one considers the acts of his youth he wonders why he was ever young; or if he ponders his later vices he asks himself why he is still alive. In what manner is Messalina superior to the puma, or is anyone any better than a beetle which takes such pleasure in the fungus, called the English phallus, which has a most odious smell. The testicles of the American lizard give off a musky odor, and the monkeys in Brazil when stroked have as pleasant a scent as Alexander of Macedon. Priam had fifty bedchambers, and despite such opulent amorous experiences had no more sense than to select as his consort the termagant Hecuba. Solomon's bed linen was fragrant with Sheba and the perspiration of a hundred concubines, but were they any dearer to the nostrils than the musky testes of the lizard? There is a paradox: the Egyptians claimed that their land was infested with scorpions until it was settled by Apis. The serpent in Eden gave Eve knowledge of the phallus, and this is the source of art, science, poetry, wisdom, and perfidy.

We weep because the human race is no better than it is. The aquatic frog has the tail of a fish until he makes a twig or a blade of grass his house, then he loses his tail and grows legs. Nature advises the frog far better than man; a noddle endeavors to employ faculties he does not possess, and the eunuch burns for Jezebel.

Where is Apollo who rested his foot on the skull of an ox; where are the wild horses, the fawn, the roe, the cubs of bears that were brought to the altars of Artemis? Shall we wed, or woo, or tremble?

Ralphs Market, Sunset & Fuller (Hollywood)

Joan Didion (1935–)

Joan Didion grew up in Sacramento. The land on which she was raised had belonged to her family for five generations. "In what way does the Holy Land resemble the Sacramento Valley?" Didion was asked by her Episcopalian Sunday school teacher. The answer: "In the type and diversity of its agricultural products."

Didion was taught an intense revisionist history that viewed the founding of California as an heroic act. In "Notes from A Native Daughter" she wrote: "Such a view of history casts a certain melancholia over those who participate in it; my own childhood was suffused with the conviction that we had long outlived our finest hour."

In 1964, Didion moved from New York to Los Angeles with her husband, writer John Gregory Dunne. They lived in a rented house on Franklin Avenue until 1971, when they moved to Trancas, 40 miles north of Los Angeles on the Pacific Coast. In

1978, they moved to Brentwood Park, California, before eventually returning to New York.

In her essay "The White Album," she writes: "I was living in a large house in a part of Hollywood that had once been expensive and was now described by one of my acquaintances as a 'senseless-killing neighborhood.' This house on Franklin Avenue was rented, and paint peeled inside and out, and pipes broke and window sashes crumbled and the tennis court had not been rolled since 1933, but the rooms were many and high-ceilinged and, during the five years that I lived there, even the rather sinistral inertia of the neighborhood tended to suggest that I should live in the house indefinitely."

from *Play It As It Lays* (1970)

CHAPTER 35

"I don't know if you noticed, I'm mentally ill," the woman said. The woman was sitting next to Maria at the snack counter in Ralph's Market. "I'm talking to you."

Maria turned around. "I'm sorry."

"I've been mentally ill for seven years. You don't know what a struggle it is to get through a day like this."

"This is a bad day for you," Maria said in a neutral voice.

"What's so different about this day."

Maria looked covertly at the pay phones but there was still a line. The telephone in the apartment was out of order and she had to report it. The line at the pay phones in Ralph's Market suddenly suggested to Maria a disorganization so general that the norm was to have either a disconnected telephone or some clandestine business to conduct, some extramarital error. She had to have a telephone. There was no one to whom she wanted to talk but she had to have a telephone. If she could not be reached it would happen, the peril would find Kate. Beside her the woman's voice rose and fell monotonously.

"I mean you can't fathom the despair. Believe me I've thought of ending it. Kaput. Over. Head in the oven."

"A doctor," Maria said.

"*Doctor.* I've talked to doctors."

"You'll feel better. Try to feel better." The girl now using the nearest telephone seemed to be calling a taxi to take her home from Ralph's. The girl had rollers in her hair and a small child in her basket and Maria wondered whether her car had been repossessed or her husband had left her or just what had happened, why was she calling a taxi from Ralph's. "I mean you have to try, you can't feel this way forever."

"I'll say I can't." Tears began to roll down the woman's face. "You don't even want to talk to me."

"But I do." Maria touched her arm. "I do."

"*Get your whore's hands off me,*" the woman screamed.

CHAPTER 36

There's some principle I'm not grasping, Maria," Carter said on the telephone from New York. "You've got a $1,500-a-month house sitting empty in Beverly Hills, and you're living in a furnished apartment on Fountain Avenue. You want to be closer to Schwab's? Is that it?"

Maria lay on the bed watching a television news film of a house about to slide into the Tujunga Wash. "I'm not living here, I'm just staying here."

"I still don't get the joke."

She kept her eyes on the screen. "Then don't get it," she said at the exact instant the house splintered and fell.

After Carter had hung up Maria wrapped her robe close and

smoked part of a joint and watched an interview with the woman whose house it had been. "You boys did a really outstanding camera job," the woman said. Maria finished the cigarette and repeated the compliment out loud. The day's slide and flood news was followed by a report of a small earth tremor centered near Joshua Tree, 4.2 on the Richter Scale, and, of corollary interest, an interview with a Pentecostal minister who had received prophecy that eight million people would perish by earthquake on a Friday afternoon in March. The notion of general devastation had for Maria a certain sedative effect (the rattlesnake in the playpen, that was different, that was particular, that was punitive), suggested an instant in which all anxieties would be abruptly gratified, and between the earthquake prophecy and the marijuana and the cheerful detachment of the woman whose house was in the Tujunga Wash, she felt a kind of resigned tranquillity. Within these four rented walls she was safe. She was more than safe, she was all right: she had seen herself on *Interstate 80* just before the news and she looked all right. Warm, content, suffused with tentative small resolves, Maria fell asleep before the news was over.

But the next morning when the shower seemed slow to drain she threw up in the toilet, and after she had stopped trembling packed the few things she had brought to Fountain Avenue and, in the driving rain, drove back to the house in Beverly Hills. There would be plumbing anywhere she went.

Mid-200 block Bunker Hill Ave. (non-existent, "redeveloped")

John Fante (1909–1983)

John Fante was born in Colorado in 1909. He attended the University of Colorado and later Long Beach City College. He began writing in 1929 and published his first story in H.L. Mencken's *The American Mercury* in 1932. His first novel, *Wait for Spring, Bandini*, appeared in 1938, with *Ask the Dust* following in 1939.

He spent much of his professional life writing screenplays for Hollywood, which included *Full of Life, Jean Eagles, My Man and I, The Reluctant Saint, Something for a Lonely Man, My Six Loves* and *Walk on the Wild Side*. Fante was stricken with diabetes in 1955 and its complications brought about his blindness in 1978. His last novel, *Dreams from Bunker Hill* (1982), was dictated to his wife. *John Fante and H.L. Mencken: a Personal Correspondence* appeared in 1989.

In the 1980 reprint of *Ask the Dust*, Charles Bukowski writes: "Then one day I pulled a book down and opened it, and there it was. I stood for a moment, reading. Then like a man who had found gold in the city dump, I carried the book to a table. The lines rolled easily across the page, there was a flow. Each line had its own energy and was followed by another like it. The very substance of each line gave the page a form, a feeling of something *carved* into it and here, at last, was a man who was not afraid of emotion. The humor and the pain were intermixed with a superb simplicity. The beginning of that book was a wild and enormous miracle to me."

from *Ask the Dust* (1939)

CHAPTER ONE

One night I was sitting on the bed in my hotel room on Bunker Hill, down in the very middle of Los Angeles. It was an important night in my life, because I had to make a decision about the hotel. Either I paid up or I got out: that was what the note said, the note the landlady had put under my door. A great problem, deserving acute attention. I solved it by turning out the lights and going to bed.

In the morning I awoke, decided that I should do more physical exercise, and began at once. I did several bending exercises. Then I washed my teeth, tasted blood, saw pink on the toothbrush, remembered the advertisements, and decided to go out and get some coffee.

I went to the restaurant where I always went to the restaurant and I sat down on the stool before the long counter and ordered coffee. It tasted pretty much like coffee, but it wasn't worth the nickel. Sitting there I smoked a couple of cigarettes, read the box scores of the American League games, scrupulously avoided the box scores of National League games, and noted with satisfaction that Joe DiMaggio was still a credit to the Italian people, because he was leading the league in batting.

A great hitter, that DiMaggio. I walked out of the restaurant, stood before an imaginary pitcher, and swatted a home run over the fence. Then I walked down the street toward Angel's Flight, wondering what I would do that day. But there was nothing to do, and so I decided to walk around the town.

I walked down Olive Street past a dirty yellow apartment house that was still wet like a blotter from last night's fog, and I thought of my friends Ethie and Carl, who were from Detroit and had lived there, and I remembered the night Carl hit Ethie because she was going to have a baby, and he didn't want a baby. But they had the baby and that's all there was to that. And I remembered the inside of that apartment, how it smelled of mice and dust, and the old women who sat in the lobby on hot afternoons, and the old woman with the pretty legs. Then there was the elevator man, a broken man from Milwaukee, who seemed to sneer every time you called your floor, as though you were such a fool for choosing that particular floor, the elevator man who always had a tray of sandwiches in the elevator, and a pulp magazine.

Then I went down the hill on Olive Street, past the horrible frame houses reeking with murder stories, and on down Olive to the Philharmonic Auditorium, and I remembered how I'd gone there with Helen to listen to the Don Cossack Choral Group, and how I got bored and we had a fight because of it, and I remembered what Helen wore that day—a white dress, and how it made me sing at the loins when I touched it. Oh that Helen—but not here.

And so I was down on Fifth and Olive, where the big street cars chewed your ears with their noise, and the smell of gasoline made the sight of the palm trees seem sad, and the black pavement still wet from the fog of the night before.

So now I was in front of the Biltmore Hotel, walking along

the line of yellow cabs, with all the cab drivers asleep except the driver near the main door, and I wondered about these fellows and their fund of information, and I remembered the time Ross and I got an address from one of them, how he leered salaciously and then took us to Temple Street, of all places, and whom did we see but two very unattractive ones, and Ross went all the way, but I sat in the parlor and played the phonograph and was scared and lonely.

I was passing the doorman of the Biltmore, and I hated him at once, with his yellow braids and six feet of height and all that dignity, and now a black automobile drove to the curb, and a man got out. He looked rich; and then a woman got out, and she was beautiful, her fur was silver fox, and she was a song across the sidewalk and inside the swinging doors, and I thought oh boy for a little of that, just a day and a night of that, and she was a dream as I walked along, her perfume still in the wet morning air.

Then a great deal of time passed as I stood in front of a pipe shop and looked, and the whole world faded except that window and I stood and smoked them all, and saw myself a great author with that natty Italian briar, and a cane, stepping out of a big black car, and she was there too, proud as hell of me, the lady in the silver fox fur. We registered and then we had cocktails and then we danced awhile, and then we had another cocktail and I recited some lines from Sanskrit, and the world was so wonderful, because every two minutes some gorgeous one gazed at me, the great author, and nothing would do but I had to autograph her menu, and the silver fox girl was very jealous.

Los Angeles, give me some of you! Los Angeles come to me the way I came to you, my feet over your streets, you pretty town I loved you so much, you sad flower in the sand, you pretty town.

A day and another day and the day before, and the library with the big boys in the shelves, old Dreiser, old Mencken, all the boys down there, and I went to see them, Hya Dreiser, Hya

Mencken, Hya, hya: there's a place for me, too, and it begins with B, in the B shelf, Arturo Bandini, make way for Arturo Bandini, his slot for his book, and I sat at the table and just looked at the place where my book would be, right there close to Arnold Bennett; not much that Arnold Bennett, but I'd be there to sort of bolster up the B's, old Arturo Bandini, one of the boys, until some girl came along, some scent of perfume through the fiction room, some click of high heels to break up the monotony of my fame. Gala day, gala dream!

But the landlady, the white-haired landlady kept writing those notes: she was from Bridgeport, Connecticut, her husband had died and she was all alone in the world and she didn't trust anybody, she couldn't afford to, she told me so, and she told me I'd have to pay. It was mounting like the national debt, I'd have to pay or leave, every cent of it—five weeks overdue, twenty dollars, and if I didn't she'd hold my trunks; only I didn't have any trunks, I only had a suitcase and it was cardboard without even a strap, because the strap was around my belly holding up my pants, and that wasn't much of a job, because there wasn't much left of my pants.

"I just got a letter from my agent," I told her. "My agent in New York. He says I sold another one; he doesn't say where, but he says he's got one sold. So don't worry Mrs. Hargraves, don't you fret, I'll have it in a day or so."

But she couldn't believe a liar like me. It wasn't really a lie, it was a wish, not a lie, and maybe it wasn't even a wish, maybe it was a fact, and the only way to find out was watch the mailman, watch him closely, check his mail as he laid it on the desk in the lobby, ask him point blank if he had anything for Bandini. But I didn't have to ask after six months at that hotel. He saw me coming and he always nodded yes or no before I asked: no, three million times; yes, once.

One day a beautiful letter came. Oh, I got a lot of letters, but this was the only beautiful letter, and it came in the morning, and it said (he was talking about *The Little Dog Laughed)* he had read *The Little Dog Laughed* and liked it; he said, Mr. Bandini, if ever I saw a genius, you are it. His name was Leonardo, a great Italian critic, only he was not known as a critic, he was just a man in West Virginia, but he was great and he was a critic, and he died. He was dead when my airmail letter got to West Virginia, and his sister sent my letter back. She wrote a beautiful letter too, she was a pretty good critic too, telling me Leonardo had died of consumption but he was happy to the end, and one of the last things he did was sit up in bed and write me about *The Little Dog Laughed:* a dream out of life, but very important; Leonardo, dead now, a saint in heaven, equal to any apostle of the twelve.

Everybody in the hotel read *The Little Dog Laughed,* everybody: a story to make you die holding the page, and it wasn't about a dog, either: a clever story, screaming poetry. And the great editor, none but J. C. Hackmuth with his name signed like Chinese said in a letter: a great story and I'm proud to print it. Mrs. Hargraves read it and I was a different man in her eyes thereafter. I got to stay on in that hotel, not shoved out in the cold, only often it was in the heat, on account of *The Little Dog Laughed.* Mrs. Grainger in 345, a Christian Scientist (wonderful hips, but kinda old) from Battle Creek, Michigan, sitting in the lobby waiting to die, and *The Little Dog Laughed* brought her back to the earth, and that look in her eyes made me know it was right and I was right, but I was hoping she would ask about my finances, how I was getting along, and then I thought why not ask her to lend you a five spot, but I didn't and I walked away snapping my fingers in disgust.

The hotel was called the Alta Loma. It was built on a hillside in reverse, there on the crest of Bunker Hill, built against the decline of the hill, so that the main floor was on the level with the street but the tenth floor was downstairs ten levels. If you had room 862, you got in the elevator and went down eight floors, and if you wanted to go down in the truck room, you didn't go down but up to the attic, one floor above the main floor.

Oh for a Mexican girl! I used to think of her all the time, my Mexican girl. I didn't have one, but the streets were full of them, the Plaza and Chinatown were afire with them, and in my fashion they were mine, this one and that one, and some day when another check came it would be a fact. Meanwhile it was free and they were Aztec princesses and Mayan princesses, the peon girls in the Grand Central Market, in the Church of Our Lady, and I even went to Mass to look at them. That was sacrilegious conduct but it was better than not going to Mass at all, so that when I wrote home to Colorado to my mother I could write with truth. Dear Mother: I went to Mass last Sunday. Down in the Grand Central Market I bumped into the princesses accidentally on purpose. It gave me a chance to speak to them, and I smiled and said excuse me. Those beautiful girls, so happy when you acted like a gentleman and all of that, just to touch them and carry the memory of it back to my room, where dust gathered upon my typewriter and Pedro the mouse sat in his hole, his black eyes watching me through that time of dream and reverie.

Pedro the mouse, a good mouse but never domesticated, refusing to be petted or house-broken. I saw him the first time I walked into my room, and that was during my hey-day, when *The Little Dog Laughed* was in the current August issue. It was five months ago, the day I got to town by bus from Colorado with a hundred and fifty dollars in my pocket and big plans in my head. I had a philosophy in those days. I was a lover of man and beast alike, and Pedro was no exception; but cheese got expensive, Pedro called all his friends, the room swarmed with them, and I had to quit it and feed them bread. They didn't like bread. I had spoiled them and they went elsewhere, all but Pedro the ascetic who was content to eat the pages of an old Gideon Bible.

Ah, that first day! Mrs. Hargraves opened the door to my room, and there it was, with a red carpet on the floor, pictures of the English countryside on the walls, and a shower adjoining. The room was down on the sixth floor, room 678, up near the front of the hill, so that my window was on a level with the green hillside and there was no need for a key, for the window was always open. Through that window I saw my first palm tree, not six feet away, and sure enough I thought of Palm Sunday and Egypt and Cleopatra, but the palm was blackish at its branches, stained by carbon monoxide coming out of the Third Street Tunnel, its crusted trunk choked with dust and sand that blew in from the Mojave and Santa Ana deserts.

Dear Mother, I used to write home to Colorado, Dear Mother, things are definitely looking up. A big editor was in town and I had lunch with him and we have signed a contract for a number of short stories, but I won't try to bore you with all the details, dear mother, because I know you're not interested in writing, and I know Papa isn't, but it levels down to a swell contract, only it doesn't begin for a couple of months. So send me ten dollars, mother, send me five, mother dear, because the editor (I'd tell you his name only I know you're not interested in such things) is all set to start me out on the biggest project he's got.

Dear Mother, and Dear Hackmuth, the great editor—they got most of my mail, practically all of my mail. Old Hackmuth with his scowl and his hair parted in the middle, great Hackmuth with a pen like a sword, his picture was on my wall autographed with his signature that looked Chinese. Hya Hackmuth, I used to say, Jesus how you can write! Then the lean days came, and Hackmuth got big letters from me. My God, Mr. Hackmuth, something's wrong with me: the old zip is gone and I can't write anymore. Do you think, Mr. Hackmuth, that the climate here has anything to do with it? Please advise. Do you think, Mr. Hackmuth, that I write as well as William Faulkner? Please advise. Do you think, Mr. Hackmuth, that sex has anything to do with it, because, Mr. Hackmuth, because, because, and I told

Hackmuth everything. I told him about the blonde girl I met in the park. I told him how I worked it, how the blonde girl tumbled. I told him the whole story, only it wasn't true, it was a crazy lie—but it was something. It was writing, keeping in touch with the great, and he always answered. Oh boy, he was swell! He answered right off, a great man responding to the problems of a man of talent. Nobody got that many letters from Hackmuth, nobody but me, and I used to take them out and read them over, and kiss them. I'd stand before Hackmuth's picture crying out of both eyes, telling him he picked a good one this time, a great one, a Bandini, Arturo Bandini, me.

The lean days of determination. That was the word for it, determination: Arturo Bandini in front of his typewriter two full days in succession, determined to succeed; but it didn't work, the longest siege of hard and fast determination in his life, and not one line done, only two words written over and over across the page, up and down, the same words: palm tree, palm tree, palm tree, a battle to the death between the palm tree and me, and the palm tree won: see it out there swaying in the blue air, creaking sweetly in the blue air. The palm tree won after two fighting days, and I crawled out of the window and sat at the foot of the tree. Time passed, a moment or two, and I slept, little brown ants carousing in the hair on my legs.

4024 Jackson St., Culver City

William Faulkner (1897–1962)

"Golden Land," published in *The American Mercury* in May 1935, was written at William Faulkner's home, Rowan Oak, in Oxford, Mississippi soon after finishing his novel *Pylon*. He had recently returned home after working for Howard Hawks at MGM Studios.

In 1932, on his first major writing assignment in Hollywood, an abandoned letter read: "I am not settled good yet. I have not got used to this work. But I am as well as anyone can be in this bedlam." While there, Paramount took up their option on *Sanctuary*, providing the author with the needed income to return to Mississippi. At Rowan Oak, in late 1932, Faulkner went back on MGM's payroll for $600 a week, working out of his home until he was again taken off the payroll in May 1933.

He returned briefly to Los Angeles in July 1934, accepting another offer from Howard Hawks. By December of 1935, he was back in Los Angeles working again for Hawks – this time at 20th Century Fox – and writing *Absalom, Absalom!* This pattern would continue throughout Faulkner's life: taking a job a total of eleven times at a studio until earning enough money to allow him to return to Mississippi.

Laurence Stallings, author of *What Price Glory* and a friend of Faulkner's, remembers driving down Wilshire Blvd. when Faulkner told him that he thought that the whole of Southern California would eventually crumble away. In his biography of Faulkner, Joseph Blotner quoted Stallings in his attempt at rendering Faulkner's speech: 'A hundred yeahs from now the archaeologists will go digging around here and find nothin'. It's all too perishable to wait for the archaeologists. The only thing they'll find will be these heah iron stobs the folks from Iowa drive into the ground to pitch hoss shoes at. Funny thing, but these heah little iron pegs are all that will survive the test of time.'

In December of 1942, Faulkner wrote to his stepson, Malcolm Franklin: "There is something here for an anthropologist's notebook. This is one of the richest towns in the country. As it exists today, its economy and geography was fixed and invented by the automobile. Therefore, the automobile invented it. The automobile (for a time, anyway) is as dead as the mastodon. Therefore, the town which the automobile created, is dying."

from "*Golden Land*"

If he had been thirty, he would not have needed the two aspirin tablets and the half glass of raw gin before he could bear the shower's needling on his body and steady his hands to shave. But then when he had been thirty neither could he have afforded to drink as much each evening as he now drank; certainly he would not have done it in the company of the men and the women in which, at forty-eight, he did each evening, even though knowing during the very final hours filled with the breaking of glass and the shrill cries of drunken women above the drums and saxophones – the hours during which he carried a little better than his weight both in the amount of liquor consumed and in the number and sum of checks paid – that six or eight hours later he would rouse from what had not been sleep at all but instead that dreamless stupefaction of alcohol out of which last night's turgid and licensed uproar would die, as though without any interval for rest or recuperation, into the familiar shape of his bedroom – the bed's foot silhouetted by the morning light which entered the bougainvillaea-bound windows beyond which his painful and almost unbearable eyes could see the view which might be called the monument to almost twenty-five years of industry and desire, of shrewdness and luck and even fortitude – the opposite canyonflank dotted with the white villas halfhidden in imported olive groves or friezed by the somber spaced columns of cypress like the facades of eastern temples, whose owners' names and faces and even voices were glib and familiar in back corners of the United States and of America and of the world where those of Einstein and Rousseau and Esculapius had never sounded.

He didn't waken sick. He never wakened ill nor became ill from drinking, not only because he had drunk too long and too steadily for that, but because he was too tough even after the thirty soft years; he came from too tough stock on that day thirty-four years ago when at fourteen he had fled, on the brakebeam of a westbound freight, the little lost Nebraska town named for, permeated with, his father's history and existence – a town to be sure, but only in the sense that any shadow is larger than the object which casts it. It was still frontier even as he remembered it at five and six – the projected and increased shadow of a small outpost of sodroofed dugouts on the immense desolation of the plains where his father, Ira Ewing too, had been first to essay to wring wheat during the six days between those when, outdoors in spring and summer and in the fetid halfdark of a snowbound dugout in the winter and fall, he preached. The second Ira Ewing had come a long way since then, from that barren and treeless village which he had fled by a night freight to where he now lay in a hundred-thousand-dollar house, waiting until he knew that he could rise and go to the bath and put the two aspirin tablets into his mouth. They – his mother and father – had tried to explain it to him – something about fortitude, the will to endure. At fourteen he could neither answer them with logic and reason nor explain what he wanted: he could only flee. Nor was he fleeing his father's harshness and wrath. He was fleeing the scene itself – the treeless immensity in the lost center of which he seemed to see the sum of his father's and mother's dead youth and bartered lives as a tiny forlorn spot which nature permitted to green into brief and niggard wheat for a season's moment before blotting it all with the primal and invincible snow as though (not even promise, not even threat) in grim and almost playful augury of the final doom of all life. And it was not even this that he was fleeing because he was not fleeing: it was only that absence, removal, was the only argument which fourteen knew how to employ against adults with any hope of success. He spent the next ten years half tramp half casual laborer as he drifted down the Pacific Coast to Los Angeles; at thirty he was married, to a Los Angeles girl, daughter of a carpenter, and father of a son and a daughter and with a foothold in real estate; at forty-eight he spent fifty thousand dollars a year, owning a business which he had built up unaided and preserved intact through nineteen-twenty-nine; he had given to his children luxuries and advantages which his own father not only could not have conceived in fact but would have condemned completely in theory – as it proved, as the paper which the Filipino chauffeur, who each morning carried him into the house and undressed him and put him to bed, had removed from the pocket of his topcoat and laid on the reading table proved, with reason. On the death of his father twenty years ago he had returned to Nebraska, for the first time, and fetched his mother back with him, and she was now established in a home of her own only the less sumptuous because she refused (with a kind of abashed and thoughtful unshakability which he did not remark) anything finer or more elaborate. It was the house in which they had all lived at first, though he and his wife and children had moved within the year. Three years ago they had moved again, into the house where he now waked in a select residential section of Beverley Hills, but not once in the nineteen years had he failed to stop (not even during the last five, when to move at all in the mornings required a terrific drain on that character or strength which the elder Ira had bequeathed him, which had enabled the other Ira to pause on the Nebraska plain and dig a hole for his wife to bear children in while he planted wheat) on his way to the office (twenty miles out of his way to the office) and spend ten minutes with her. She lived in as complete physical ease and peace as he could devise. He had arranged her affairs so that she did not even need to bother with money, cash, in order to live; he had arranged credit for her with a neighboring market and butcher so that the Japanese gardener who came each day to water and tend the flowers could do her shopping for her; she never even saw the bills. And the only reason she had no servant was that even at seventy she apparently clung stubbornly to the old habit of doing her own cooking and housework. So it would seem that he had been right. Perhaps there were times when, lying in bed like this and waiting for the will to rise and take the aspirin and the gin (mornings perhaps following evenings when he had drunk more than ordinarily and when even the six or seven hours of oblivion had not been sufficient to enable him to distinguish between reality and illusion) something of the old strong harsh Campbellite blood which the elder Ira must have bequeathed him might have caused him to see or feel or imagine his father looking down from somewhere upon him, the prodigal, and what he had accomplished. If this were so, then surely the elder Ira, looking down for the last two mornings upon the two tabloid papers which the Filipino removed from his master's topcoat and laid on the reading table, might have taken advantage of that old blood and taken his revenge, not just for that afternoon thirty-four years ago but for the entire thirty-four years.

When he gathered himself, his will, his body, at last and rose from the bed he struck the paper so that it fell to the floor and lay open at his feet, but he did not look at it. He just stood so, tall, in silk pajamas, thin where his father had been gaunt with the years of hard work and unceasing struggle with the unpredictable and implacable earth (even now, despite the life which he had led, he had very little paunch) looking at nothing while at his feet the black headline flared above the row of five or six tabloid photographs from which his daughter alternately stared back or flaunted long pale shins: APRIL LALEAR BARES ORGY SECRETS. When he moved at last he stepped on the paper, walking on his bare feet into the bath; now it was his trembling and jerking hands that he watched as he shook the two tablets onto the glass shelf and set the tumbler into the rack and unstoppered the gin bottle and braced his knuckles against the wall in order to pour into the tumbler. But he did not look at the paper, not even when, shaved, he re-entered the bedroom and went to the bed beside which his slippers sat and shoved the paper aside with his foot in order to step into them. Perhaps, doubtless, he did not need to. The trial was but entering its third tabloidal day now, and so for two days his daughter's face had sprung out at him, hard, blonde and inscrutable, from every paper he opened; doubtless he had never forgot her while he slept even, that he had waked into thinking about remembering her as he had waked into the dying drunken uproar of the evening eight hours behind him without any interval between for rest or forgetting.

Nevertheless as, dressed, in a burnt orange turtleneck sweater beneath his gray flannels, he descended the Spanish staircase, he was outwardly calm and possessed. The delicate iron balustrade and the marble steps coiled down to the tile-floored and barnlike living room beyond which he could hear his wife and son talking on the breakfast terrace. The son's name was Voyd. He and his wife had named the two children by what might have been called mutual contemptuous armistice – his wife called the boy Voyd, for what reason he never knew; he in his turn named the girl (the child whose woman's face had met him from every paper he touched for two days now beneath or above the name, April Lalear) Samantha, after his own mother. He could hear them talking – the wife between whom and himself there had been nothing save civility, and not always a great deal of that, for ten years now; and the son who one afternoon two years ago had been delivered at the door drunk and insensible by a car whose occupants he did not see and, it devolving upon him to undress the son and put him to bed, whom he discovered to be wearing, in place of underclothes, a woman's brassiere and step-ins. A few minutes later, hearing the blows perhaps, Voyd's mother ran in and found her husband beating the still unconscious son with a series of towels which a servant was steeping in rotation in a basin of ice-water. He was beating the son hard, with grim and deliberate fury. Whether he was trying to sober the son up or was merely beating him, possibly he himself did not know. His wife though jumped to the latter conclusion. In his raging disillusionment he tried to tell her about the woman's garments but she refused to listen; she assailed him in turn with virago fury. Since that day the son had contrived to see his father only in his mother's presence (which neither the son nor the mother found very difficult, by the way) and at which times the son treated his father with a blend of cringing spite and vindictive insolence half a cat's and half a woman's.

He emerged onto the terrace; the voices ceased. The sun, strained by the vague high soft almost nebulous California haze, fell upon the terrace with a kind of treacherous unbrightness. The terrace, the sundrenched terra cotta tiles, butted into a rough and savage shear of canyon wall bare yet without dust, on or against which a solid mat of flowers bloomed in fierce lush myriad-colored paradox as though in place of being rooted into and drawing from the soil they lived upon air alone and had been merely leaned intact against the sustenanceless lavawall by someone who would later return and take them away. The son, Voyd, apparently naked save for a pair of straw-colored shorts, his body brown with sun and scented faintly by the depilatory which he used on arms, chest and legs, lay in a wicker chair, his feet in straw beach shoes, an open newspaper across his brown legs. The paper was the highest class one of the city, yet there was a black headline across half of it too, and even without pausing, without even being aware that he had looked, Ira saw there too the name which he recognized. He went on to his place; the Filipino who put him to bed each night, in a white service jacket now, drew his chair. Beside the glass of orange juice and the waiting cup lay a neat pile of mail topped by a telegram. He sat down and took up the telegram; he had not glanced at his wife until she spoke:

"Mrs. Ewing telephoned. She says for you to stop in there on your way to town."

5521 Amistoy Ave., Encino (demolished)

F. Scott Fitzgerald (1896–1940)

In 1925, Fitzgerald had written Maxwell Perkins that if *The Great Gatsby* "will support me with no more intervals of trash I'll go on as a novelist. If not, I'm going to quit, come home, go to Hollywood and learn the movie business." In 1927, with Zelda, he visited Los Angeles for the first time, staying in the fashionable Ambassador Hotel and working at First National (later Warner Bros.). One evening, Fitzgerald asked a clerk at the Ambassador for one hundred dollars in coins. He threw handfuls of silver up against the hotel windows, shouting "It's money, it's money, it's money! It's free!"

Flying into Los Angeles, looking out over the city at night, Fitzgerald said the lights looked like "fireworks" and they gave him a "feeling of new worlds to conquer."

His first screenplay was a failure. It read like a short story, not a script. It opened: "School was over. The happy children, their books swinging carelessly at a strap's end, tripped out into the Spring fields – Wait a minute, that's the wrong story." By all accounts, Fitzgerald was, by this time, a sickly sober man, filled with the false modesty of the recovered alcoholic. His dashingly youthful poses were gone.

He was back in 1931, working for Irving Thalberg at MGM, the man about which he would later write *The Last Tycoon*. He would lose his job again, after a disastrous party in which he embarrassed himself in front of the most powerful people in Hollywood. He would be back again, until leaving the studios for good in 1938.

Charles W. Warren wrote to Fitzgerald, "Lower your high-brow & help on some trash. They buy trash here – they're quite willing to pay high for it ... If you would forget originality and finesse and think in terms of cheap melo-theatrics you would probably have made a howling success of your visits here and would likewise have no financial worries now."

At a party thrown by Dorothy Parker, Fitzgerald was phoned by producer Hunt Stromberg who demanded Scott drive to his home and work on the script for "Marie Antoinette." Fitzgerald wrote a note which he sent over by messenger:

Stromberg sent for Poppa
Tho' Poppa hadn't et,
To do what Jesus couldn't –
Save Marie Antoinette

He was removed from the "Madame Curie" project at MGM, which he had started writing with Aldous Huxley, who had quit the studios shortly after the project had begun. Dorothy Parker eventually worked on the script as well. Fitzgerald died of a heart attack at age 44 while in the process of writing *The Last Tycoon*.

At a Los Angeles mortuary after his death, Parker stood over the casket and said the same elegy for Fitzgerald which Owl Eyes had pronounced for Gatsby: "Poor son of a bitch."

from *The Last Tycoon* (1941)

When we went into the airport Mr. Schwartz was along with us, too, but he seemed in a sort of dream. All the time we were trying to get accurate information at the desk, he kept staring at the door that led out to the landing field, as if he were afraid the plane would leave without him. Then I excused myself for a few minutes and something happened that I didn't see, but when I came back he and White were standing close together, White talking and Schwartz looking twice as much as if a great truck had just backed up over him. He didn't stare at the door to the landing field any more. I heard the end of Wylie White's remark ...

' – I told you to shut up. It serves you right.'

'I only said – '

He broke off as I came up and asked if there was any news. It was then half past two in the morning.

'A little,' said Wylie White. 'They don't think we'll be able to start for three hours anyhow, so some of the softies are going to an hotel. But I'd like to take you out to the Hermitage, Home of Andrew Jackson.'

'How could we see it in the dark?' demanded Schwartz.

'Hell, it'll be sunrise in two hours.'

'You two go,' said Schwartz.

'All right – you take the bus to the hotel. It's still waiting – *he's* in there.' Wylie's voice had a taunt in it. 'Maybe it'd be a good thing.'

'No, I'll go along with you,' said Schwartz hastily.

We took a taxi in the sudden country dark outside, and he seemed to cheer up. He patted my knee-cap encouragingly.

'I should go along,' he said, 'I should be chaperon. Once upon a time when I was in the big money, I had a daughter – a beautiful daughter.'

He spoke as if she had been sold to creditors as a tangible asset.

'You'll have another,' Wylie assured him. 'You'll get it all back. Another turn of the wheel and you'll be where Cecilia's papa is, won't he Cecilia?'

'Where is this Hermitage?' asked Schwartz presently. 'Far away at the end of nowhere? We will miss the plane?'

'Skip it,' said Wylie. 'We ought to've brought the stewardess along for you. Didn't you admire the stewardess? I thought she was pretty cute.'

We drove for a long time over a bright level countryside, just a road and a tree and a shack and a tree, and then suddenly along a winding twist of woodland. I could feel even in the darkness that the trees of the woodland were green – that it was all different from the dusty olive-tint of California. Somewhere we passed a Negro driving three cows ahead of him, and they mooed as he scattered them to the side of the road. They were real cows, with warm, fresh, silky flanks, and the Negro grew gradually real out of the darkness with his big brown eyes staring at us close to the car, as Wylie gave him a quarter. He said '*Thank* you – thank you,' and stood there, and the cows mooed again into the night as we drove off.

I thought of the first sheep I ever remember seeing – hundreds of them, and how our car drove suddenly into them on the back lot of the old Laemmle studio. They were unhappy about being in pictures, but the men in the car with us kept saying:

'Swell!'

'Is that what you wanted, Dick?'

'Isn't that swell?' And the man named Dick kept standing up in the car as if he were Cortez or Balboa, looking over that grey fleecy undulation. If I ever knew what picture they were in, I have long forgotten.

We had driven an hour. We crossed a brook over an old rattly iron bridge laid with planks. Now there were roosters crowing and blue-green shadows stirring every time we passed a farmhouse.

'I told you it'd be morning soon,' said Wylie. 'I was born near here – the son of impoverished southern paupers. The family mansion is now used as an outhouse. We had four servants – my father, my mother and my two sisters. I refused to join the guild, and so I went to Memphis to start my career, which has now reached a dead end.' He put his arm around me: 'Cecilia, will you marry me, so I can share the Brady fortune?'

He was disarming enough, so I let my head lie on his shoulder.

'What do you do, Cecilia. Go to school?'

'I go to Bennington. I'm a junior.'

'Oh, I beg your pardon. I should have known, but I never had the advantage of college training. But a *ju*nior – why I read in *Esquire* that juniors have nothing to learn, Cecilia.'

'Why do people think that college girls – '

'Don't apologize – knowledge is power.'

'You'd know from the way you talk that we were on our way to Hollywood,' I said. 'It's always years and years behind the times.'

He pretended to be shocked.

'You mean girls in the East have no private lives?'

'That's the point. They *have* got private lives. You're bothering me, let go.'

'I can't. It might wake Schwartz, and I think this is the first sleep he's had for weeks. Listen, Cecilia: I once had an affair with the wife of a producer. A very short affair. When it was over she said to me in no uncertain terms, she said: "Don't you ever tell about this or I'll have you thrown out of Hollywood. My husband's a much more important man than you!" '

I liked him again now, and presently the taxi turned down a long lane fragrant with honeysuckle and narcissus, and stopped beside the great grey hulk of the Andrew Jackson house. The driver turned around to tell us something about it, but Wylie shushed him, pointing at Schwartz, and we tiptoed out of the car.

'You can't get into the Mansion now,' the taxi man told us politely.

Wylie and I went and sat against the wide pillars of the steps.

'What about Mr. Schwartz?' I asked. 'Who is he?'

'To hell with Schwartz. He was the head of some combine once – First National? Paramount? United Artists? Now he's down and out. But he'll be back. You can't flunk out of pictures unless you're a dope or a drunk.'

'You don't like Hollywood,' I suggested.

'Yes I do. Sure I do. Say! This isn't anything to talk about on the steps of Andrew Jackson's house – at dawn.'

'I *like* Hollywood,' I persisted.

'It's all right. It's a mining town in lotus land. Who said that? I did. It's a good place for toughies, but I went there from Savannah, Georgia. I went to a garden party the first day. My host shook hands and left me. It was all there – that swimming pool, green moss at two dollars an inch, beautiful felines having drinks and fun –

' – And nobody spoke to me. Not a soul. I spoke to half a dozen people but they didn't answer. That continued for an hour, two hours – then I got up from where I was sitting and ran out at a dog trot like a crazy man. I didn't feel I had any rightful identity until I got back to the hotel and the clerk handed me a letter addressed to me in my name.'

Naturally I hadn't ever had such an experience, but looking back on parties I'd been to, I realized that such things could happen. We don't go for strangers in Hollywood unless they wear a sign saying that their axe has been thoroughly ground elsewhere, and that in any case it's not going to fall on our necks – in other words, unless they're a celebrity. And they'd better look out even then.

'You should have risen above it,' I said smugly. 'It's not a slam at *you* when people are rude – it's a slam at the people they've met before.'

'Such a pretty girl – to say such wise things.'

There was an eager to-do in the eastern sky, and Wylie could see me plain – thin with good features and lots of style, and the kicking foetus of a mind. I wonder what I looked like in that dawn, five years ago. A little rumpled and pale, I suppose, but at that age, when one has the young illusion that most adventures are good, I needed only a bath and a change to go on for hours.

Wylie stared at me with really flattering appreciation and then suddenly we were not alone. Mr Schwartz wandered apologetically into the pretty scene.

'I fell upon a large metal handle,' he said, touching the corner of his eye.

Wylie jumped up.

'Just in time, Mr. Schwartz,' he said. 'The tour is just starting. Home of Old Hickory – America's tenth president. The victor of New Orleans, opponent of the National Bank, and inventor of the Spoils System.'

Schwartz looked towards me as towards a jury. 'There's a writer for you,' he said. 'Knows everything and at the same time he knows nothing.'

'What's that?' said Wylie, indignant.

It was my first inkling that he was a writer. And while I like writers – because if you ask a writer anything, you usually get an answer – still it belittled him in my eyes. Writers aren't people exactly. Or, if they're any good, they're a whole *lot* of people trying so hard to be one person. It's like actors, who try so pathetically not to look in mirrors, who lean *back*ward trying – only to see their faces in the reflecting chandeliers.

'Ain't writers like that, Cecilia?' demanded Schwartz. 'I have no words for them. I only know it's true.'

Wylie looked at him with slowly gathering indignation. 'I've heard that before,' he said. 'Look, Manny, I'm a more practical man than you any day! I've sat in an office and listened to some mystic stalk up and down for hours spouting tripe that'd land him on a nut-farm anywhere outside of California – and then at the end tell me how *practical* he was, and I was a dreamer – and would I kindly go away and make sense out of what he'd said.'

Mr. Schwartz's face fell into its more disintegrated alignments. One eye looked upwards through the tall elms. He raised his hand and bit without interest at the cuticle on his second finger. There was a bird flying about the chimney of the house, and his glance followed it. It perched on the chimney pot like a raven, and Mr. Schwartz's eyes remained fixed upon it as he said: 'We can't get in, and it's time for you two to go back to the plane.'

It was still not quite dawn. The Hermitage looked like a nice big white box, but a little lonely and vacated still after a hundred years. We walked back to the car. Only after we had gotten in, and Mr Schwartz had surprisingly shut the taxi door on us, did we realize he didn't intend to come along.

'I'm not going to the Coast – I decided that when I woke up. So I'll stay here, and afterwards the driver could come back for me.'

'Going back East?' said Wylie with surprise. 'Just because – '

'I have decided,' said Schwartz, faintly smiling. 'Once I used to be a regular man of decision – you'd be surprised.' He felt in his pocket, as the taxi driver warmed up the engine. 'Will you give this note to Mr. Smith?'

'Shall I come in two hours?' the driver asked Schwartz.

'Yes ... sure. I shall be glad to entertain myself looking around.'

I kept thinking of him all the way back to the airport trying to fit him into that early hour and into that landscape. He had come a long way from some Ghetto to present himself at that raw shrine. Manny Schwartz and Andrew Jackson – it was hard to say them in the same sentence. It was doubtful if he knew who Andrew Jackson was as he wandered around, but perhaps he figured that if people had preserved his house Andrew Jackson must have been someone who was large and merciful, able to understand. At both ends of life man needed nourishment: a breast – a shrine. Something to lay himself beside when no one wanted him further, and shoot a bullet into his head.

Of course we did not know this for twenty hours. When we got to the airport we told the purser that Mr. Schwartz was not continuing, and then forgot about him. The storm had wandered away into Eastern Tennessee and broken against the mountains, and we were taking off in less than an hour. Sleepy-eyed travelers appeared from the hotel, and I dozed a few minutes on one of those Iron Maidens they use for couches. Slowly the idea of a perilous journey was recreated out of the debris of our failure: a new stewardess, tall, handsome, flashing dark, exactly like the other except she wore seersucker instead of French red-and-blue, went briskly past us with a suitcase. Wylie sat beside me as we waited.

1056 De Garmo Dr. (City Terrace)

Chester Himes (1909–1984)

Born in 1909, in Jefferson City, Missouri, Himes moved with his parents to St. Louis and later to Cleveland. After two semesters at Ohio State University and more than seven years at Ohio State Penitentiary, in 1941 Himes and his wife Jean were hired by best-selling novelist Louis Bromfield to work as butler and cook on the novelist's farm near Cleveland. Later that year the Himeses followed him to Hollywood where Bromfield had been hired to write a screenplay.

As Himes recalls in his autobiography, *The Quality of Hurt*: "Los Angeles hurt me racially as much as any city I have ever known – much more than any city I remember in the South. It was the lying hypocrisy that hurt me." Himes goes on to say, "The only thing that surprised me about the race riots in Watts in 1965 was that they waited so long to happen. We are a very patient people."

Himes' biographers, Erward Margolies and Michel Fabre, describe this period as one of continual shock and humiliation. Because of large influxes of southern whites fleeing the depression, as well as thousands of soldiers and sailors who had never lived outside of segregated regions of the country, the atmosphere in Los Angeles "was tense and would worsen throughout the war years – roughly the length of Himes' stay." His Hollywood experiences were no different, going from studio to studio, in a series of rejections. "At one point he was on the verge of being hired as a reader for screenplays," Margolies and Fabre note, "but was afterward told that Jack Warner 'didn't want any niggers on his lot.' At another studio where he was being considered for a publicity position, he learned that the all-Negro cast of *Cabin in the Sky* was excluded from the whites-only commissary."

Himes sums up the experience: "I had lived in the South, I had fallen down an elevator shaft, I had been kicked out of college, I had served seven and one half years in prison, I had survived the humiliating last five years of the Depression in Cleveland; and still I was entire, complete, functional; my mind was sharp, my reflexes were good, and I was not bitter. But under the mental corrosion of race prejudice in Los Angeles I became bitter and saturated with hate."

After several apartments in South Central Los Angeles, Chester and Jean Himes moved to a little house evacuated by a Nisei family on a hilltop in City Terrace. It was there he began *If He Hollers Let Him Go*. In a 1962 letter, Himes wrote: "It was an isolated house next to a reservoir, with only a Mexican couple for neighbors and I used to keep my Winchester rifle within reach at all times."

Himes received a Rosenwald Foundation grant in 1944 and was soon off to New York to finish his novel. He concludes: "I was thirty-one and whole when I went to Los Angeles and thirty-five and shattered when I left to go to New York."

Chester Himes

from *If He Hollers Let Him Go*

CHAPTER ONE

I dreamed a fellow asked me if I wanted a dog and I said yeah, I'd like to have a dog and he went off and came back with a little black dog with stiff black gold-tipped hair and sad eyes that looked something like a wire-haired terrier. I was standing in front of a streetcar that was just about to start and the fellow led the dog by a piece of heavy stiff wire twisted about its neck and handed me the end of the wire and asked me if I liked the dog. I took the wire and said sure I liked the dog. Then the dog broke loose and ran over to the side of the street trailing the wire behind him and the fellow ran and caught it and brought it back and gave it to me again.

"About the – " I began. I wanted to ask him how much it cost because I didn't have any money.

But he cut me off. "Now about the pay. It'll cost you a dollar and thirty-five cents."

I said, "I haven't got any money now but I'll give it to you on Monday."

"Sure, that's all right," he said.

I took the dog and got on the streetcar. I liked the little dog; but when I got home nobody else seemed to like it.

Then I turned over and dreamed on the other side.

I was working in a war plant where a white fellow named Frankie Childs had been killed and the police were there trying to find out who did it.

The police lieutenant said, "We got to find a big tall man with strong arms, big hands, and a crippled leg."

So they started calling in the colored fellows. The first one to be called was a medium-sized, well-built, fast-walking, dark brown man of about thirty-five. He was dressed in a faded blue work shirt and blue denim overall pants tied about the waist with a cord. He came up from the basement and walked straight to the lieutenant and looked him in the eye, standing erect and unflinching.

The lieutenant asked, "Can you stand the test?"

"What test?" the colored fellow wanted to know.

"Can you go up to the third floor and look the dead body of Frankie Childs in the face?"

The colored fellow said, "Frankie Childs! Sure, I can go up and look at that bastard dead or alive." He had a fine, scholarly voice, carrying but unmusical. He turned and started up the stairs three at a time. Suddenly I began to laugh.

"Oh!" I said to the lieutenant. "You gonna keep 'em running upstairs until you find out what one's crippled.' I fell out and rolled all over the floor laughing.

Then I turned over and dreamed on my back.

I was asking two white men for a job. They looked as if they didn't want to give me the job but didn't want to say so outright. Instead they asked me if I had my tools. I said I didn't have any tools but I could do the job. They began laughing at me, scornfully and derisively. One said, "He ain't got no tools," and they laughed like hell.

I didn't mind their not giving me the job, but their laughing at me hurt. I felt small and humiliated and desperate, looking at the two big white men laughing at me.

Suddenly I came awake. For a time I laid there without thought, suspended in a vacancy. There was no meaning to anything; I didn't even remember having dreamed.

The alarm went off again; I knew then that it had been the alarm that had awakened me. I groped for it blindly, shut it off; I kept my eyes shut tight. But I began feeling scared in spite of hiding from the day. It came along with consciousness. It came into my head first, somewhere back of my closed eyes, moved slowly underneath my skull to the base of my brain, cold and hollow. It seeped down my spine, into my arms, spread through my groin with an almost sexual torture, settled in my stomach like butterfly wings. For a moment I felt torn all loose inside, shriveled, paralyzed, as if after a while I'd have to get up and die.

Every day now I'd been waking up that way, ever since the war began. And since I'd been made a leaderman out at the Atlas Shipyard it was really getting me. Maybe I'd been scared all my life, but I didn't know about it until after Pearl Harbor. When I came out to Los Angeles in the fall of '41, I felt fine about everything. Taller than the average man, six feet two, broad-shouldered, and conceited, I hadn't a worry. I knew I'd get along. If it had come down to a point where I had to hit a paddy I'd have hit him without any thought. I'd have busted him wide open because he was a paddy and needed busting.

Race was a handicap, sure, I'd reasoned. But hell, I didn't have to marry it. I went where I wanted and felt good about it. I'd gotten refused back in Cleveland, Ohio, plenty of times. Cleveland wasn't the land of the free or the home of the brave either. That was one reason why I left there to come to Los Angeles; I knew if I kept on getting refused while white boys were hired from the line behind me I'd hang somebody as sure as hell. But it'd never really gotten me down. Once I threatened to sue a restaurant and got a hundred dollars. I'd even thought about making a business of it. Most times when I got refused I just went somewhere else, put it out of my mind, forgot about it.

They shook that in Los Angeles. It wasn't being refused employment in the plants so much. When I got here practically the only job a Negro could get was service in the white folks' kitchens. But it wasn't that so much. It was the look on the people's faces when you asked them about a job. Most of 'em didn't say right out they wouldn't hire me. They just looked so goddamned startled that I'd even asked. As if some friendly dog had come in through the door and said, "I can talk." It shook me.

Maybe it had started then, I'm not sure, or maybe it wasn't until I'd seen them send the Japanese away that I'd noticed it.

Little Riki Oyana singing "God Bless America" and going to Santa Anita with his parents next day. It was taking a man up by the roots and locking him up without a chance. Without a trial. Without a charge. Without even giving him a chance to say one word. It was thinking about if they ever did that to me, Robert Jones, Mrs. Jones's dark son, that started me to getting scared.

After that it was everything. It was the look in the white people's faces when I walked down the streets. It was that crazy, wild-eyed, unleashed hatred that the first Jap bomb on Pearl Harbor let loose in a flood. All that tight, crazy feeling of race as thick in the street as gas fumes. Every time I stepped outside I saw a challenge I had to accept or ignore. Every day I had to make one decision a thousand times: *Is it now? Is now the time?*

I was the same color as the Japanese and I couldn't tell the difference. "A yeller-bellied Jap" coulda meant me too. I could always feel race trouble, serious trouble, never more than two feet off. Nobody bothered me. Nobody said a word. But I was tensed every moment to spring.

I carried it as long as I could. I carried my muscle as high as my ears. But I couldn't keep on carrying it. I lost twenty pounds in two weeks and my hands got to trembling. I was working at the yard then as a mechanic and every time my white leaderman started over toward me I drew up tight inside. I got so the only place I felt safe was in bed asleep.

I was even scared to tell anybody. If I'd gone to a psychiatrist he'd have had me put away. Living every day scared, walled in, locked up. I didn't feel like fighting any more; I'd take a second thought before I hit a paddy now. I was tired of keeping ready to die every minute; it was too much strain. I had to fight hard enough each day just to keep on living. All I wanted was for the white folks to let me alone; not say anything to me; not even look at me. They could take the goddamned world and go to hell with it.

Suddenly the baby started bawling in the next room and I heard the bed squeak as Ella Mae got up to feed him. I wondered if they knew how well I could hear them through the thin partition. If they did they didn't let it bother them. I heard Henry mutter sleepily, "Goddamnit! Goddamnit!" Then all I could hear was the sound of the baby sucking greedily, and I thought if they really wanted to give him a break they'd cut his throat and bury him in the back yard before he got old enough to know he was a nigger. Then I was ashamed. Ella Mae loved that baby. If anything happened to him she'd die.

Parts of my dream started coming back and I remembered vaguely about a little black dog with gold-tipped hair, and the police lieutenant looking for a big crippled man who must be colored. I remembered saying in my dream, "Oh, you gonna keep 'em running upstairs until you find out what one's crippled." Suddenly it struck me as funny, and I began laughing. But right in the middle of the laugh I felt a crazy impulse to cry. I wanted to just lie there and cry.

Hell, I oughta stay home today, I thought. I oughta go over and see Susie and take a quart of rum. She was fine if you were drunk enough. Once she told me, "I'm not pretty but I'm wonderful." I could picture her ducky black body with the tiny waist and round, bucket-shaped hips. I knew if I kept thinking about her I'd get up and go over and play it out and to hell with my job.

I tried to force my mind to a blank. I had to get myself together; I had to get up.

I could hear the baby still sucking. Lucky little rascal, I thought, didn't know how lucky he was. I wished I had Ella Mae in bed with me; I could lose myself with her too. I remembered how she used to let me in the evenings when Henry was at work. That was during the time I was having so much trouble trying to get my journeyman's rating at the yard and used to come home so burnt up all the time. When I found out she'd done it just because she felt sorry for me I quit speaking to her for a week. But she hadn't let it bother her one way or the other.

I'd gone to the Lincoln Theatre last night and I began thinking of how the audience had applauded so loudly for the two white acrobats. The other acts had been all-colored – singing and dancing and black-face comedy. I thought at the time how the white folks were still showing everybody how strong they were and how we spooks were still trying to prove how happy we were. But what got me was the way the colored audience clapped their hands off for the white acrobats – not so much just because they were white, although that was reason enough in itself, I thought – but because one of the boys was blind.

"He's blind," I heard some woman in back of me whisper. "He is? Which one?"

"The little one."

"Is dat so? Well, ain't he spry?"

It went all through the audience: The little one's blind.

We're a wonderful, goddamned race, I thought. Simple-minded, generous, sympathetic sons of bitches. We're sorry for everybody but ourselves; the worse the white folks treat us the more we love 'em. Ella Mae laying me because I wasn't married and she figured she had enough for me and Henry too; and a black audience clapping its hands off for a blind white acrobat.

I thought of Ben telling Conway out at the yard, "I was just asking the man a question, fellow, I ain't going to steal your white man. I know that's the one thing a Negro won't forgive you for – that's stealing his prize white man."

What I was trying to do now was to keep from thinking about Alice, just to drift on my thoughts as long as they didn't touch her. I was scared if I thought about her now I'd begin to wonder, maybe to doubt her. She'd broken a date with me last night; that's why I'd gone to the Lincoln.

The next thing I knew I had opened my eyes and was looking at her picture on my dressing table. It was as if I was trying to catch some telltale expression in her eyes. But it wasn't there; she had the same warm, intelligent, confident look. I just looked at her and didn't think about her at all – I just laid there and enjoyed looking at a really fine chick. She had one of those heart-shaped faces with a cupid's-bow mouth, and coal-black hair parted in the middle and pulled tight down over her ears.

Now I didn't mind thinking about her – who she was, her position as supervisor of case work in the city welfare department. Her father was a doctor – Dr. Wellington L.-P. Harrison. He was the kind of pompous little guy you'd expect to have a hyphenated name, one of the richest Negroes in the city if not on the whole West Coast.

I jumped out of bed and went over and picked up the picture. It set me up to have a chick like her. It gave me a personal pride to have her for my girl. And then I was proud of her too. Proud of the way she looked, the appearance she made among white people; proud of what she demanded from white people, and the credit they gave her; and her position and prestige among her own people. I could knock myself out just walking along the street with her; and whenever we ran into any of the white shipyard workers downtown somewhere I really felt like something.

I didn't want to think about her breaking our date. She'd called and said she ought to attend a sorority meeting she'd forgotten all about – she was president of the local chapter. And would I really mind? Of course I couldn't mind; that was where the social conventions had me. If she'd been Susie I could have said, "Hell yes, I mind," but I had to be a gentleman with Alice. And I really wanted to be. Only thinking about it now gave me a tight, jealous feeling. Started me to wondering why she'd want to marry a guy like me – two years of college and a shipyard job – when she could pick any number of studs with both money and position. But she was trying so hard to make me study nights so I could go back to college after the war and study law, she had to be serious, I reassured myself.

Before I lost it again I put the picture down on the dresser and went into the kitchen to make some coffee. I didn't know Ella Mae was there; I was barefooted and my pyjamas were open. She was standing before the small gas range and when I came in she turned to face me. Her robe was hanging open but at sight of me she pulled it together and fastened it, not hurried, but with finality.

"I was just getting ready to wake you," she said.

She was a full-bodied, slow-motioned home girl with a big broad flat face, fiat-nosed and thick-lipped; yellow but not bright. She had the big, brown, glassy eyes that went along with the rest of her; and her hair was short and straightened and she had it in curlers.

"Good morning, *Mrs.* Brown," I said facetiously, then, lowering my voice, I added, "I was just thinking about you, baby."

She smiled self-consciously, but her look made me button my pyjamas. "Your clock woke the baby up," she said.

"He's cute," I said. "I heard him."

She turned back to the stove so I couldn't see her face. "She's a *she,"* she corrected.

"I forgot." I ran my finger down her spine.

She pulled away and began making coffee in her silex.

"Go on and get dressed," she said. "You'll be late again." When I didn't move she added, "I'm making your coffee. You want anything else?"

"Yeah," I said. She didn't answer. "I'd get married if I could find somebody like you," I went on. "Then I wouldn't mind waking up in the mornings."

"Go on and get dressed," she said again. I made another pass at her and she said, "Oh, go on, Bob! You'll be over it in a minute. Everybody wakes up like that."

"So!" I said, putting my arm about her waist and trying to pull her to me. "You oughtn' to told me that, baby." I put my right hand on her shoulder and tried to face her to me. "Come on, baby, be sweet."

She gave me a hard push, sent me off balance. "Go on now! Don't be so crazy. Hurry up or you'll be late."

I stood back and looked at her with a sudden hard soberness. "Do you ever wake up scared?" I asked.

She turned and looked at me then. There was a queer expression on her flat yellow face. She stepped over to me, reached up, and put her hands about my head, drew me down to kiss her. Then she pushed me away again, saying, "Now hurry up, you'll make all your riders late too."

"Okay, little sister," I said. "When Henry's gone to the Army and you get all hot and bothered and come running to me, just remember."

She gave a slow laugh and stuck out her tongue. I felt differently now. All the tightness and scare, even the lingering traces of jealousy, had gone out of me. I just felt pressed for time.

I hurried back to my room and put on my shirt and shorts, crossed the kitchen to the bathroom, still barefooted. It was a small, four-room cottage sitting back in a court off of Wall Street in the middle fifties, and the rooms opened into one another so there wasn't any way of getting out of a certain casual intimacy, even if I'd never had Ella Mae. My room was in the back, off from the kitchen, and the bathroom was on the other side. Their bedroom was on one side of the front, and the parlor on the other.

When I'd finished brushing my teeth and washing up I started back through the kitchen in my underwear and almost bumped into Ella Mae as she was returning to bed. I patted her on the hips and said, "Stingy." She switched on through the parlor into her bedroom.

I got a clean pair of coveralls out of the dresser drawer, slipped them on over my underwear, pulled on my high-heeled, iron-toed boots, slanted my "tin" hat on the back of my head, and slipped into my leather jacket. Something about my working clothes made me feel rugged, bigger than the average citizen, stronger than a white-collar worker – stronger even than an executive. Important too. It put me on my muscle. I felt a swagger in my stance when I stepped over to the dresser to get my keys and wallet, identifications, badge, handkerchief, cigarettes. I looked to see if I had enough money, saw a ten and some ones. Then I went into the kitchen and drank two cups of black coffee. All of a sudden I began rushing to get to work on time.

1320 N. 701 S. Amalfi Dr., Pacific Pallisades

Aldous Huxley (1894–1963)

The Huxleys arrived in Los Angeles in late 1937, driving across the 700 miles of desert and mountains that separated New Mexico from Los Angeles. They came to Hollywood after Jake Zeitlin left his book shop in Los Angeles to visit them on D.H. Lawrence's ranch in Taos where they were staying. Zeitlin spoke of the many distinguished writers working in Hollywood. The Huxley's "visit" would last for the next 20 years.

The first trip was a visit to see the place and test the waters of the Hollywood industry. "Even then Aldous is horrified, though fascinated, by the prospect of being tied to this horrible (studio) life," Maria Huxley wrote to a friend. And in another of Maria's letters: "Aldous will perhaps go to work in California – that is, if he's wanted and they pay him enormously."On Easter Sunday 1938, the Huxleys were walking on the Santa Monica beach with Thomas and Katia Mann, considering whether to join the growing cadre of European intellectuals in exile. Maria noticed vaguely suggestive shapes on the sand, suddenly realizing that thousands of condoms were spread across the beach. Aldous, with his always-failing eyesight, mistook them for flowers.

In 1938 Huxley worked for MGM, where he began writing, with F. Scott Fitzgerald, "Madame Curie," designed for Greta Garbo. Huxley left the studio before the script was completed, and eventually Fitzgerald too was removed from the project. Salka Viertel, who for a time picked up the project, remembered asking MGM executive Bernie Hyman what had happened to the Huxley-Fitzgerald script. "Embarrassed, he admitted that he had had no time to read it but had given it to Goldie, his secretary, who told him 'it stinks.'" In *Hanging on in Paradise,* Fred Guiles wrote of the German and British intellectuals who landed in Hollywood in the late 1930s: "Your fame had taken you among other elite of the world to the moon, and there were short men chewing on dead cigars who ruled the planet."

Huxley, who had compared Hollywood to the court of Louis XIV – "because people are always losing their heads" – was invited back to work at MGM a week after finishing *After Many A Summer Dies The Swan.*

from *After Many a Summer Dies the Swan* (1939)

A few minutes later they were on their way. Cradled in the back seat of the car, out of range, he hoped, of the chauffeur's conversation, Jeremy Pordage abandoned himself to the pleasure of merely looking. Southern California rolled past the windows; all he had to do was to keep his eyes open.

The first thing to present itself was a slum of Africans and Filipinos, Japanese and Mexicans. And what permutations and combinations of black, yellow and brown! What complex bastardies! And the girls – how beautiful in their artificial silk! "And Negro ladies in white muslin gowns." His favorite line in The Prelude. He smiled to himself. And meanwhile the slum had given place to the tall buildings of a business district. The population took on a more Caucasian tinge. At every corner there was a drug-store. The newspaper boys were selling headlines about Franco's drive on Barcelona. Most of the girls, as they walked along, seemed to be absorbed in silent prayer; but he supposed, on second thought, it was only gum that they were thus incessantly ruminating. Gum, not God. Then suddenly the car plunged into a tunnel and emerged into another world, a vast, untidy, suburban world of filling stations and billboards, of low houses in gardens, of vacant lots and waste paper, of occasional shops and office buildings and churches – primitive Methodist churches built, surprisingly enough, in the style of the Cartuja at Granada, Catholic churches like Canterbury Cathedral, synagogues disguised as Hagia Sophia, Christian Science churches with pillars and pediments, like banks. It was a winter day and early in the morning; but the sun shone brilliantly, the sky was without a cloud. The car was traveling westwards and the sunshine, slanting from behind them as they advanced, lit up each building, each sky sign and billboard as though with a spot-light, as though on purpose to show the new arrival all the sights.

EATS. COCKTAILS. OPEN NITES.

JUMBO MALTS.

DO THINGS, GO PLACES WITH CONSOL SUPER-GAS!

AT BEVERLY PANTHEON FINE FUNERALS ARE NOT EXPENSIVE.

The car sped onwards, and here in the middle of a vacant lot was a restaurant in the form of a seated bulldog, the entrance between the front paws, the eyes illuminated.

"Zoomorph," Jeremy Pordage murmured to himself, and again, "zoomorph." He had the scholar's taste for words. The bulldog shot back into the past.

ASTROLOGY, NUMEROLOGY, PSYCHIC READINGS.

DRIVE IN FOR NUTBURGERS – whatever they were. He resolved at the earliest opportunity to have one. A nutburger and a jumbo malt.

STOP HERE FOR CONSOL SUPER-GAS.

Surprisingly, the chauffeur stopped. "Ten gallons of Super-Super," he ordered; then, turning back to Jeremy, "This is our company," he added. "Mr. Stoyte, he's the president." He pointed to a billboard across the street. CASH LOANS IN FIFTEEN MINUTES, Jeremy read; CONSULT COMMUNITY SERVICE FINANCE CORPORATION. "That's another of ours," said the chauffeur proudly.

They drove on. The face of a beautiful young woman, distorted, like a Magdalene's, with grief, stared out of a giant billboard. BROKEN ROMANCE, proclaimed the caption. SCIENCE PROVES THAT 73 PERCENT OF ALL ADULTS HAVE HALITOSIS.

IN TIME OF SORROW LET BEVERLY PANTHEON BE YOUR FRIEND.

FACIALS, PERMANENTS, MANICURES.

BETTY'S BEAUTY SHOPPE.

Next door to the beauty shoppe was a Western Union office. That cable to his mother.... Heavens, he had almost forgotten! Jeremy leaned forward and, in the apologetic tone he always used when speaking to servants, asked the chauffeur to stop for a moment. The car came to a halt. With a preoccupied expression on his mild, rabbit-like face, Jeremy got out and hurried across the pavement, into the office.

"Mrs. Pordage, The Araucarias, Woking, England," he wrote, smiling a little as he did so. The exquisite absurdity of that address was a standing source of amusement. "The Araucarias, Woking." His mother, when she bought the house, had wanted to change the name, as being too ingenuously middle-class, too much like a joke by Hilaire Belloc. "But that's the beauty of it," he had protested. "That's the charm." And he had tried to make her see how utterly right it would be for them to live at such an address. The deliciously comic incongruity between the name of the house and the nature of its occupants! And what a beautiful, topsy-turvy appositeness in the fact that Oscar Wilde's old friend, the witty and cultured Mrs. Pordage, should write her sparkling letters from The Araucarias, and that from these same Araucarias, these Araucarias, mark you, at *Woking*, should come the works of mingled scholarship and curiously rarefied wit for which her son had gained his reputation. Mrs. Pordage had almost instantly seen what he was driving at. No need, thank goodness, to labor your points where she was concerned. You could talk entirely in hints and anacoluthons; she could be relied on to understand. The Araucarias had remained The Araucarias.

Having written the address, Jeremy paused, pensively frowned and initiated the familiar gesture of biting his pencil – only to find, disconcertingly, that this particular pencil was tipped with brass and fastened to a chain. "Mrs. Pordage, The Araucarias, Woking, England," he read out loud, in the hope that the words would inspire him to compose the right, the perfect message – the message his mother expected of him, at once tender and witty, charged with a genuine devotion ironically worded, acknowledging her maternal domination, but at the same time making fun of it, so that the old lady could salve her conscience by pretending that her son was entirely free, and herself, the least tyrannical of mothers. It wasn't easy – particularly with this pencil on a chain. After several abortive essays he decided, though it was definitely unsatisfactory, on: "Climate being sub-tropical shall break vow re underclothes. Stop. Wish you were here my sake not yours as you would scarcely appreciate this unfinished Bournemouth indefinitely magnified. Stop."

"Unfinished what?" questioned the young woman on the further side of the counter.

"B-o-u-r-n-e-m-o-u-t-h," Jeremy spelled out. He smiled; behind the bifocal lenses of his spectacles his blue eyes twinkled, and, with a gesture of which he was quite unconscious, but which he always automatically made when he was about to utter one of his little jokes, he stroked the smooth bald spot on the top of his head. "*You* know," he said, in a particularly fluty tone, "the bourne to which no traveler goes, if he can possibly help it."

The girl looked at him blankly then, inferring from his expression that something funny had been said and remembering that Courteous Service was Western Union's slogan, gave the bright smile for which the poor old chump was evidently asking, and went on reading: "Hope you have fun at Grasse. Stop. Tendresses. Jeremy."

It was an expensive message; but luckily, he reflected, as he took out his pocketbook, luckily Mr. Stoyte was grossly overpaying him. Three months' work, six thousand dollars. So damn the expense.

He returned to the car and they drove on. Mile after mile they went, and the suburban houses, the gas stations, the vacant lots, the churches, the shops went along with them, interminably. To right and left, between palms, or pepper trees, or acacias, the streets of enormous residential quarters receded to the vanishing point.

CLASSY EATS. MILE HIGH CONES.

JESUS SAVES.

HAMBURGERS.

Yet once more, the traffic lights turned red. A paperboy came to the window. "Franco claims gains in Catalonia," Jeremy read, and turned away. The frightfulness of the world had reached a point at which it had become for him merely boring. From the halted car in front of them, two elderly ladies, both with permanently waved white hair and both wearing crimson trousers descended, each carrying a Yorkshire terrier. The dogs were set down at the foot of the traffic signal. Before the animals could make up their minds to use the convenience, the lights had changed. The Negro shifted into first, and the car swerved forward, into the future. Jeremy was thinking of his mother. Disquietingly enough, she too had a Yorkshire terrier.

FINE LIQUORS.

TURKEY SANDWICHES.

GO TO CHURCH AND FEEL BETTER ALL THE WEEK.

WHAT IS GOOD FOR BUSINESS IS GOOD FOR YOU.

Another zoomorph presented itself, this time a real estate agent's office in the form of an Egyptian sphinx.

JESUS IS COMING SOON.

YOU TOO CAN HAVE ABIDING YOUTH WITH THRILL-PHORM BRASSIERES.

BEVERLY PANTHEON, THE CEMETERY THAT IS DIFFERENT...

With the triumphant expression of Puss in Boots enumerating the possessions of the Marquis of Carabas, the Negro shot a glance over his shoulder at Jeremy, waved his hand towards the billboard and said, "That's ours, too."

"You mean, the Beverly Pantheon?"

The man nodded. "Finest cemetery in the world, I guess," he said; and added, after a moment's pause, "Maybe you's like to see it. It wouldn't hardly be out of our way."

"That would be very nice," said Jeremy with upperclass English graciousness. Then, feeling that he ought to express his acceptance rather more warmly and democratically, he cleared his throat and, with a conscious effort to reproduce the local vernacular, added that it would be *swell*. Pronounced in his Trinity College Cambridge voice, the word sounded so unnatural that he began to blush with embarrassment. Fortunately, the chauffeur was too busy with the traffic to notice.

They turned to the right, sped past a Rosicrucian Temple, past two cat-and-dog hospitals, past a School for Drum-Majorettes and two more advertisements of the Beverly Pantheon. As they turned to the left on Sunset Boulevard, Jeremy had a glimpse of a young woman who was doing her shopping in a hydrangea-blue strapless-bathing suit, platinum curls and a black fur jacket. Then she too was whirled back into the past.

The present was a road at the foot of a line of steep hills, a road flanked by small, expensive-looking shops, by restaurants, by night-clubs shuttered against the sunlight, by offices and apartment houses. Then they too had taken their places in the irrevocable. A sign proclaimed that they were crossing the city limits of Beverly Hills. The surroundings changed. The road was flanked by the gardens of a rich residential quarter. Through trees, Jeremy saw the facades of houses, all new, almost all in good taste – elegant and witty pastiches of Lutyens manor houses, of Little Trianons, of Monticellos; lighthearted parodies of Le Corbusier's solemn machines-for-living-in; fantastic adaptations of Mexican haciendas and New England farms.

They turned to the right. Enormous palm trees lined the road. In the sunlight, masses of mesembryanthemums blazed with an intense magenta glare. The houses succeeded one another, like the pavilions at some endless international exhibition. Gloucestershire followed Andalusia and gave place in turn to Touraine and Oaxaca, Düsseldorf and Massachusetts.

"That's Harold Lloyd's place," said the chauffeur, indicating a kind of Boboli. "And that's Charlie Chaplin's. And that's Pickfair."

The road began to mount, vertiginously. The chauffeur pointed across an intervening gulf of shadow at what seemed a Tibetan lamasery on the opposite hill. "That's where Ginger Rogers lives. Yes, *sir,*" he nodded triumphantly, as he twirled the steering wheel.

Five or six more turns brought the car to the top of the hill. Below and behind lay the plain, with the city like a map extending indefinitely into a pink haze.

...Before and to either hand were mountains – ridge after ridge as far as the eye could reach, a desiccated Scotland, empty under the blue desert sky.

The car turned a shoulder of orange rock, and there all at once, on a summit hitherto concealed from view, was a huge sky sign, with the words BEVERLY PANTHEON, THE PERSONALITY CEMETERY, in six-foot neon tubes and, above it, on the very crest, a full-scale reproduction of the Leaning Tower of Pisa – only this one didn't lean.

"See that?" said the Negro impressively. "That's the Tower of Resurrection. Two hundred thousand dollars, that's what it cost. Yes, *sir*." He spoke with an emphatic solemnity. One was made to feel that the money had all come out of his own pocket.

434 Sycamore Rd., Santa Monica

Christopher Isherwood (1904–1986)

Isherwood arrived, famously, with friend W.H. Auden in New York in the beginning of 1939. Three months later, he boarded a bus headed for Los Angeles, with a vague interest in the pacifism of his countrymen Aldous Huxley and Gerald Heard.

In Los Angeles, Isherwood felt at home in what he called the city's "theatrical impermanence." Gerald Heard introduced him to Swami Prabhavananda, a Hindu monk who had established a center for Vedanta philosophy in a secluded house on Ivar Avenue off of Hollywood Boulevard.

In 1940, Isherwood began work at MGM studios, insisting that his contract allow an option to terminate without notice. He would take writing jobs at the studios intermittingly throughtout his life. He spent most of the war years living in Prabhavananada's monastery and contemplated becoming a monk. Eventually he left the monastery, though he helped his swami translate a new version of the Bhagavad-Gita and wrote a biography of Ramakrishna.

In the early 1960s Isherwood taught at Los Angeles State College, with the experience providing material for the novel *A Single Man*, in which he commented about Southern California living: "We've retired to live inside our advertisements, like hermits going into caves to contemplate." In his *Diaries*, he noted: "What was there, on this shore, a hundred years ago?Practically nothing. And which, of all these flimsy structures, will be standing a hundred years from now? Probably not a single one. Well, I like that thought. It is bracingly realistic. In such surroundings, it is easier to remember and accept the fact that you won't be here, either."

from *A Single Man* (1965)

Sitting on the john, he can look out of the window. (They can see his head and shoulders from across the street, but not what he is doing.) It is a gray lukewarm California winter morning; the sky is low and soft with Pacific fog. Down at the shore, ocean and sky will be one soft, sad gray. The palms stand unstirred and the oleander bushes drip moisture from their leaves.

This street is called Camphor Tree Lane. Maybe camphor trees grew here once; there are none now. More probably the name was chosen for its picturesqueness by the pioneer escapists from dingy downtown Los Angeles and stuffy-snobbish Pasadena who came out here and founded this colony back in the early twenties. They referred to their stucco bungalows and clapboard shacks as cottages, giving them cute names like "The Fo'c'sle" and "Hi Nuff." They called their streets lanes, ways or trails, to go with the woodsy atmosphere they wanted to create. Their utopian dream was of a subtropical English village with Montmartre manners: a Little Good Place where you could paint a bit, write a bit, and drink lots. They saw themselves as rear-guard individualists, making a last-ditch stand against the twentieth century. They gave thanks loudly from morn till eve that they had escaped the soul-destroying commercialism of the city. They were tacky and cheerful and defiantly bohemian, tirelessly inquisitive about each other's doings, and boundlessly tolerant. When they fought, at least it was with fists and bottles and furniture, not lawyers. Most of them were lucky enough to have died off before the Great Change.

The Change began in the late forties, when the World War Two vets came swarming out of the East with their just-married wives, in search of new and better breeding grounds in the sunny Southland, which had been their last nostalgic glimpse of home before they shipped out to the Pacific. And what better breeding ground than a hillside neighborhood like this one, only five minutes' walk from the beach and with no through traffic to decimate the future tots? So, one by one, the cottages which used to reek of bathtub gin and reverberate with the poetry of Hart Crane have fallen to the occupying army of Coke-drinking television watchers.

The vets themselves, no doubt, would have adjusted pretty well to the original bohemian utopia; maybe some of them would even have taken to painting or writing between hangovers. But their wives explained to them, right from the start and in the very clearest language, that breeding and bohemianism do not mix. For breeding you need a steady job, you need a mortgage, you need credit, you need insurance. And don't you dare die, either, until the family's future is provided for.

So the tots appeared, litter after litter after litter. And the small old schoolhouse became a group of big new airy buildings. And the shabby market on the ocean front was enlarged into a super. And on Camphor Tree Lane two signs were posted. One of them told you not to eat the watercress which grew along the bed of the creek, because the water was polluted. (The original colonists had been eating it for years; and George and Jim tried some and it tasted delicious and nothing happened.) The other sign – those sinister black silhouettes on a yellow ground – said CHILDREN AT PLAY.

•

It is one of the marvels and blessings of the Los Angeles freeway system that you can now get from the beach to San Tomas State College in fifty minutes, give or take five, instead of the nearly two hours you would have spent, in the slow old days, crawling from stop light to stop light clear across the downtown area and out into the suburbs beyond.

George feels a kind of patriotism for the freeways. He is proud that they are so fast, that people get lost on them and even sometimes panic and have to bolt for safety down the nearest cutoff. George loves the freeways because he can still cope with them; because the fact that he can cope proves his claim to be a functioning member of society. He can still *get by.*

(Like everyone with an acute criminal complex, George is hyperconscious of all bylaws, city ordinances, rules and petty regulations. Think of how many Public Enemies have been caught just because they neglected to pay a parking ticket! Never once has he seen his passport stamped at a frontier, his driver's license accepted by a post-office clerk as evidence of identity, without whispering gleefully to himself, *Idiots – fooled them again!*)

He will fool them again this morning, in there, in the midst of the mad metropolitan chariot race – Ben-Hur would certainly chicken out – jockeying from lane to lane with the best of them, never dropping below eighty in the fast left lane, never getting rattled when a crazy teen-ager hangs on to his tail or a woman (it all comes of letting them go first through doorways) cuts in sharply ahead of him. The cops on their motorcycles will detect nothing, yet, to warn them to roar in pursuit flashing their red lights, to signal him off to the side, out of the running, and thence to escort him kindly but ever so firmly to some beautifully ordered nursery-community where Senior Citizens ("old," in our country of the bland, has become nearly as dirty a word as "kike" or "nigger") are eased into senility, retaught their childhood games but with a difference: it's known as "passive recreation" now. Oh, by all means let them screw, if they can still cut the mustard; and, if they can't, let them indulge without inhibitions in babylike erotic play. Let them get married, even – at eighty, at ninety, at a hundred – who cares? Anything to keep them busy and stop them wandering around blocking the traffic.

•

There's always a slightly unpleasant moment when you drive up the ramp which leads onto the freeway and become what's called "merging traffic." George has that nerve-crawling sensation which can't be removed by simply checking the rearview mirror: that, inexplicably, invisibly, he's about to be hit in the back. And then, next moment, he has merged and is away, out in the clear, climbing the long, easy gradient toward the top of the pass and the Valley beyond.

And now, as he drives, it is as if some kind of auto-hypnosis exerts itself. We see the face relax, the shoulders unhunch themselves, the body ease itself back into the seat. The reflexes are taking over; the left foot comes down with firm, even pressure on the clutch pedal, while the right prudently feeds in gas. The left hand is light on the wheel; the right slips the gearshift with precision into high. The eyes, moving unhurriedly from road to mirror, mirror to road, calmly measure the distances ahead, behind, to the nearest car.... After all, this is no mad chariot race – that's only how it seems to onlookers or nervous novices – it is a river, sweeping in full flood toward its outlet with a soothing power. There is nothing to fear, as long as you let yourself go with it; indeed, you discover, in the midst of its stream-speed, a sense of indolence and ease.

And now something new starts happening to George. The face is becoming tense again, the muscles bulge slightly at the jaw, the mouth tightens and twitches, the lips are pressed together in a grim line, there is a nervous contraction between the eyebrows. And yet, while all this is going on, the rest of the body remains in a posture of perfect relaxation. More and more it appears to separate itself, to become a separate entity: an impassive anonymous chauffeur-figure with little will or individuality of its own, the very embodiment of muscular co-ordination, lack of anxiety, tactful silence, driving its master to work.

And George, like a master who has entrusted the driving of his car to a servant, is now free to direct his attention elsewhere. As they sweep over the crest of the pass, he is becoming less and less aware of externals – the cars all around, the dip of the freeway ahead, the Valley with its homes and gardens opening below, under a long brown smear of smog, beyond and above which the big barren mountains rise. He has gone deep down inside himself.

What is he up to?

On the edge of the beach, a huge, insolent highrise building which will contain one hundred apartments is growing up within its girders; it will block the view along the coast from the park on the cliffs above. A spokesman for this project says, in answer to objections, Well, that's progress. And anyhow, he implies, if there are people who are prepared to pay $450 a month for this view by renting our apartments, why should you park-users (and that includes George) get it for free?

A local newspaper editor has started a campaign against sex deviates (by which he means people like George). They are everywhere, he says; you can't go into a bar any more, or a men's room, or a public library, without seeing hideous sights. And they all, without exception, have syphilis. The existing laws against them, he says, are far too lenient.

A senator has recently made a speech, declaring that we should attack Cuba right now, with everything we've got, lest the Monroe Doctrine be held cheap and of no account. The senator does not deny that this will probably mean rocket war. We must face this fact; the alternative is dishonor. We must be prepared to sacrifice three quarters of our population (including George).

It would be amusing, George thinks, to sneak into that apartment building at night, just before the tenants moved in, and spray all the walls of all the rooms with a specially prepared odorant which would be scarcely noticeable at first but which would gradually grow in strength until it reeked like rotting corpses. They would try to get rid of it with every deodorant known to science, but in vain; and when they had finally, in desperation, ripped out the plaster and woodwork, they would find that the girders themselves were stinking. They would abandon the place as the Khmers did Angkor; but its stink would grow and grow until you could smell it clear up the coast to Malibu. So at last the entire structure would have to be taken apart by workers in gas masks and ground to powder and dumped far out in the ocean.... Or perhaps it would be more practical to discover a kind of virus which would eat away whatever it is that makes metal hard. The advantage that this would have over the odorant would be that only a single injection in one spot would be necessary, for the virus would then eat through all the metal in the building. And then, when everybody had moved in and while a big housewarming party was in progress, the whole thing would sag and subside into a limp tangled heap, like spaghetti.

605 S. Normandie Ave. (Wilshire District)

Malcolm Lowry (1909–1957)

Lowry arrived in New York in 1934, he used to say, with nothing but a football shirt and a copy of *Moby Dick*. He had actually followed his American bride to the States, who already had left Paris for home. He arrived by bus in Los Angeles in 1936. Soon, he and his wife settled in Acapulco, then Cuernavaca, then Oaxaca, then Mexico City. He returned to his wife in Los Angeles in 1938, who had left him in Mexico, after repeatedly failing to keep Lowry away from his self-destructive behavior. Upon arriving, his wife asked Lowry what he wanted. "The sea," he mumbled, so they borrowed a car and drove to Malibu.

After drying out in a clinic in La Crescenta, Lowry moved into the Normandie Hotel, a location found for him by the lawyer who was running Lowry's affairs, along with the lawyer representing the writer's father in England. Lowry saved his 25 cents a day allowance, given him for phone calls and streetcar fares, and spent the money instead on fortified wines that cost 50 cents a gallon. He persuaded the hotel clerk to add the costs of the cables he sent to his bill. Friends who visited him at the Normandie would dispose of the empty bottles spread across the room. There he worked with a twenty-two year-old typist, Carol Phillips, revising *Under The Volcano* from a dog-eared, hand-written, double-sided, 100 page manuscript.

In July 1939, two days before his 30th birthday, Lowry's Visa expired. He left Los Angeles and drove north to Canada, where he continued to rewrite *Under The Volcano*. His idea was to apply for visa reinstatement, but it would be more than six years before Lowry would again set foot again on American soil.

from *Under the Volcano* (1958)

Beside the Consul Hugh took out a cigarette, tapped it on his thumbnail, noted it was the last in the package, and placed it between his lips. He put his feet up on the back of the seat beneath him and leaned forward, resting his elbows on his knees, frowning down into the arena. Then, fidgeting still, he struck a match, drawing his thumbnail across it with a crackle like a small cap-pistol, and held it to the cigarette, cupping his quite beautiful hands, his head bent ... Hugh was coming toward her this morning, in the garden, through the sunlight. With his rolling swagger, his Stetson hat on the back of his head, his holster, his pistol, his bandolier, his tight trousers tucked inside the elaborately stitched and decorated boots, she'd thought, just for an instant, that he was – actually! – Bill Hodson, the cowboy star, whose leading lady she'd been in three pictures when she was fifteen. Christ, how absurd! How marvelously absurd! *The Hawaiian Islands gave us this real outdoor girl who is fond of swimming, golf, dancing, and is also an expert horsewoman! She* ... Hugh hadn't said one word this morning about how well she rode, though he'd afforded her not a little secret amusement by explaining that her horse miraculously didn't want to drink. Such areas there are in one another we leave, perhaps forever, unexplored! – She'd never told him a word about her movie career, no, not even that day in Robinson ... But it was a pity Hugh himself hadn't been old enough to interview her, if not the first time, that second awful time after Uncle Macintyre sent her to college, and after her first marriage, and the death of her child, when she had gone back once more to Hollywood. *Yvonne the Terrible! Look out, you sarong sirens and glamour girls, Yvonne Constable, the "Boomp Girl," is back in Hollywood! Yes, Yvonne is back, determined to conquer Hollywood for the second time. But she's twenty-four now, and the "Boomp Girl" has become a poised exciting woman who wears diamonds and white orchids and ermine – and a woman who has known the meaning of love and tragedy, who has lived a lifetime since she left Hollywood a few short years ago. I found her the other day at her beach home, a honey-tanned Venus just emerging from the surf. As we talked she gazed out over the water with her slumbrous dark eyes and the Pacific breezes played with her thick dark hair. Gazing at her for a moment it was hard to associate the Yvonne Constable of to-day with the rough-riding serial queen of yesteryear, but the torso's still terrific, and the energy is still absolutely unparalleled! The Honolulu Hellion, who at twelve was a war-whooping tomboy, crazy about baseball, disobeying everyone but her adored Dad, whom she called "The Boss-Boss," became at fourteen a child actress, and at fifteen, leading lady to Bill Hodson. And she was a powerhouse even then. Tall for her age, she had a lithe strength that came from a childhood of swimming and surfboarding in the Hawaiian breakers. Yes, though you may not think it now, Yvonne has been submerged in burning lakes, suspended over precipices, ridden horses down ravines, and she's an expert at "double pick-offs." Yvonne laughs merrily to-day when she remembers the frightened determined girl who declared she could ride very well indeed, and then, the picture in progress, the company on location, tried to mount her horse from the wrong side! A year later she could do a "flying mount" without turning a hair. "But about that time I was rescued from Hollywood," as she smilingly puts it, "and very unwillingly too, by my Uncle Macintyre, who literally swooped down, after my father died, and sailed me back to Honolulu!" But when you've been a "Boomp Girl" and are well on your way to being an "Oomph Girl" at eighteen and when you've just lost your beloved "Boss-Boss," it's hard to settle down in a strict loveless atmosphere. "Uncle Macintyre," Yvonne admits, "never conceded a jot or tittle to the tropics. Oh, the mutton broth and oatmeal and hot tea!" But Uncle Macintyre knew his duty and, after Yvonne had studied with a tutor, he sent her to the University of Hawaii. There – perhaps, she says, "because the word 'star' had undergone some mysterious transformation in my mind" – took a course in astronomy! Trying to forget the ache in her heart and its emptiness, she forced an interest in her studies and even dreamed briefly of becoming the "Madame Curie" of astronomy! And there too, before long, she met the millionaire playboy, Cliff Wright. He came into Yvonne's life at a moment when she was discouraged in her University work, restless under Uncle Macintyre's strict regime, lonely, and longing for love and companionship. And Cliff was young and gay, his rating as an eligible bachelor was absolutely blue ribbon. It's easy to see how he was able to persuade her, beneath the Hawaiian moon, that she loved him, and that she should leave college and marry him.* ("Don't tell me for Christ sake about this Cliff," the Consul wrote in one of his rare early letters, "I can see him and I hate the bastard already: short-sighted and promiscuous, six foot three of gristle and bristle and pathos, of deep-voiced charm and casuistry." The Consul had seen him with some astuteness as a matter of fact – poor Cliff! – one seldom thought of him now and one tried not to think of the self righteous girl whose pride had been so outraged by his infidelities – "business-like, inept and unintelligent, strong and infantile, like most American men, quick to wield chairs in a fight, vain, and who, at thirty still ten, turns the act of love into a kind of dysentery ...") *Yvonne has already been a victim of "bad press" about her marriage and in the inevitable divorce that followed, what she said was misconstrued, and when she didn't say anything, her silence was misinterpreted. And it wasn't only the press who misunderstood: "Uncle Macintyre," she says ruefully, "simply washed his hands of me."* (Poor Uncle Macintyre. It was fantastic, it was almost funny – it was screamingly funny, in a way, as one related it to one's friends. She was a Constable through and through, and no child of her mother's people! Let her go the way of the Constables! God knows how many of them had been caught up in, or invited, the same kind of meaningless tragedy, or half-tragedy, as herself and her father. They rotted in asylums in Ohio or dozed in dilapidated drawing rooms in Long Island with chickens pecking among the family silver and broken teapots that would be found to contain diamond necklaces. The Constables, a mistake on the part of nature, were dying out. In fact, nature meant to wipe them out, having no further use for what was not self-evolving. The secret of their meaning, if any, had been lost.) *So Yvonne left Hawaii with her head high and a smile on her lips, even if her heart was more achingly empty than ever before. And now she's back in Hollywood and people who know her best say she has no time in her life now for love, she thinks of nothing but her work. And at the studio they're saying the tests she's been making recently are nothing short of sensational. The "Boomp Girl" has become Hollywood's greatest dramatic actress! So Yvonne Constable, at twenty-four, is well on the way for the second time to becoming a star.*

– But Yvonne Constable had not become a star for the second time. Yvonne Constable had not even been on her way to becoming a star. She had acquired an agent who managed to execute some excellent publicity – excellent in spite of the fact that publicity of any kind, she persuaded herself, was one of her greatest secret fears – on the strength of her earlier rough-riding successes; she received promises, and that was all. In the end she walked alone down Virgil Avenue or Mariposa beneath the dusty dead shallow planted palms of the dark and accursed City of the Angels without even the consolation that her tragedy was no less valid for being so stale. For her ambitions as an actress had always been somewhat spurious: they suffered in some sense from the dislocations of the functions – she saw this – of womanhood itself. She saw it, and at the same time, now it was all quite hopeless (and now that she had, after everything, *outgrown* Hollywood), saw that she might under other conditions have become a really first-rate, even a great artist. For that matter what was she if not that now (if greatly directed) as she walked or drove furiously through her anguish and all the red lights, seeing, as might the Consul, the sign in the Town House window "Informal Dancing in the Zebra Room" turn "Infernal" – or "Notice to Destroy Weeds" become "Notice to Newlyweds." While on the hoarding – "Man's public inquiry of the hour" – the great pendulum on the giant blue clock swung ceaselessly. Too late! And it was this, it was all this that had perhaps helped to make meeting Jacques Laruelle in Quauhnahuac such a shattering and ominous thing in her life. It was not merely that they had the Consul in common, so that through Jacques she had been mysteriously able to reach, in a sense to avail herself of, what she had never known, the Consul's innocence; it was only to him that she'd been able to talk of Hollywood (not always honestly, yet with the enthusiasm with which close relatives may speak of a hated parent and with what relief!) on the mutual grounds of contempt and half-admitted failure. Moreover they discovered that they were both there in the same year, in 1932, had been once, in fact, at the same party, outdoor-barbecue-swimming-pool-and-bar; and to Jacques she had shown also, what she had kept hidden from the Consul, the old photographs of Yvonne the Terrible dressed in fringed leather shirts and riding breeches and high-heeled boots, and wearing a ten-gallon hat, so that in his amazed and bewildered recognition of her this horrible morning, she had wondered was there not just an instant's faltering – for surely Hugh and Yvonne were in some grotesque fashion transposed! ... And once too in his studio, where the Consul was so obviously not going to arrive, M. Laruelle had shown her some stills of his old French films, one of which it turned out – good heavens! – she'd seen in New York soon after going east again. And in New York she'd stood once more (still in Jacques' studio) on that freezing winter night in Times Square – she was staying at the Astor – watching the illuminated news aloft traveling around the Times Building, news of disaster, of suicide, of banks failing, of approaching war, of nothing at all, which, as she gazed upward with the crowd, broke off abruptly, snapped off into darkness, into the end of the world, she had felt, when there was no more news. Or was it – Golgotha? A bereaved and dispossessed orphan, a failure, yet rich, yet beautiful, walking, but not back to her hotel, in the rich fur trappings of alimony, afraid to enter the bars alone whose warmth she longed for then, Yvonne had felt far more desolate than a streetwalker; walking – and being followed, always followed – through the numb brilliant jittering city – *the best for less*, she kept seeing, or *Dead End*, or *Romeo and Juliet*, and then again, *the best for less* – that awful darkness had persisted in her mind, blackening still further her false wealthy loneliness, her guilty divorced dead helplessness. The electric arrows thrust at her heart – yet they were cheating: she knew, increasingly frightened by it, that darkness to be still there, in them, of them. The cripples jerked themselves slowly past. Men muttered by in whose faces all hope seemed to have died. Hoodlums with wide purple trousers waited where the icy gale streamed into open parlors. And everywhere, that darkness, the darkness of a world without meaning, a world without aim – *the best for less* – but where everyone save herself, it seemed to her, however hypocritically, however churlish, lonely, crippled, hopeless, was capable, if only in a mechanical crane, a cigarette butt plucked from the street, if only in a bar, if only in accosting Yvonne herself, of finding some faith ... *Le Destin de Yvonne Griffaton* ... And there she was – and she was still being followed – standing outside the little cinema in Fourteenth Street which showed revivals and foreign films. And there, upon the stills, who could it be, that solitary figure, but herself, walking down the same dark streets, even wearing the same fur coat, only the signs above her and around her said: *Dubonnet, Amer Picon, Les 10 Frattelinis, Moulin Rouge*. And "Yvonne, Yvonne!" a voice was saying at her entrance, and a shadowy horse, gigantic, filling the whole screen, seemed leaping out of it at her: it was a statue that the figure had passed, and the voice, an imaginary voice, which pursued Yvonne Griffaton down the dark streets, and Yvonne herself too, as if she had walked straight out of that world outside into this dark world on the screen, without taking breath.

437 N. Oakhurst (Beverly Hills)

Lewis MacAdams (1944–)

Born in San Angelo, Texas and raised in Dallas, MacAdams was educated at Princeton, where he received a BA in English in 1966, and U. of New York at Buffalo, MA English, 1968. MacAdams, in his own words, "blew into L.A. Jan. 1, 1980."

He is the author of 10 books of poetry, including *The Poetry Room, Live At The Church, News From Niman Farm* and *Africa and The Marriage of Walt Whitman and Marilyn Monroe*, from which this selection is taken. A new collection, *The River, Books 1–2*, appeared in 1998. He has read and performed his works in clubs, bars, bookstores, libraries, theaters, and auditoriums throughout the U.S. and Europe. For three years in the mid 1970s he was the Director of the Poetry Center at San Francisco State University, and remains a member of its Board of Directors. He is a two-time winner of the World Heavyweight Poetry Championship bout in Taos, New Mexico.

As a journalist, in the early '80s, he was the American correspondent for the popular French magazine *Actuel*. From 1980 to 1982, he was the editor of *WET*, "the Magazine of Gourmet Bathing and Beyond," a Los-Angeles-based, internationally-circulated bi-monthly. Since the mid-1980s he has been a contributing editor of the *L.A. Weekly*, producing at least a dozen cover stories and hundreds of other shorter pieces on a wide variety of subjects. He also writes regularly on culture and ecology for *Rolling Stone*, and on business personalities for *Los Angeles Magazine*.

In 1985, he founded Friends of The Los Angeles River, a "40 year art work" to bring the Los Angeles River back to life. In the years since, FoLAR has become the River's most important and influential advocate, with a quarterly newsletter, *The Current News* that reaches 3,000 people, a 12 member Board of Directors, a widely-respected Technical Advisory Board. Among FoLAR's many projects are an annual river clean-up, the "Gran Limpieza," which brings 1500 people down to the river to clean up every Spring; an on-going series of conferences and planning workshops dealing with every aspect of the river.

MacAdams lives with his wife JoAnne Klabin, Director of the Sweet Relief Musician's Fund, and their daughter Natalia Grace, in Silver Lake, just northwest of downtown Los Angeles, and near the river.

L FUCKIN' A

for Bob & Bob

"this is biologically the most austere
and seismically the most stable place
on the face of the globe," Schneider said.

"Wastes here can truly be placed
out of sight and out of mind."

The bus depot lobby clock told me I had twenty-five minutes to wait, so I walked outside and picked up a *Newsweek* at the newstand. The newsboy eyed me from his stool. I turned to page 2, and the newsboy approached me with his hands bunched into his change apron, jingling his coins. He walked up to me so close I could smell his breath. "Yessir," he said, "can I help you?" I put the *Newsweek* back on the rack and picked up a Wall Street Journal. "Will this paper get me rich?" I asked. "A lot of people swear by it," said the newsboy. "How much is it?" "Twenty-five cents." "If I don't buy it, then I'll be richer by a quarter," I concluded, replacing the paper. "Very funny," said the newsboy, as his eyes narrowed. There was an arcade round the bus station and I decided to explore. Twenty minutes until rendezvous.

Fifteen minutes. Flies and bees buzzed in and out of open garbage cans strewn at the entrance to the souvenir stalls. In a filthy display window a dummy modeled a dusty bathing suit next to a deflated beach ball.

Ten minutes. At the back of the bus station was a taxi rank. The cabbies were snoozing in the heat, their visors with their "off-duty" signs turned down to shield their eyes from the light. I kept walking.

On the south side of the station I was drawn to a postcard stand. I looked through the cards for a few minutes until I found some great ones, then took them inside to pay. Five minutes.

Once inside, I realized this was more than a souvenir stand. Suspended from the old-fashioned ceiling as scrolls, pinned to all the walls, and draped over work tables and display counters were many dozens, perhaps hundreds of beautifully brushed calligraphy, exquisitely painted hermit sages in bamboo forests, roaring tigers, cabins at the bases of waterfalls at the feet of mountains that disappeared into the mists. One particular tiger was so beautifully rendered that each brush stroke seemed to transcend the roaring tiger's roar. There was a large work area near the back of the shop where several assistants looked busily at work turning out new calligraphies, and portraits in various steps toward completion. The old proprietor put down his work and came toward the counter. I handed him my quarter. He reached out for the money with his right hand while taking hold of my hand with his left. He held my hand and looked at me.

"You make very beautiful calligraphy here," I told him.

"Oh, you know calligraphy?"

"A little. Not really."

"I'm glad you like it. Would you like to try some?"

I felt pressed. I was looking for the exit, but he was holding all the cards. I thought Paul might be outside already, circling the block.

"Would you like to try?"

Uh, well. OK."

The man went and fetched some thin pieces of paper and a slender brush, which he dipped into a bottle of ink.

"What is your name?"

I told him.

He painted a pair of characters. That is your name," he said, continuing to draw. "This is your life," he continued, without looking up. "This is your house." He nodded. "It will be found, because it is not entirely lost." He looked up at me above his glasses. "But this time you will have to work at it much harder." He finished painting and smiled at me. "This is the Japanese character for the home. I'm putting it next to your name. OK?"

"For sure," I replied, and he rang up the sale.

Dazed, I pocketed my cards and went outside to look for Paul. "What the fuck? What the fuck?" I kept saying to myself, "Who was that guy, and how did he know who I was? Is this really Los Angeles?" I asked myself. "It sure is," I answered, looking 6th Street up and down. "And it's High Noon."

MOGULS AND MONKS

A dollar-green Cadillac limousine
pulls from the gate at Paramount
and turns down Melrose.
The mogul passenger leans his bald head
back on his head rest and smiles,
his face a mass of pure contentment

as two Buddhist monks bow by,
waiting at the corner for the light to change
so they can bow across Gower.
Though they don't
see each other, I am them both
as I turn up Highland, cruising
in the twelve spiritual
directions, with the
thirteen calls for cash.

But last night I met someone who was fine.

Fates, be kind.

Malraux says to love someone is not to
hold that someone for marvelous,
but for indispensable.

L.A. EXILE

The way seabreezes
skirt along the edge of the continent
that's how I want to reach you,
slip inside you like
a coastal
weather change, à la
anything interesting happening over there, dearie?
Dammit, why don't you write me? C'mon, honey.
One fire, one desire.

THE MEANING OF THE UNIVERSE AT NIGHT

TV on in every room,
on each screen a news. The phone rings
and Saturday night draws me down to the
China Club. Got any problems?
Ask Sy Chen. We chat it up
until I spot you coming toward me.
Gulp. But what's done is done, hon',
and can't be undone.
And when the credits rolls
we'll *see* who rides to retail eminence
and who's propelled outwards on a vein of fire.

Still, pleased to meet, we touch cheek to cheek
and smile; and after the bar closes
we see each other to the door. And,
though the world sends us into the night
our separate ways, we can still be graceful in our parting
and grateful for our instant. Even though the world
sends us off into the night alone.

Lewis MacAdams

Two Lebanese boys
in broken twilight,
half in Arabic,
discuss the Super Bowl.
A lunatic old man
raves at the entrance
to the L.A. times.
Six bells at Saint Vibiana's.
The 4th Street Viaduct lamps
flicker on; and underneath,
an SP diesel
pulls a string of empties
along the concrete river.
At the bus stop are
so many tired faces.
It's hard to keep
the dream awake
when night falls on the city.

1550 San Remo Drive, Pacific Pallisades

Thomas Mann (1875–1955)

In a letter to Erich von Kahler, Mann writes: "We ourselves thought at first that we belonged to Brentwood, and added Los Angeles to our address for good measure. But we were repeatedly corrected by the post office until we resigned ourselves to living nowhere else but Pacific Palisades, California, although I did not consider that a town name at all – and in fact it probably isn't a township but a landscape with a few colonial homes and ocean view."

The Manns helped many other German refugees – musicians, literati, film and theater people – move to California. To some extent, it felt like home. As Katja wrote: "In the world of émigrés everyone has an open house, and so in California we saw more German writers than we had in Munich." Thomas Mann and Bertolt Brecht, however, didn't get along with each other. Upon reading one of Brecht's plays, he commented: "Just imagine, the monster has talent." Thomas and Katja Mann received their American citizenship on June 23, 1944, in Los Angeles.

In writing *Dr. Faustus*, Mann went to Theodor W. Adorno for advice on musical matters. Adorno would later believe that he was the actual author of the book, not Mann. Once, when asked to wait for Thomas Mann and his guests to finish dinner before visiting, Adorno replied, "That you should make me wait here like this is such an affront to Thomas Mann that I really can't accept it. It's incomprehensible."

Dr. Faustus also caused resentment on the part of Arnold Schoenberg – the invention of the twelve-tone system attributed in the novel to Adrian Leverkühn. Schoenberg was finally appeased when Mann included a correction, in the second printing of the book, crediting Schoenberg as its inventor. *Dr. Faustus*, begun in 1943, was finished in 1946 and published the following year to generally favorable reviews.

On May 28, 1946, Mann returned to Pacific Palisades from a lung operation in Chicago: "It was the loveliest time of the year. The garden had been beautifully looked after by Vattaru, and every stroll amidst its rich display of flowers, every view over valley and hills to the clearly outlined chain of the Sierra [*ed. note*: more probably the San Gabriel Mountains, the Sierra beginning about 200 or more miles to the northeast) and over the tops of the palm trees on the other side to Catalina and the ocean – all these paradisaical scenes and colors enraptured me." Though Mann's lifelong project remained exclusively German and European, it is interesting to note that in *Dr. Faustus* the writer's exile *from* Europe becomes the narrator's exile *within* the "European fortress."

from *Dr. Faustus* (1947)

I wish to state quite definitely that it is by no means out of any wish to bring my own personality into the foreground that I preface with a few words about myself and my own affairs this report on the life of the departed Adrian Leverkühn. What I here set down is the first and assuredly very premature biography of that beloved fellow-creature and musician of genius, so afflicted by fate, lifted up so high, only to be so frightfully cast down. I intrude myself, of course, only in order that the reader – I might better say the future reader, for at this moment there exists not the smallest prospect that my manuscript will ever see the light unless, by some miracle, it were to leave our beleaguered European fortress and bring to those without some breath of the secrets of our prison-house – to resume only because I consider that future readers will wish to know who and what the author is do I preface these disclosures with a few notes about myself. Indeed, my mind misgives me that I shall only be awakening the reader's doubt whether he is in the right hands: whether, I mean, my whole existence does not disqualify me for a task dictated by my heart rather than by any true competence for the work.

I read over the above lines and cannot help remarking in myself a certain discomfort, a physical oppression only too indicative of the state of mind in which I sit down today in my little study, mine these many years, at Freising on the Isar, on the 27th of May 1943, three years after Leverkühn's death (three years, that is, after he passed from deep night into the deepest night of all), to make a beginning at describing the life of my unhappy friend now resting – oh, may it be so! – now resting in God. My words, I say, betray a state of mind in anguished conflict between a palpitating impulse to communicate and a profound distrust of my own adequacy. I am by nature wholly moderate, of a temper, I may say, both healthy and humane, addressed to reason and harmony; a scholar and *conjuratus* of the "Latin host," not lacking all contact with the arts (I play the viola d'amore) but a son of the Muses in that academic sense which by preference regards itself as descended from the German humanists of the time of the "Poets."

Heir of a Reuchlin, a Crotus of Dornheim, of Mutianus and Eoban of Hesse, the dæmonic, little as I presume to deny its influence upon human life, I have at all times found utterly foreign to my nature. Instinctively I have rejected it from my picture of the cosmos and never felt the slightest inclination rashly to open the door to the powers of darkness arrogantly to challenge, or if they of themselves ventured from their side, even to hold out my little finger to them. To this attitude I have made my sacrifices, not only ideally but also to my practical disadvantage: I unhesitatingly resigned my beloved teaching profession, and that before the time when it became evident that it could not be reconciled with the spirit and claims of our historical development. In this respect I am content with myself. But my self-satisfaction or, if you prefer, my ethical narrow-mindedness can only strengthen my doubt whether I may feel myself truly called to my present task.

Indeed, I had scarcely set my pen in motion when there escaped it a word which privately gave me a certain embarrassment. I mean the word "genius": I spoke of the musical genius of my departed friend. Now this word "genius," although extreme in degree, certainly in kind has a noble, harmonious, and humane ring. The likes of me, however far from claiming for my own person a place in this lofty realm, or ever pretending to have been blest with the *divinis influxibus ex alto*, can see no reasonable ground for shrinking, no reason for not dealing with it in clear-eyed confidence. So it seems. And yet it cannot be denied (and has never been) that the dæmonic and irrational have a disquieting share in this radiant sphere. We shudder as we realize that a connection subsists between it and the nether world, and that the reassuring *epitheta* which I sought to apply: "sane, noble, harmonious, humane," do not for that reason quite fit, even when – I force myself, however painfully, to make this distinction – even when they are applied to a pure and genuine, God-given, or shall I say God-inflicted genius, and not to an acquired kind, the sinful and morbid corruption of natural gifts, the issue of a horrible bargain...

Here I break off, chagrined by a sense of my artistic shortcomings and lack of self-control. Adrian himself could hardly – let us say in a symphony – have let such a theme appear so prematurely. At the most he should have allowed it to suggest itself afar off, in some subtly disguised, almost imperceptible way. Yet to the reader the words which escaped me may seem but a dark, distrustable suggestion, and to me alone like a rushing in where angels fear to tread. For a man like me it is very hard, it affects him almost like wanton folly, to assume the attitude of a creative artist to a subject which is dear to him as life and burns him to express; I know not how to treat it with the artist's easy mastery. Hence my too hasty entry into the distinction between pure and impure genius, a distinction the existence of which I recognize, only to ask myself at once whether it has a right to exist at all. Experience has forced me to ponder this problem so anxiously, so urgently, that at times, frightful to say, it has seemed to me that I should be driven beyond my proper and becoming level of thought, and myself experience an "impure" heightening of my natural gifts.

Again I break off, in the realization that I came to speak of genius, and the fact that it is in any case dæmonically influenced, only to air my doubt whether I possess the necessary affinity for my task. Against my conscientious scruples may the truth avail, which I always have to bring into the field against them, that it was vouchsafed me to spend many years of my life in close familiarity with a man of genius, the hero of these pages; to have known him since childhood, to have witnessed his growth and his destiny and shared in the modest role of adjuvant to his creative activity. The libretto from Shakespeare's comedy *Love's Labour's Lost*, Leverkühn's exuberant youthful composition, was my work; I also had something to do with the preparation of the texts for the grotesque opera suite *Gesta Romanorum* and the oratorio *The Revelation of St. John the Divine.* And perhaps there was this, that, and the other besides. But also I am in possession of papers, priceless sketches, which in days when he was still in health, or if that is saying too much, then in comparatively and legally sound ones, the deceased made over to me, to me and to no other; on these I mean to base my account, yes, I intend to select and include some of them direct. But first and last – and this justification was always the most valid, if not before men, then before God – I loved him, with tenderness and terror, with compassion and devoted admiration, and but little questioned whether he in the least returned my feeling.

That he never did – ah, no! In the note assigning his sketches and journals there is expressed a friendly, objective, I might almost say a gracious confidence, certainly honorable to me, a belief in my conscientiousness, loyalty, and scrupulous care. But love? Whom had this man loved? Once a woman, perhaps. A child, at the last, it may be. A charming trifler and winner of hearts, whom then, probably just because he inclined to him, he sent away – to his death. To whom had he opened his heart, whomever had he admitted into his life? With Adrian that did not happen. Human devotion he accepted, I would swear often unconsciously. His indifference was so great that he was hardly ever aware what went on about him, what company he was in. The fact that he very seldom addressed by name the person he spoke with makes me conjecture that he did not know the name, though the man had every reason to suppose he did. I might compare his absentness to an abyss, into which one's feeling towards him dropped soundless and without a trace. All about him was coldness – and how do I feel, using this word, which he himself, in an uncanny connection, once also set down? Life and experience can give to single syllables an accent utterly divorcing them from their common meaning and lending them an aura of horror, which nobody understands who has not learned them in that awful context.

2714 Marsh St. (Elysian Valley, demolished)

Thomas McGrath (1916–1990)

Thomas McGrath was born on a North Dakota farm in 1916. He attended the University of North Dakota, Louisiana State University, New College, and was a Rhodes Scholar at Oxford University. McGrath served in the Air Force in the Aleutian Islands during World War II. He worked as a documentary film script-writer and labor organizer, and taught at Colleges and Universities in Maine, California, New York, North Dakota, and Minnesota. He was the founder and first editor of the poetry magazine *Crazy Horse*.

In 1953, the House Committee on Un-American Activities began an investigation of Communist activities in the motion picture and educational fields in Los Angeles, when McGrath, teaching at Los Angeles State College, was called to testify. At the hearing, he stated: "As a poet I must refuse to cooperate with the Committee on what I can only call aesthetic grounds. The view of life which we receive through the great works of art is a privileged one – it is a view of life according to probability or necessity, not subject to the chance and accident of our real world and therefore in a sense truer than the life we see lived all around us."

Later McGrath was forced out of his teaching position, when he refused to sign the infamous California State "Loyalty Oath." Five years later, he wrote to friend E.P. Thompson, "Since the Committee got my teaching job, I've been working at several things, most very tiring and dull – and also bad paying. A very hard period. I wrote a long poem – about 150 pages – last year." This was the start of his narrative epic, *Letter to An Imaginary Friend,* which he would work on for 30 years, publishing "Part One" in 1963 and finishing "Part Four" in 1985. Of this work, Philip Levine has said, "I hope I can someday give this country or the few poetry lovers of this country something as large, soulful, honest, and beautiful as McGrath's great and still unappreciated epic of our mad and lyric century, *Letter to an Imaginary Friend*, a book from which we can draw hope and sustenance for as long as we last."

from *Letter to an Imaginary Friend* (1970)

PART ONE

I

1

– "From here it is necessary to ship all bodies east."
I am in Los Angeles, at 2714 Marsh Street,
Writing, rolling east with the earth, drifting toward Scorpio,
                                                                                    thinking
Hoping toward laughter and indifference.
"They came through the passes,
                    they crossed the dark mountains in a month of snow,

Finding the plain, the bitter water,
                                        the iron rivers of the black North.
Horsemen,
Hunters of the hornless deer in the high plateaus of that country,
They traveled the cold year, died in the stone desert."

Aye, long ago. A long journey ago,
Most of it lost in the dark, in a ruck of tourists,
In the night of the compass, companioned by tame wolves, plagued
By theories, flies, visions, by the anthropophagi...

I do not know what end that journey was toward.
– But I am its end. I am where I have been and where
I am going. The journeying destination – at least that...
But far from the laughter.
                                        So. Writing:
"The melt of the pig pointed to early spring.
The tossed bones augered an easy crossing.
North, said the mossy fur of the high pines.
West, said the colored stone at the sulphur pool."

4
Took them? They came –
Past the Horn, Cape Wrath, Oxford and Fifth and Main
Laughing and mourning, snug in the two seater buggy,
Jouncing and bouncing on the gumbo roads
Or slogging loblolly in the bottom lands –
My seven tongued family.
How could I escape? Strapped on the truckle bars
Of the bucking red-ball freights or riding the blinds cold
Or sick and sea-sawed on the seven seas
Or in metal and altitude, drilling the high blue
I fled.

I heard them laughing at the oarsmen's bench.
Conched in cowcatchers, they rambled at my side.
The seat of the buggy was wider than Texas
And slung to the axles were my rowdy cousins;
Riding the whippletrees: aunts, uncles, brothers,
Second cousins, great aunts, friends and neighbors
All holus-bolus, piss-proud, all sugar-and-shit
A goddamned gallimaufry of ancestors.
The high passes?
Hunter of the hornless deer?

5

A flickering of gopher light. The Indian graves...
And then the river.
                                        Companioned, and alone,
Five, ten, or twenty, I followed the coulee hills
Into the dreaming green of the river shade,
The fish-stinking cow-dunged dark of the cattle-crossing,
The fox-barking, timber-wolf country, where...
The cicada was sawing down the afternoon:
Upstream a beaver was spanking Nature:
The cows were wilder:
Horses carnivorous.

The kittycorner river cut through the buggy
Through Dachau and Thaelmann
Rolfe in Spain
Through the placid, woodchuck-coughing afternoon
Drifting
Past Greenwich, Baton Rouge, Sheldon, Rome
And past Red Hook and Mobile where the rivers mourn
Old Thames, Missouri, Rio Hondo. Now
In far Los Angeles I hear

L.A. EXILE

The Flying Dutchman in the dry river
Mourning. Mourning.
Ancestral night....

•

Passages of the dark; streets with no known turning
Beyond the sleepy midnight and the metaphysical summer
Leading here. Here. Here, queerly here.
To the east slant light of the underground moon, and the rusty garde
Empty.
                                        Bounded by ghosts.
                                                            Empty except for footnotes
Of journeying far friends near.

                                                                        Enter now,
O bird on the green branch of the dying tree, singing
Sing me toward home:
Toward the deep past and inalienable loss:
Toward the gone stranger carrying my name
In the possible future
                                                            – enter now:
Purlieus and stamping grounds of the hungering people
O enter

"They died in the stone desert
They crossed the dark mountain in the month of snow.
Finding the plain, the bitter water, the iron rivers of the black North.
Horns on the freeway. Footsteps of strangers,
Angelinos: visitations in the metropolitan night.

"Hunters of the hornless deer."

Ancestral baggage....

XII

5

Now, toward midnight, the rain ends.
The flowers bow and whisper and hush;
the clouds break
And the great blazing constellations rush up out of the dark
To hang in the flaming North....
Arcturus, the Bear, the Hunter
Burning.....

Now, though the Furies come, my furious Beast,
I have heard the Laughter,
And I go forward from catastrophe to disaster
Indifferent: singing:
My great ghosts and the Zodiac of my dead
Swing round my dream.

Star-shine steady over this house where I sit writing this down –
2714 Marsh Street –
Drifting toward Gemini...
Night, pure crystal,
coils in my ear like
song...

Los Angeles, 1955

PART TWO

II

1

Fictional breakfasts, feasts of illusionary light!
"Poo ine

L.A. EXILE

O dromos sto horyo where is the lonesome road
To the village where is it the hydroaeroplano leaves
For Buenos Aires?"
I'll cut for sign...
mark of the blazed tree
Where I left the note and the colored stone in the hopeful intervals
Between cyclones and water spouts, while the firing squads
Were taking a five minute break...
" – was right here, someplace...
– place where I left it..."
Patience.
I am the light. I'm
Wearing my blazer...
Begun before Easter in the holy sign
Of the Fish.
Dakota.
The farm house...
– but before that...

•

Ten years – doing time in detention camps of the spirit,
Grounded in Twin Plague Harbor with comrades Flotsom & Jetsom:
Wreckage of sunken boats becalmed in Horse Latitudes
Windless soul's doldrums Los Angeles Asia Minor of the intellect
Exile.

I arrived in the form of a dream, the dream formed
Journey begun in love and hunger, Dakota, the Old
Dominion of darkness...
from labor
ignitable books
unsettled

Thomas McGrath

Terms of a murderous century
dynamite
the eternal bourgeois
Verities of poverty and money – to voyage forth toward the light...

Got there by way of War and His cousin Personal Misery.
And of that journey and time and the records thereof kept
As of books written logs tallies maps manifestoes
As of resolutions past or not passed in aforementioned intervals
Between stampedes shipwrecks log jams battles with hostiles
Catatonic inventions hellsfire attacks of personal and spurious
Revelation –
Tokens:
stone
marked tree
immortal
Blazonings...

2

Windless city built on decaying granite, loose ends
Without end or beginning and nothing to tie to, city down hill
From the high mania of our nineteenth century destiny – what's loose
Rolls there, what's square slides, anything not tied down
Flies in...
kind of petrified shitstorm.
Retractable
Swimming pools.
Cancer farms.
Whale dung
At the bottom of the American night refugees tourists elastic
Watches...

Vertical city shaped like an inverse hell:

L.A. EXILE

At three feet above tide mark, at hunger line, are the lachrymose
Cities of the plain weeping in the sulphurous smog; Anaheim:
South Gate (smell of decaying dreams in the dead air)
San Pedro Land's End...
                                          – where the color of labor is dark –
(Though sweat's all one color) around Barrio No Tengo,
Among the Nogotnicks of the Metaphysical Mattress Factory, where
          the money is made.

And the second level: among the sons of the petty B's –
The first monkey on the back of South Gate, labor – at the ten
Thousand a year line (though still in the smog's sweet stench)
The Johnny Come Earlies of the middling class:
                                                                      morality
                                                                                      fink-size
Automatic rosaries with live Christs on them and cross-shaped purloined
Two-car swimming pools full of holy water...
                                                                  From here God goes
Uphill.
          Level to level.
                                       Instant escalation of money – up!
To Cadillac country.

                                       Here, in the hush of the long green,
The leather priests of the hieratic dollar enclave to bless
The lush-workmg washing machines of the Protestant Ethic ecumenical
Laundries: to steam the blood from the bills – O see O see how
Labor His Sublime Negation streams in the firmament!
Don't does all here; whatever is mean is clean.

And to sweep their mountain tops clear of coyotes and currency climbers
They have karate-smokers and judo-hypes, the junkies of pain,
Cooking up small boys' fantasies of mental muscles, distilling
A magic of gouged eyes, secret holds, charm

Of the high school girls demi-virginity and secret weapon
Of the pudenda pachucas (takes a short hair type
For a long hair joke) power queers; socially-acceptable sadists –
Will tear your arm off for a nickel and sell it back for a dime.

And these but the stammering simulacra of the Rand Corpse wise men –
Scientists who have lost the good of the intellect, mechanico-humanoids
Antiseptically manufactured by the Faustian humunculus process.
And how they dream in their gelded towers these demi-men!
(Singing of overkill, kriegspiel, singing of blindfold chess –
Sort of ainaleckshul rasslin matches to sharpen their fantasies
Like a scout knife.)
                    Necrophiles.
                                        Money protectors...
– They dream of a future founded on fire, on a planned coincidence
Of time and sulphur...
                              Heraclitian eschatology...

And over it all, god's face,
                                  or perhaps a baboon's ass
In the shape of an IBM beams toward another war.
One is to labor, two is to rob, three is to kill.
Executive
          legislative
                      judiciary...
                                        – muggery, buggery, and thuggery
All Los Angeles
                America
                          is divided into three parts.

2041 Alvarado St. (Echo Park)

Carey McWilliams (1905–1980)

McWilliams grew up on a cattle ranch in Colorado, riding his horse to school. His father was one of the pioneer settlers of northwestern Colorado, who had built a minor cattle empire before being wiped out in the post-WWI collapse of that market.

McWilliams wrote: "I arrived in Los Angeles in the first years of the 1920 decade. No migrant ever arrived in the region knowing less about it than I did. I had never visited the state before I came to live there. I remember that I left Denver for Los Angeles in a blizzard a day or two after St. Patrick's Day, 1922. The snow storm is an important detail because those who set out for Southern California under such circumstances are always the more impressed by the warm and affable climate they encounter on arrival. The bit about St. Patrick's Day is also of minor importance. I had celebrated the occasion much too enthusiastically, certainly, for a freshman who was already on probation at the University of Denver for some similar, and earlier antics. So the authorities, deeply imbued as they were in those days with the Methodist ethos, were naturally, and justifiably, a bit nettled, and suggested that the time had come for me to leave. And where do you go when you leave Colorado? I did what many other residents of the Rocky Mountain states were doing in the 1920s (although for different reasons), I set out for Southern California."

He has said of Los Angeles in that period, "Then suddenly, beginning in the 1920s, it achieved great-city status through a process of forced growth based on booster tactics and self-promotion." Later, he was to add, "To say that my first reactions to Los Angeles were negative would be a gross understatement. I loathed the place. Gradually I began to acquire a relish for this strange new scene. Long before the end of the decade, I came to feel that I had a ringside seat at a year-round circus."

He worked at the *L.A. Times* while attending USC, chasing down delinquent advertising bills. He writes: "Near the *Times* was the old Music and Arts Building. I got to know the building and its tenants as perhaps no one else knew them. The place was alive with colorful fakers and con-men. The various "studios" were occupied by a constantly changing collection of voice teachers, "masseurs," swamis, mind readers, graphologists, yogis, divine teachers, faith healers, spiritualists, old thespians who wanted to teach neophytes, fake publishers, fake literary agents, and other exotic types. And this was merely one building, one collection. In our frantic efforts to minimize the *Times*' losses from running advertising it should never have accepted in the first place and certainly not unless accompanied by a certified check, we came to know a fine cross-section of men and women "on the make," mostly recent migrants to Los Angeles, enticed there by dreams of health, fame, and easy money. Some of our adversaries later became prominent figures in the business and financial life of the community – in motion pictures, oil, and real estate. Men who later became millionaire "realtors" and joined the California Club feuded with us as though we were revenue officers at war with moonshiners."

McWilliams left Los Angeles in 1951 to work as the editor of *The Nation.*

from *Southern California Country: an Island on the Land* (1946)

"On the road to old L.A.,
Where the tin-can tourists play
And a sign says 'L.A. City Limits'
At Clinton, Ioway."

CHAPTER IX: "I'm a Stranger Here Myself"

In 1890 native-born Californians constituted 25% of the residents of Los Angeles; in 1900, 27%; in 1910, 25%; in 1920, 20%; and in 1930, 20%. Visiting Los Angeles in 1930, Garet Garrett noted that "you have to begin with the singular fact that in a population of a million and a quarter, every other person you see has been there less than five years. More than nine in every ten you see have been there less than fifteen years. Practically, therefore, the whole population is immigrant, with the slowly changing sense of home peculiar to non-indigenous life. The mind is first adjusted, then the conscious feelings; but for a long time – for the rest of the immigrant's life perhaps – there will be in the cells a memory of home that was elsewhere."

An excellent statement of a major aspect of life in Southern California, this observation requires some refinement. While retaining a "memory of home," the newcomer in Southern California is not really an exile for he and his kind have always constituted a dominant majority of the population. In such a unique situation, the newcomer is generally able to find, somewhere in the vast recesses of Los Angeles, others of his kind. Association with them enables him to keep alive his memory of home. Out of this situation has been improvised a unique social institution, "the state society," which has functioned among out-of-state Americans in Southern California much as an immigrant-aid society functions in foreign-born communities. It assists the newcomer in making an adjustment by placing him in touch with others of his kind, thereby assuaging the aching loneliness – the really terrible loneliness – that for years has been so clearly apparent in the streets and parks, the boarding houses and hotels, the cafeterias and "lonely clubs" of Los Angeles. In fact, there is no more significant Southern California institution than the state society.

I. SHEPHERD OF THE LONELY

> *"For Southern California's balmy days,*
> *Movie sets and palm-lined ways,*
> *Snow-capped peaks and azure bays –*
> *Land of fortune, land of rest –*
> *For you alone we journeyed west."*

The first state society was formed in Los Angeles on November 16, 1882, when Col. C.H. Haskins assembled the Pennsylvanians and organized a club. A tradition survives that Maine was the first state to organize, which may very probably have been the case, but I have been unable to verify the statement. In part, the state societies had their genesis in the colony system of settlement, whereby colonists were recruited from a particular region or community to form new townsites in Southern California. At the outset, the motivation was purely social, as shown by a resolution adopted by the Illinois Association at a meeting held on December 18, 1886:

> Whereas we, the members of the Illinois Association, having endured the tortures inseparably connected with life in a region of ice and snow, and having fled from our beloved State to this favored land;
>
> Resolved: That we sympathize with our friends and former fellow citizens of Illinois who still endure the ills they have, rather than fly to pleasures that they know not of;
>
> Resolved: That in this grand country we have the tallest mountains, the biggest trees, the crookedest railroads, the dryest rivers, the loveliest flowers, the smoothest ocean, the finest fruits, the mildest lives, the softest breezes, the purest air, the heaviest pumpkins, the best schools, the most numerous stars, the most bashful real estate agents, the brightest skies, and the most genial sunshine to be found anywhere in the United States;
>
> Resolved: That we heartily welcome other refugees from Illinois and will do all in our power to make them realize that they are sojourning in a City of Angels, where their hearts will be irrigated by the healing waters flowing from the perennial fountains of health, happiness, and longevity.

Iowans were among the first to form a state society and the first group to establish the practice of holding picnic meetings. A notation in one of the annals mentions a picnic meeting in Lincoln Park on January 1, 1887, which was attended by 408 Iowans. It was an Iowan, C.H. Parsons, who, on April 24, 1909, sponsored the formation of the Federation of State Societies of which he remained the guiding influence until his death a few years ago. (The federation was not formally incorporated until January 10, 1913, by which time a society had been formed for every state in the union.) By the late 'twenties, the federation boasted a membership of 500,000, representing every state in the union and every province in Canada. Centering in Los Angeles, the movement began to spread throughout Southern California. Branch state societies were formed in Ventura, Riverside, San Diego, Pasadena, Long Beach, and Santa Paula (the home of the people from Maine.) Today the Iowa Society, long the dominant group in the federation, has branches throughout the region.

In his memoirs, Parsons tells of the first Iowa Society picnic he attended, in Pasadena, on January 18, 1900. It was, he noted, "no pickle and cold-coffee affair," but a real picnic. Here it was that he first sensed the wave of the future, or, as he put it, that he first heard "the steady oncoming tread of the dauntless Iowans, whose faces were toward the Setting Sun." At this meeting 3,000 Iowans were present; the next year saw 6,000 on hand, then 12,000, 18,000, and, finally, in the 'twenties, when the picnic ground had been transferred to Bixby Park in Long Beach, 150,000 Iowans answered the roll call. In the early 'twenties, writes Parsons, it was a thrilling experience to hear "the tramp of Iowa's mustered hosts," as people set out for the picnic grounds. On Iowa Day, "a singular excitement was in the air, when, from far and near, the tribes begin to assemble ... a sight not to be matched in any commonwealth of the world." For years all roads in Southern California, on Iowa Day, led to the picnic grounds. "On the morning of the Great Reunion," wrote Parsons, "there is wont to be a light on land and sea that must impress newcomers with the glory of the home of their adoption: a light that flashes along the purple embattlements of the Sierra Madres, touching dark canyons and scarred mountain walls, leaping along foothills that ripple to the plains; a light that brings into relief the bright green of the wide reaches thus carpeted in mid-winter, and that finally dances out and out, in elfish beauty, to caress the waves of the Pacific." On Iowa Day, the jealous Native Son found himself standing outside the picnic grounds or morbidly paced deserted streets.

This man Parsons was, perhaps, the first real sociologist in Southern California. He had an uncanny insight into the acute loneliness that haunted the region. Out of this insight, he created a social institution that perfectly answered a need sensed by thousands of residents. To be sure, the federation became, and to some extent still remains, a promotion agency, giving information to tourists and homeseekers, routing newcomers to the right real-estate offices and banks, and indirectly sponsoring the "right" candidates for public office. But, essentially, the state society was an innocent conception, a purely spontaneous folk affair.

Parsons also had a great flair for organization. Under this leadership, the Iowa Society became a thing of beauty and an object of wonder. Beginning around 1920, he broke the bulky Iowa Society down into its component parts by forming county societies within the larger state society. At the Iowa picnic, signs directed visitors to ninety-nine sacred spots in the park, each designation representing one of the counties of Iowa. Polk County, he noted, always had the largest attendance, followed by Lynn, Scott, Woodbury, and Marshall. The cost of the picnic was largely financed by the sale of ribbons, and, here again, the genius of Parsons was revealed. For the ribbons were not alike. Red ribbons, representing "the life blood that must be sold only to natives," went to those born in Iowa, blue ribbons were sold to those "who have merely lived in Iowa" (the color blue, said Parsons, symbolized "the feeling of blueness for not having been born there"), while yellow ribbons were sold to the visitors, the yellow symbolizing the "jaundice of envy" of those who were not Hawkeyes. Still later, a white ribbon was sold as a badge of glory to those haughty pioneers who had lived in Iowa for fifty years or more. The official "button" of the society, sold in vast quantities, consisted of a white background with an ear of corn in the center, bearing along its length a picture of a fat pig, with the caption: "Hog and hominy."

Not content with this masterly organizational apparatus, Parsons proceeded to form Iowa college-reunion societies so that the graduates of the thirty-five colleges in Iowa could meet beneath particular trees designated by the various college flags and pennants. So famous did these Iowa picnics become that people came from all over the world just to attend them. Notices of the meetings were, of course, mailed to all Iowans listed in Parsons' voluminous records. In addition, notices appeared in all the newspapers published south of Tehachapi, giving the time and place of the meeting, and, in later years, most of the Iowa newspapers carried notices and stories of the meetings. Mrs. Parsons informs me that Iowa families have for years made a practice of planning their winter vacation so that they could be present in Los Angeles on Iowa Day. The picnic became the established form of meeting largely because, as Parsons put it, there was no hall in all Southern California large enough to house the Iowans.

A small, modest little man, "inconspicuously dressed as a field mouse," Parsons was known as "the man who makes half a state feel at home," and, as "the man who meets a million cordially." While he could not remember all the Iowans, he knew thousands of them by name, and all of them knew him. He felt, and rightly, that the state societies had served an enormously important function in anchoring people in Southern California. As he put it, the state societies "liquidated the blues." After they had formed a state society, the Iowans, he noted, began to speak affectionately of Southern California and "settled themselves down in its warm sunshine like kittens under a kitchen range." Parsons took the keenest delight, as he wrote, in watching "the long line of Iowa's hosts swinging down the curving walk, ten, fifteen abreast, in endless serpentines." Only he knew how valuable the new social form was to these newcomers. "I've seen a lot of thrilling scenes," he wrote, "of brother meeting brother for the first time in years; of friends standing, hands clasped, tears on their cheeks, greeting each other for the first time in ten, twenty, thirty or forty years."

As loyal to California as a Native Son, Parsons always insisted that the state-society movement did not alienate the affections of the newcomers. "People don't like California less," he stoutly contended, "merely because they like to gather together and reminisce." Gifted with rare sociological insight, Parsons observed that Middle Westerners invariably identified themselves in terms of the states or counties in which they had lived, never by towns. The expression heard among them was, "I'm a Polk County man." He used to amuse himself by asking them to name the capital of the state from which they came and noted that, in most instances, they did not know the answer. On the other hand, Easterners always say "I'm from Boston," or "I'm a New Yorker."

Those who have never attended an Iowa picnic cannot possibly imagine the scene, when, the hilarity of the picnic over, gnarled old hands and beaming faces would answer the roll call of the counties. The societies were, and to some extent still are, more than one-party annual affairs. On the contrary, for twenty-five years these societies each averaged one regular monthly meeting, all announced, planned, and arranged by Parsons and his delightful wife. "For a quarter of a century," wrote Parsons, "I averaged six nights out a week attending state-society functions." Obviously these societies were a powerful integrating force, making for a sense of social solidarity and cohesiveness. In fact, I believe it fair to say that the state societies constituted ersatz communities, communities within a community, workable substitutes for the lack of real communities. The federation of state societies, for example, functioned, for many purposes, as a community. For many years, the federation was a major political force in Southern California, with politicians clamoring to be "introduced" at the picnics and eagerly identifying themselves with one or another of the state societies. The Iowa Society elected one of its members, Frank Merriam, governor of California and placed a number of its members on the bench.

One could make a book of the Iowa jokes heard in Southern California. It was proposed, for example, that Southern California be known as Caliowa. Long Beach has been known for years as Iowa's Sea Port. On meeting in Southern California, strangers were supposed to inquire: "What part of Iowa are you from?" The transcontinental trains were supposed to run non-stop excursions directly from Iowa to Bixby Park on Iowa Day. Whether the expression, "I'm a stranger here myself," actually originated in Los Angeles or not, it aptly expresses the reality of loneliness that was responsible for Parsons' great success. When he first began to devote full time to the federation, he did so, he said, because he had so frequently heard the expression, "If I could only run into some one I know," in the streets of Los Angeles. In Darwin Teilhet's novel, *Journey to the West*, the section on Southern California is entitled "The Iowa Coast."

444 Ocampo Dr., Pacific Pallisades

Henry Miller (1891–1980)

Born in Brooklyn in 1891, Miller's career was quite varied before he started living as a writer in Paris. In New York City he worked for Atlas Portland Cement, from 1909–11; traveled throughout the western United States working at odd jobs in 1913; worked with his father back home in their tailor shop in 1914; sorted mail for the War Department in 1917; with Bureau of Economic Research in 1919; Western Union Telegraph in Manhattan, from 1920–24, starting as a messenger and eventually becoming employment manager; sold prose-poems from door to door, 1925; opened speakeasy in Greenwich Village, 1927; toured Europe, 1928; returned to New York in 1929; and then back to Europe and Paris, where he lived from 1930–1939.

His books about his expatriate days in France, *Tropic of Cancer*, *Tropic of Capricorn*, and *Black Spring*, were first published in Paris in the 1930s. In her preface to his first book, *Tropic of Can-*

cer (1934), a publication for which she was largely responsible, Anais Nin writes, "In a world grown paralyzed with introspection and constipated by delicate mental meals this brutal exposure of the substantial body comes as a vitalizing current of blood." It was not until 1961 that Miller was able to publish this work in the U.S., with his legal victory over the censorship of the 1961 Grove Press edition of *Tropic of Cancer*.

After first visiting California while writing *The Air-Conditioned Nightmare*, Henry Miller moved there in 1942. He stayed for a time with friends in a cottage in the Beverly Glen section of Los Angeles. Among his first impressions of California he mentioned: "This is the vital spot (for people like us) in America. It is quite unexhaustible." In 1943 Miller mailed, from Los Angeles, his "Open Letter to All and Sundry" – a forceful plea for money from his prominent friends. He also began to earn some money selling his watercolors.

In 1963, Miller moved into the house on 444 Ocampo Drive in Pacific Pallisades. Three years later he met a 26 year old Japanese jazz singer, Hiroko Tokuda (who sang at a restuarant in Chinatown). Hoki sang love songs in five languages – English, French, Spanish, Italian and Japanese. Night after night Miller drove to the restaurant to hear her sing. Hoki repeatedly resisted Miller's advances, until the U.S. Immigration Office informed her that she was to leave the country. The two were married soon thereafter, in 1967.

A torturous two years followed, in which Hoki would stay out all night with friends and disappear for days at a time. In desperation, Miller wrote *Insomnia or the Devil at Large*. Ms. Tokuda moved out of Miller's house two years after their marriage, and left for good in 1974.

from *Insomnia or The Devil at Large* (1974)

Night after night it was the bar. Sometimes it began with dinner — upstairs. I would watch her eat with the same attention as later I listened to her play and sing. Often I was the first one at the bar. How lovely, how enchanting to receive exclusive attention! (It could have been any one else, he would have received the same attention. First come, first served.)

Those same songs night after night — how can any one do it and not go mad? And always with feeling, as

(10.)

if delivering her very soul. So that's the life of an entertainer! I used to say to myself. Same tunes, same faces, same responses — and same headaches. Given the chance, I would change all that. Surely she must be fed up with it. So I thought.

An entertainer is never fed up with the game. At the worst she gets bored. But never for long. Life without approval, without applause, without acclaim is meaningless to her. There must always be a sea of faces, silly faces, stupid faces, drunken faces — no matter! But faces. There must always be that starry-eyed idiot who appears for the first time and, with tears in his eyes, exclaims — "You're wonderful! You're marvelous! Please sing it again!" And she will sing it again, as if to him only and never again. And if he is a man of means, perhaps a shoe manufacturer, he

(11.)

will ask her to go to the races. And she will accept the invitation, as if he had bestowed a great honor on her.

Sitting there at the bar, playing the part of Mr. Nobody, I had a wonderful insight into the whole show. Forgetting, of course, that I was a part of it, perhaps the saddest part. One by one they would confess to me, tell me how much they loved her, and I, I would listen as if immune, but always sympathetic and full of understanding.

"Love must have the power to find its own way to certainty...." (Hermann Hesse)

First though one has to learn to battle with the powers that rule the base of the spine, viz. Kundalini's brothers and sisters-in-law.

"Good morning, Fröken, is it permitted to touch your puff to-day?" (my alter ego, Herr Nagel, speaking.)

All those beautiful tunes rolling around in my noodle as I roll along in the cab. "What would you like me to sing?" Like Madame

(12.)

Yamaguchi begging permission to remove her drunken husband's shoes. Why not "Irish Eyes are Smiling"? Or, "By Killarney's Lakes and Dells?" Anything with a smile in it so that I can pretend I'm happy. "There are smiles that make you happy, there are smiles...." And why not a dash of Bitters? Sometimes I smiled so much it wouldn't come off when I went to bed. I would lie there with eyes closed, smiling back. Now and then I'd get up and do a low bow—the bow of extreme humility. (They have a good word for it in Japanese—I forget what it is now.) Anyway, it's a back-breaker. What's more, it keeps you in trim for the next day's insults. Never lose face! If you meet with prevarication, indignation, procrastination, hallucination, falsification, vacillation, or even constipation, keep smiling, keep bowing.

Despite all the chicanery, all the frivolity, and mendacity, I believed

(13.)

in her. I believed even when I knew she was lieing to me. For every wrong, stupid, treacherous thing she did I could make excuses. Wasn't I a bit of a liar myself? Wasn't I too a cheat, a humbug, a traitor? If you love you must believe, and if you believe you understand and forgive. Yeah, I could do all that but — I couldn't forget. Part of me is a sublime idiot and another part is detective, judge and executioner. I can listen like an obedient child and sing Yankee Doodle Dandy backwards at the same time. I could remember weeks later unfinished phrases and sentences, and fill in the missing parts at will — with variations. Only I refrained from doing so. I wanted to see, and I lay in wait to see, what she would remember to remember.

But she wasn't much for recalling or remembering. She always opened up new fields of exploration, like covering the coffin with spades full of dirt to bury

(14.)

the past. Now it's buried, let's dance!
Now it's dead, let's make merry! "What
are you doing to-morrow? I'll call you
around four, O.K.?" "O.K." But there
never was a to-morrow. It was always yesterday.

The day before yesterday was another
matter. I mean her life with others, her
love life, so to speak. Somehow all that
seemed locked in the vault of memory.
Only a stick of dynamite could open it.
Besides, was it really important, really
necessary to go into all that? "Love
must have the power, etc. etc. etc."
Maybe I only thought I was in love.
Maybe I was simply hungry, lonely, a
clay pigeon any one could put away
with a toy pistol.

I try to think — when did I first
fall in love with her? Not the first time
we met, that's definite. If I had never
met her again it wouldn't have bothered me in the least. I remember
how surprised I was when she called

(15.)

me the next day, or the day after. I didn't even recognize her voice. "Hello! This is your little friend from Tokyo speaking." That's how it really began. Over the telephone. Me wondering why I should be honored with a call. Maybe she was lonesome. She had only arrived a few weeks before. Maybe some one had tipped her off that I was crazy about the Orient, particularly about Oriental women. More particularly about the Japanese woman.

"You really dig them, don't you?" a pal of mine keeps saying.

The ones I dig most are still in Japan, I guess. Like Lawrence said in "Twilight in Italy" — "The whistlers go to America." There are people who are born out of time and there are people who are born out of country, caste and tradition. Not loners exactly but exiles, voluntary exiles. They're not always romantic either: they just don't belong. And I mean — nowhere.

2247 Hidalgo St. (SilverLake)

Anais Nin (1903–1977)

Of the many American expatriates in Paris in the twenties and thirties, Anais Nin was one of the few repatriates. She was born in Neuilly to artistic parents: father, Joaquin, a pianist and composer; mother Rosa, a singer. Joaquin deserted the family when Anais was eleven, and Rosa took her children, Anais, Joaquin, and Thorvald, to New York. During the separation from her father, Nin wrote him a letter that would evolve into her most famous and important work, her *Diary*. Nin quit high school and continued her studies at home and in the public libraries.

Around age 21, she married Hugh Guiler, a banker (later known as Ian Hugo, a film maker and illustrator of Nin's books), and, sometime before 1930, she returned to France, where she stayed until the War forced her back to the U.S. In Paris, in 1931, she met the unknown, unpublished writer Henry Miller, who became her most intimate friend throughout the Paris years, and with whom she remained close to until her death. After the War, she also married Rupert Pole who lived in Los Angeles.

Nin's first impressions of Los Angeles, like most, were strong. In a letter to Lawrence Durrell, she wrote: "I live a divided life. One in New York with Hugo-the-father, graceful apartment, chic clothes, white heat living, many friends, café life in the Village, trips to Mexico, business. And another life here with Rupert-the-son, grandson of Frank Lloyd Wright, nature man, beach man, a professor by mistake, by temperament a guitar player hating work ... have friends but colorless because California is colorless, like a cheap drug that has been mixed with bicarbonate and toothpaste, a pseudo-tranquilizer."

Part of Nin's unease might have been because of the double life (the "Trapeze," as she called it) she was leading, with husbands in both New York and Los Angeles. She would shuttle between the two, covertly, for the next 30 years.

She lived on a steep hillside on "the wrong side of Silver Lake" overlooking the reservoir that gave the district its name (which Raymond Chandler dismissively referred to as "Gray Lake"). Rupert Pole (Frank Lloyd Wright's grandson) had built the house himself, which was designed by Pole's father, Lloyd Wright.

from *The Diary of Anais Nin: 1966–1974* (1981)

Last night, in Los Angeles, Henry Jaglom came. He has long hair, the most intelligent, aware eyes behind eyeglasses, with super vision, one feels. A genuine, open smile. He is magnificently articulate. His descriptions of his parents and his relationships to them complete. His father "the most interesting man in the world," powerful, convinced he is always right because he has always made the right decisions. A Russian Jew, he left Germany at the right time, influenced and dominated influential people and cannot believe he can ever be wrong.

But with Henry he found the most diabolically effective way of tyranny: love. He loves his son. "I know I should let you make your own mistakes, but I love you and if I see you about to fall out of a window I must hold you back." He came to see *A Safe Place*. He was proud that he could look at it as if it were made by somebody else, not his son. "Yes, it is like you, crazy, but it has something, it has some quality at moments...." A quality which made him dream that night and remember his dream for the first time in his life. Henry is almost overwhelmed by the significance of this subliminal influence we both practice, he is ready to weep. The shell has cracked, at last. He dreamed that Henry was the girl, dreamed it was Henry's life. But just as Henry expects more, fearing to have crossed the border into the irrational the father will not concede to, he adds that the dream was probably due to a pillow that kept sliding behind the bed.

His mother is beautiful and intelligent. They understand each other. When homesick for Europe after they came to America in 1940, she played *La Mer* over and over again while pregnant with Henry, and later when he chose the music for *A Safe Place*, he selected the pieces which made him weep. One of them was *La Mer*. He has been taping all his conversations with his parents for five years (to keep, conserve, preserve what may vanish). This, in a period when links to parents are so often broken, amazes his contemporaries. I saw his diary, a real date book. He makes entries in different colors, mostly designs indicating color of person or place. Calligraphy, Pop Art, one word, a name, to remind him.

In Israel he met a man who asked him if he knew my work and then offered the information that he was Dr. Mann in *Collages*. I told Henry his real name. But he introduced himself: "I am Doctor Mann."

People connect his film with my work. There are affinities.

Discovered word "Numinous." We looked it up in the dictionary. It pleased Henry Jaglom. "Spiritually elevated. The strange numinous sense of presentness, like a spell. From 'numen,' the presiding divinity or spirit of a place. Creative energy regarded as a genius or demon dwelling within one."

Before Henry's visit I had a difficult week. Illness, depression. The day before I emerged from the doldrums I had a dream: I was condemned to die. I was lying on a board and I was going to be electrocuted. First I was given a sedative, which did not have any effect. The man who was going to execute me finally could not do it. He loved me. He freed me and I knew he was going to pamper me. It was after this dream that I awakened well and began spiraling upward.

Wakened at seven and began work on article for *Westways*. Since I returned I had to answer letters, take care of the "business" part of writing. With Henry Jaglom's visit I was inspired again.

Outside in the world the climate is suffocating. Everyone watches Watergate on television from seven AM to two PM. They call it a morality play. At last the evil is exposed, the corruption being judged.

But I refuse to spend my day in the company of such a low breed of men. I rejoiced wildly when Ellsberg was free, but newspapers and television give me the feeling that people are nourishing themselves on garbage. I find history repellent, not worthy of attention. It is an escape from the real tasks. Ha ha, they called the artist an escapist but the real escapists are the spectators of history, avoiding the active tasks of changing themselves, because the men being tried were chosen by them when they voted for Nixon.

Nature was kind to me. First of all, sensual love can continue as long as emotional love is alive. In my case my body was never distorted. My feet are unchanged – the ankles not swollen. I have no varicose veins. I have kept my weight at 120 pounds and wear the same size dress I wore at sixteen. I hold myself erect and walk lithely, swiftly. The only signs of age which were ugly were wrinkles on the throat. I have no frown lines between the eyes. I have wrinkles around my eyes, laugh wrinkles, but no pouches. My forehead is smooth. My legs are slim, and I can wear miniskirts. The flesh under my forearm is a little loose. But my breasts are like a young girl's, the nipples pink. I have a slim, indented waistline.

When you love someone for a long time, the expression of the body, its presence, takes on emotional attributes; and lovers do not lose desire because of the signs of age. Deep love grows deeper with the loved one's flowering. The body changes but so does the spirit, and its numinous qualities increase.

I am youthful when friends come, and I talk with brightness and catch all that is being said. I am a tireless walker and I walk fast.

It is not so definable – age, desire and love. I still arouse desire and receive love letters.

At Robert Snyder's suggestion, International Community College asked Lawrence Durrell and me to take a few writing students. This "university without walls" uses the old guild system of a master teacher working with each student on a "one to one" basis. Their offices are in Westwood Village, next to UCLA, but they now have teachers all over the world.

I wrote for their catalogue:

> Anaïs Nin, Los Angeles, California, will accept ten students, graduate or undergraduate, for individual, independent study in diary and fiction writing. The following expresses Anaïs Nin's philosophy of teaching writing:
>
> "The summation of my methods of inspiring writers is contained in *The Novel of the Future.* It means studying all the ways of revivifying writing and reuniting it with the

rhythm of life itself. It means discovering the ever-renewed sources of its vitality and power. It means restoring its lost influence to help us out of the desperate loneliness of silence, out of the anxieties of alienation. It means giving a voice once again to the deep sources of metaphysical and numinous qualities contained in human beings and inhibited by our cultures. I think of writing as the ultimate instrument for explorations of new forms of consciousness, as a means to ecstasy, to a wider range of experience, to a deep way of communicating with other human beings. That is why I wish to teach both diary writing, which keeps us in close contact with the personal, and fiction writing, which is the expansion of what we have learned and experienced into myth and poem. I teach writing as a way of reducing distance between human beings, opening vision into experience, deepening understanding of others, as a way to touch and reach the depths of human beings, as nourishment; as a means of linking the content of the dream to our actions so that they become harmonious and interactive. I teach the source of writing, which is ever fertile, the images of dreams, how to use them, how they can become the starting point of a saga, an adventure, a drama. By the interaction of diary writing and fiction, I show how experience can be heightened, expanded, developed. The image of the Japanese paper flower which expands in a glass of water is apt in this case. I teach writing as a way to reintegrate ourselves when experience shatters us, as a center of gravity, as an exercise in creative will, as an exercise in synthesis, as a means to create a world according to our wishes, not those of others, as a means of creating the self, of making the inner journey, of giving birth to ourselves. I teach the value of the personal relationships to all things because it creates intimacy, and intimacy creates understanding,

understanding creates love and love conquers loneliness. Before becoming a perfect novelist, I teach it is important to possess empathy and identification. I advise whoever wishes to study with me to read *The Novel of the Future* in order to understand what I believe writing can become and the vital role of the writer."

My sweetest moments are spent in the pool. I swim two or three times a day throughout the year. Though it is right next to the house, the pool with its dark green color, with plants growing over its sides, with huge red sandstone boulders at the corners, becomes part of the garden. While swimming, you can look out over the edge and see the lake below. The trees give me complete privacy so I can swim *au naturel*. On the rare occasions of a writing block, often I can float it away in the pool. The side of the house facing the pool is glass, and sometimes when it is raining I leave my tiny writing cell and write in the large room like a Buddhist monk meditating in front of his reflecting pool, hypnotized by the lacework of interlocking circles formed by the raindrops. Fortunately (even though it *never* rains in the summer in Los Angeles), it rained a little one day that Robert Snyder was making his film and Baylis Glascock was able to capture this with his camera. The Garden of Eden effect is enhanced by the perfume from the forest of pittosporum trees, like a blend of lemon and jasmine.

I am beginning to appreciate Los Angeles. True, Frank Lloyd Wright called it a lot of suburbs looking for a city (he also said the United States tilts to the southwest and everything loose ended up in Southern California), and I still resent the long drives on the freeways. But I now feel this is the only large cosmopolitan city where I can be warm all year, close to the sea and still create my own small paradise just five minutes from downtown.

Garden of Allah, Sunset & Crescent Heights (demolished & "redeveloped")

Dorothy Parker (1893–1967)

Parker arrived in Los Angeles in 1931 for a three-month writing stint at MGM. She lived with her husband and writing partner Alan Campbell at the Garden of Allah, a bungalow complex hidden among four acres of exotic palms, banana, bamboo, cedar, grapefruit and orange trees. The complex featured John Barrymore's drunken midnight dives into the pool fully-clothed, Tallulah Bankhead's naked cavorting at 5:00 AM, and other antics by its extrovert-residents that earned it a notorious reputation. The place became known as "the uterus of Flickerland".

Parker wrote to her sister: "Aside from the work, which I hate like holy water, I love it here." Interviewed about her experiences in Hollywood, she said: "I just sat in a cell-like office and did nothing. I would imagine the Klondike would be like that –

a place where people rush for gold." At script conferences, her dog at her feet, she would knit through the meeting unable or unwilling to hide her extreme boredom.

Parker would return for long stretches in Los Angeles for most of her life. Asked by the *L.A. Times* how she liked being back at work in Hollywood, she replied, "It's alright. You make a little money and get caught up on your debts. We're up to 1912 now." She wrote of the industry:

> Oh, come my love, and join with me
> The oldest infant industry.
> Come, seek the bourne of palm and pearl
> The lovely land of boy-meets-girl.
> Come, grace the lotus-laden shore,
> The isle of Do-What's-Done-Before,
> Come, curb the new and watch the old win
> Out where the streets are paved with Goldwyn ...

While living in Los Angeles, she became increasingly politically active. In 1933 she became one of the chief organizers of the Screen Writers' Guild. "I am a Communist," she declared in 1934. In 1936 she helped form the Anti-Nazi League. Addressing the Left-Wing Congress of American Writers in 1939, she said that in Hollywood "... the word 'sophisticate' means, very simply, 'obscene.' A sophisticated story is a dirty story. Some of that meaning was wafted eastward and got itself mixed up into the present definition. So that a 'sophisticate' means: one who dwells in a tower made of a DuPont substitute for ivory and holds a glass of flat champagne in one hand and an album of dirty post cards in the other."

In 1947, the House Sub-Commitee on Un-American Activities (HUAC) named Parker as an alleged Communist. Throughout the hearing, Parker exhibited disdain for the proceedings.

When asked the infamous question "Are you now or have you ever been a member of the Communist party?" she replied, "I was and am many things, to myself and to my friends. But I am not a traitor and I will not be involved in this obscene inquisition." HUAC quietly dropped the case.

TOMBSTONES IN THE STARLIGHT

I. *The Minor Poet*

His little trills and chirpings were his best.
    No music like the nightingale's was born
Within his throat; but he, too, laid his breast
    Upon a thorn.

II. *The Pretty Lady*

She hated bleak and wintry things alone.
    All that was warm and quick, she loved too well –
A light, a flame, a heart against her own;
    It is forever bitter cold, in Hell.

III. *The Very Rich Man*

He'd have the best, and that was none too good;
    No barrier could hold, before his terms.
He lies below, correct in cypress wood,
    And entertains the most exclusive worms.

IV. *The Fisherwoman*

The man she had was kind and clean
  And well enough for every day,
But, oh, dear friends, you should have seen
  The one that got away!

V. *The Crusader*

Arrived in Heaven, when his sands were run,
  He seized a quill, and sat him down to tell
The local press that something should be done
  About that noisy nuisance, Gabriel.

VI. *The Actress*

Her name, cut clear upon this marble cross,
  Shines, as it shone when she was still on earth;
While tenderly the mild, agreeable moss
  Obscures the figures of her date of birth.

MIDNIGHT

The stars are soft as flowers, and as near;
  The hills are webs of shadow, slowly spun;
No separate leaf or single blade is here –
  All blend to one.

No moonbeam cuts the air; a sapphire light
  Rolls lazily, and slips again to rest.
There is no edgèd thing in all this night,
  Save in my breast.

1421 SummitRidge, Beverly Hills

P.M. Pasinetti (1913–)

P.M. Pasinetti was born and grew up in Venice, Italy. In 1935, he came to study in the United States, where his first published fiction appeared in *The Southern Review.* He had been writing pieces for magazines and newspapers in Italy since the age of eighteen. His first book, three novelettes, was published in 1942.

After lectureships at Goettingen and Stockholm, where he spent most of the war years, he returned to the United States in 1946. He taught briefly at Bennington College before receiving a doctorate in Comparative Literature (the first ever awarded) from Yale. In 1949 he arrived in Los Angeles to take a position in the Italian Department at UCLA. In 1964, he was appointed to the Institute for Creative Arts at UCLA. Since 1958, he has lived in Beverly Hills, in a house designed by the Romanian architect Harlan Georgesco. He has continued since then to split his time yearly between his native city, Venice, and his adopted, if curious metropolis; where Pasinetti has remained, as his protagonist notes, "rather nicely settled in a small house among subtropical vegetation," with "a wide view of mountains and ocean from [his] bedroom window."

Gore Vidal has written of Pasinetti's work: "The world he has created or recreated is not less complex than that of Proust, Joyce, or Mann. But his passions are as different as Venice is from Paris, Dublin, or Lubeck."

from *From the Academy Bridge* (1970)

CHAPTER ONE

GILBERTO ROSSI:

That stretch of the Pacific Highway which runs southward from Palos Rojos to Bradley in the direction of the Mexican border, has on the inland side an unbroken chain of mountains with colors that go from that of burnt earth to that of fog, while on the outside it has a series of beaches, very narrow and slanting at some points while at other points they are smooth, white and wide like piazzas, under the heavy sun.

So the coastal highway stretches on, glittering between beaches and mountains, four lanes north-south and four south-north. To climb up to our Institute you can turn from the highway into any of the three canyons between Palos Rojos and Bradley: Palos Rojos Canyon, Bitter Canyon, Bradley Canyon. I almost always choose Bitter, whether I come from the north or from the south; it is the narrowest and stoniest, nearly always deserted between precipices. In that abandoned silence the squirrel jumps, the lizard moves jerkily forward, blazed; and every now and then you discover bushes of flowers with colors of a blinding intensity.

It is rather tortuous and at first it is all caught between steep walls, then as you go on climbing, the landscape opens up, like an immense dry flower revealing petal by petal the successive layers of mountains, the nearest ones brown, the farther ones bluish, and every once in a while, sudden and very, very far down below, slabs of ocean water. Bitter Canyon at some point joins Palos Rojos Canyon, larger and more important, all nicely paved with asphalt. Three quarters of a mile from this crossing there are wide plateaulike spaces which have been obtained by sawing off a few mountain tops. Various new university buildings have been placed up here, while in the small town of Palos Rojos down in the valley there is still the university center, the old campus, white stucco and brick-colored tiled roofs, little cloisters and patios among the palm trees.

Up here, instead, a prevalence of glass and steel: the Center for Business Statistics, with its own telephone exchange and the latest in electronic computers; the Subtropical Horticulture Station; and, of course, our Institute, the Institute for Language and Communication Analysis.

From the time when, having obtained my immigration visa for the United States, I accepted the offer of employment extended to me by director Alphonse Rossi, this has been my office address; to make the proper impression it should be typewritten, single-spaced, on an oblong envelope:

Mr. Gilberto Rossi,
Palos Rojos Institute for Language and
Communication Analysis,
University of Palos Rojos,
Palos Rojos, Calif. 92099.

Occasionally I type that address all by myself on an envelope or on a white piece of paper and then I keep staring at it with stings of astonishrment.

So here I am, I, born at Portogruaro, raised in Portogruaro and Venice, graduated from the University of Milan a couple of years before the war, obtaining 102/110 points (a very undistinguished grade), variously engaged in the common political and martial sufferings and in modest cultural professions between youth and ripe age – here I am now on the Pacific Coast, being part of one of those study centers where "the world of yesterday and of today is being analyzed to prepare for the world of tomorrow," or some such key phrase; I am rather nicely settled in a small house among subtropical vegetation; I have a wide view of mountains and ocean from my bedroom window; I also have a comfortable office at the Institute and a small metal desk reserved at the library; sufficient salary; abundant research tools: all of this to analyze documents of history of the last fifty years, particularly Italian. Theoretically, in my area, I should also decide about problems to be programmed for the electronic computer which Business Statistics allows us to use for some segments of time.

The Opportunity to come to the Pacific had presented itself when my life in Italy seemed silently and unobtrusively to be falling apart. I suddenly noticed that we were racing toward the end of the twenty-year period from the conclusion of the war; in our office at the Di Gaetano publishing house (myself and two other employees), I was the only one to notice that. I also realized that there would be, after that, another period of twenty years, much quicker that the first one, so as to pass almost unobserved. And that would carry me, in terms of age close to seventy. For all practical purposes, I felt I was as good as seventy already.

My military service during the Second World War, I would tell myself, casting glances over my past and attempting recapitulations, was perfectly indistinguishable from that of millions of others; the first postwar twenty-year stretch has been ninety-five percent dull. What am I, I would ask myself, Gilberto Rossi, as a human fact, as a unique and unrepeatable event? And consequently, what am I as a social individual, as a citizen? I am a democrat, in the broadest sense of the term. Backed up by a passable education and carried on by my natural disposition, I have become a professional of culture. What do you mean by that, Gilberto? Well, let's say – a man who attempts to express and divulge, in one way or another, certain particular visions of what he considers to be the truth. Or something of the sort. I would tell myself this, and then I would think that for about twenty years I had been an obscure and hardly influential employee at a publishing house, one day on top of the other, one clay on top of the other, with brief hopes and long frustrations in my work; pleasantness and disheartenment, love and egotism in my private life. So I had accumulated these twenty years and had now come to see the clear necessity for a renewed contact with myself, a jolt, a crisis.

I saw in my past professional life only two brief periods that had been slightly out of the ordinary: that academic year, at the beginning of the war, when I taught Italian at a German university, and that solar year, at the beginning of the postwar era, when I was a member of a little jazz band in Venice.

•

I flew from Italy direct to the Pacific Coast, without changing planes. From the moment you entered the jet, you were already in a transatlantic atmosphere: the crashing noises and jolts of Mediterranean life were being replaced by swishing noises, well-oiled gestures, calm – in other words, the main American characteristics. In comparison, for example, with a Roman street, these motions and noises made you feel as though you were living under water.

The first person who took care of me was Alphonse's factotum secretary. It was she who had typed my appointment letter, which at the bottom bore the double formula *AR/dp. AR* for Alphonse Rossi, and her name was Diane Peck. I say "was," because her last name is different since her marriage to a young scientist. In the first few days, for several hours every day, our */dp* took me around in her convertible, helping me find a place to stay and make domestic purchases. In our thoughtlessness in those first days up these canyons, we exchanged a few kisses which now, seen from the present perspective, appear wholly unreal to me, as they must to the young lady who meanwhile has married this astrophysicist of Polish origin.

What I shall finally accomplish here naturally remains to be seen. I work a lot; I always involve myself deeply in the things I do. At the present rate of exchange I earn perhaps a third of what, for example, Ceroni does, but never mind, I hope to live a more original and droll life than he has. He is considered one of the two top Petrarch scholars in Italy; as long as I was in his presence, this fact used to paralyze me, but now I am beginning to see it with greater equanimity. The day I found the right lodgings and made them mine with a regular lease, I sent Ceroni an impulsive post card, a view of this coast in vivid colors, with palm and cactus trees; as a text I chose that nostalgic line of the patriotic Italian poet Carducci in which, dreaming of his youthful love, he says: *"Marrying you, fair Maria, would have been better,"* only instead of "better" I wrote "worse," signing it simply "Gilbert." Infantile stupidity on my part? Will I regret this some day? Well, that's too bad.

117 Paloma Ave., Venice

Stuart Z. Perkoff (1930–1974)

For the West Coast and particularly that Southern California colony called Venice West, Stuart Z. Perkoff was one of the most respected, if too-little-known, poets of the Beat era. His readings are recalled with almost religious enthusiasm by survivors of the Venice scene. Perkoff's various addictions, from books to heroin, remain legend among friends and acquaintances for their intensity. Even for some personalities in the entertainment industry of the period – Perkoff appeared on the Groucho Marx and Steve Allen shows – Perkoff was the quintessential Beat poet.

Almost as notorious among his friends and admirers were stories about the great number of unpublished poems that vanished during Perkoff's rather erratic career. Testimonies abound as to work lost in countless moves from pad to pad, several arrests and confiscations of property, numerous untaped improvisations to jazz, and the many enraptured readings which departed from the written page. In retrospect, it seems ironic that Perkoff was fond of mentioning how he and his poet friends, Frank Rios and Tony Scibella, would gather and write poems to the muse (or "The Lady," as they called her) and then end the session by burning the manuscripts.

Perkoff was born in St Louis in 1930, the son of a book-maker. His first poems were published in 1951 in the second issue of Cid Corman's *Origin* magazine. In 1956, Jonathan Williams published Perkoff's first book, *The Suicide Room*. He was one of the poets included in Donald Allen's seminal 1960 anthology, *The New American Poetry*. In 1966, he was arrested for possession of marijuana and heroin, and spent the next five years at the Terminal Island Federal Penitentiary. Upon his release in 1971, he relocated to Northern California, where he tried to establish a bookstore – one of his lifelong desires – before returning to Venice in 1973. He died of a sudden cancer at the age of 44 in 1974. *Voices of the Lady*, Perkoff's collected poems, was published in 1998 by the National Poetry Foundation (University of Maine).

A COLLAGE FOR TRISTAN TZARA

broken the
broken the
wood iron coal steel
an art gallery that sells collages in which there is a collage
        with a photograph of an art gallery that sells
        collages like the quaker oats man torn from a
        newpaper

tzara i am building this collage
of actual things because i no longer know

L.A. EXILE

what is a poem
& because you are tristan tzara

heroin, tzara
marijuana
dreams & fears in many colors, dont forget them

on my wall it says:

wyatt earp
john garfield
dr fu manchu
pooh the poet
dr doolittle
dashiell hammett
the land of oz
i j singer
erich von stroheim
charlie chan
orson welles
captain midnite
the shadow
ben turpin
buñuel
alex berkman
the man who invented heroin
charlie parker
thelonius sphere monk
henry fonda
raymond chandler
tennyson
yeats
eliot
charlie brown

johnnie mack brown
pound
john ford
wordsworth
sherlock holmes
jackson pollock
ma perkins
rembrandt
chaucer
raggedy ann
cocteau
dostoyevsky
edgar allen poe
michael gold
patchen
bob (curley) steele
robert creeley
kurt schwitters
　　people i dig
　　in no special order
　　She knows them all
& it says:
　"remove the shoes which clothe yr feet, & you
　will find that the ground upon which you stand
　even now is holy ground." – buber

into the collage with them, tzara, along with
MAN COMMITS SUICIDE WHEN HE DISCOVERS
　WORD WILL NOT DESTROY
RIPPED RIPPED RIPPED ANYTHING CD HAVE BE A
　BABY'S FOOT
MAYBE OR ANGEL WING TEAR TORN SLASHED

along with /
piles of bones
theatre tickets

do you think you recognise this collage, tzara?
no. it is the similarity of all chaos.

let me put me into the collage
tzara. let me put you in it
also.

tzara, they are glueing us
down. tzara, we are hanging in
a gallery. tzara, a fat rich woman is buying
us. for her house.

how's that, eh, tzara? never can tell
which way a collage
will go

IN MEMORIAM: GARY COOPER

coop because i know you
dont care i'll tell you
all my poems
are movies america electric blink blink blink
flashing neon zeon flics flickering
heros heros heros big as the bond clothing people
on broadway or heads on rush
more

hey, coop! whoa! hey! shitkicking toe
no more.
dead.
great clumps of
hollywood burned the day you were
shot down by a warped orgone ray
yet old man reich died in federal jail for inventing
cancer but they wdnt have called
him in for you anyway cancer is sure
all american way to go coop
small consolation
doped up dieing while those ugly i mean to say
rich
houses under that
now dirty sign on that dirty brown hill:
            HOLLYWOOD
went to
flame
& you
just
went. toe digging dirty sly
eyeing jean arthur

dirty old man
jockstrap kept yr crotch flat
when the injuns were going to
burn you had you hanging
flat crotch hot katy jurado cdnt touch
yr lonely official tick tock cock at the
railroad train of terror
                        pure loo –
king cockless all
the way you

L.A. EXILE

recognize me the director? my head turned
backwards legs tucked
tight into my feer? i dont know why
bother now y're dead
cancer eating your flesh like
a ranch breakfast flapjacks potatoes
bullets mimeographed scripts lots
of syrup eggs & no one puts
anything in the coffee
whoa hi ho
makes me so jolly not just
the houses
burning burning burning
but the way you cancered so softly into
                                        (did you gulp 'yup' just one more time?)
being dead is a
laugh, a big, tough (i'm laffing)
cowboy (i'm
laffing) you know
cant
die in bed while hollywood burns.
                                                            you
come back spit the fires
dead swoop on all out
laws & horses while yodelling
the canterbury tales & i'll
give you a comeback
role in the 'kowboy pomes'

dont pay much, but
beats dieing.
maybe.
anyway, so
long, coop
yup!

LETTER TO JACK HIRSCHMAN

jack, let's talk
abt
the streets. OK? where
it's all
happening, right?

what do we want from them? not
more blood, no graduate courses
in human capabilities. dachau
was the streets. how many more
such roads
must we travel?

let's insist on vision
i will accept nothing less than miracles
all men are unhappy
camus sd
& everyone dies. a street
all share

L.A. EXILE

perhaps it is a matter
of language
                                    the sage says: man
is the language of
god. what creature or monster
forms our world
in its mouth?

where we walk
we know the dangers. if
the choice is between the streets
& literature
there is no choice

maybe we shd be talking
abt "joy". is that what you mean
by "streets" jack?

217 33rd St, Manhattan Beach

Thomas Pynchon (1937–)

"Tom was then living in a two-room studio with kitchen," wrote his friend Jules Seigel in a 1977 *Playboy* article, "that had evidently been converted from a garage. It was on a side street a couple of blocks up from the beach... A built-in bookcase had rows of piggy banks on each shelf and there was a collection of books and magazines about pigs. The kitchen cabinets contained not groceries but many empty Hills Brothers coffee cans in orderly array, as if displayed on supermarket shelves. His desk sat next to a window in the small living room. It had a clutter of miscellaneous papers, letters from obscure publications pleading for articles, an Olivetti portable typewriter, a thick stack of that graph paper covered with his fine script – the draft of *Gravity's Rainbow*, which he was in the process of typing and rewriting. He felt that he had rushed through *The Crying of Lot 49* in order to get the money. He was taking no such chance with the new book, apparently having begun it soon after the publication of *V.*, interrupting it to write *The Crying of Lot 49*. Much of the draft was done in Mexico. 'I was so fucked up while I was writing it,' he said, 'that now I go back over some of those sequences and I can't figure out what I could have meant.'"

Thomas Pynchon is a writer who has famously guarded his privacy to such an extent that his existence has been called into question. In his essay, "Slow Learner" Pynchon wrote: "Somewhere I had come up with the notion that one's personal life had nothing to do with fiction, when the truth, as everyone knows, is nearly the direct opposite." Pynchon's biography is sketchy. It is known that after a childhood in Glen Cove, New York, he studied at Cornell from 1953 to 1959 – interrupted by a two-year stint in the Navy. In 1960, he began work for Boeing, in Seattle, as a technical writer. In December 1960, he published an article in *Aerospace Safety Magazine* (a Air Force publication) titled, "Togetherness," about the potential risks involved in moving unarmed missiles to launch sites. In September 1962, Pynchon left Boeing.

By the beginning of 1963, he was living in Manhattan Beach. In the months that preceded the move, he is presumed to have been living in Mexico City. (Where he once jumped out of a window to avoid being photographed and where, as is rumored, he had a friend in Greenwich Village running to the library to look up data in the World Almanac for his first novel, *V.*) Pynchon probably left the Los Angeles area in the early 70s to return some years later, before moving to Northern California at the end of the decade. He is now said to be living in Manhattan.

Thomas Pynchon

from *The Crying of Lot 49* (1966)

San Narciso lay further south, near L.A. Like many named places in California it was less an identifiable city than a grouping of concepts—census tracts, special purpose bond-issue districts, shopping nuclei, all overlaid with access roads to its own freeway. But it had been Pierce's domicile, and headquarters: the place he'd begun his land speculating in ten years ago, and so put down the plinth course of capital on which everything afterward had been built, however rickety or grotesque, toward the sky; and that, she supposed, would set the spot apart, give it an aura. But if there was any vital difference between it and the rest of Southern California, it was invisible on first glance. She drove into San Narciso on a Sunday, in a rented Impala. Nothing was happening. She looked down a slope, needing to squint for the sunlight, onto a vast sprawl of houses which had grown up all together, like a well-tended crop, from the dull brown earth; and she thought of the time she'd opened a transistor radio to replace a battery and seen her first printed circuit. The ordered swirl of houses and streets, from this high angle, sprang at her now with the same unexpected, astonishing clarity as the circuit card had. Though she knew even less about radios than about Southern Californians, there were to both outward patterns a hieroglyphic sense of concealed meaning, of an intent to communicate. There'd seemed no limit to what the printed circuit could have told her (if she had tried to find out); so in her first minute of San Narciso, a revelation also trembled just past the threshold of her understanding. Smog hung all round the horizon, the sun on the bright beige countryside was painful; she and the Chevy seemed parked at the center of an odd, religious instant. As if, on some other frequency, or out of the eye of some whirlwind rotating too slow for her heated skin even to feel the centrifugal coolness of, words were being spoken. She suspected that much. She thought of Mucho, her husband, trying to believe in his job. Was it something like this he felt, looking through the soundproof glass at one of his colleagues with a headset clamped on and cueing the next record with movements stylized as the handling of chrism, censer, chalice might be for a holy man, yet really tuned in to the voice, voices, the music, its message, surrounded by it, digging it, as were all the faithful it went out to; did Mucho stand outside Studio A looking in, knowing that even if he could hear it he couldn't believe in it?

She gave it up presently, as if a cloud had approached the sun or the smog thickened, and so broken the "religious instant," whatever it might've been; started up and proceeded at maybe 70 mph along the singing blacktop, onto a highway she thought went toward Los Angeles, into a neighborhood that was little more than the road's skinny right-of-way, lined by auto lots, escrow services, drive-ins, small office buildings and factories whose address numbers were in the 70 and then 80,000s. She had never known numbers to run so high. It seemed unnatural. To her left appeared a prolonged scatter of wide, pink buildings, surrounded by miles of fence topped with barbed wire and interrupted now and then by guard towers: soon an entrance whizzed by, two sixty-foot missiles on either side and the name YOYODYNE lettered conservatively on each nose cone. This was San Narciso's big source of employment, the Galactronics Division of Yoyodyne, Inc., one of the giants of the aerospace industry. Pierce, she happened to know, had owned a large block of shares, had been somehow involved in negotiating an understanding with the county tax assessor to lure Yoyodyne here in the first place. It was part, he explained, of being a founding father.

Barbed wire again gave way to the familiar parade of more beige, prefab, cinderblock office machine distributors, sealant makers, bottled gas works, fastener factories, warehouses, and whatever. Sunday had sent them all into silence and paralysis, all but an occasional real estate office or truck stop. Oedipa resolved to pull in at the next motel she saw, however ugly, stillness and four walls having at some point become preferable to this illusion of speed, freedom, wind in your hair, unreeling landscape—it wasn't. What the road really was, she fancied, was this hypodermic needle, inserted somewhere ahead into the vein of a freeway, a vein nourishing the mainliner L.A., keeping it happy, coherent, protected from pain, or whatever passes, with a city, for pain. But were Oedipa some single melted crystal of urban horse, L.A., really, would be no less turned on for her absence.

Still, when she got a look at the next motel, she hesitated a second. A representation in painted sheet metal of a nymph holding a white blossom towered thirty feet into the air; the sign, lit up despite the sun, said "Echo Courts." The face of the nymph was much like Oedipa's, which didn't startle her so much as a concealed blower system that kept the nymph's gauze chiton in constant agitation, revealing enormous vermilion-tipped breasts and long pink thighs at each flap. She was smiling a lipsticked and public smile, not quite a hooker's but nowhere near that of any nymph pining away with love either. Oedipa pulled into the lot, got out and stood for a moment in the hot sun and the dead-still air, watching the artificial windstorm overhead toss gauze in five-foot excursions. Remembering her idea about a slow wind, words she couldn't hear.

The room would be good enough for the time she had to stay. Its door opened on a long courtyard with a swimming pool, whose surface that day was flat, brilliant with sunlight. At the far end stood a fountain, with another nymph. Nothing moved. If people lived behind the other doors or watched through the windows gagged each with its roaring air-conditioner, she couldn't see them.

L.A. EXILE

from *Gravity's Rainbow* (1973)

ORPHEUS PUTS DOWN HARP

LOS ANGELES (PNS) – Richard M. Zhlubb, night manager of the Orpheus Theatre on Melrose, has come out against what he calls "irresponsible use of the harmonica." Or, actually, "harbodica," since Manager Zhlubb suffers from a chronic adenoidal condition, which affects his speech. Friends and detractors alike think of him as "the Adenoid."

Anyway, Zhlubb states that his queues, especially for midnight showings, have fallen into a state of near anarchy because of the musical instrument.

"It's been going on ever since our Bengt Ekerot / Maria Casarès Film Festival," complains Zhlubb, who is fiftyish and jowled, with a permanent five-o'clock shadow (the worst by far of all the Hourly Shadows), and a habit of throwing his arms up into an inverted "peace sign," which also happens to be semaphore code for the letter U, exposing in the act uncounted yards of white French cuff.

"Here, Richard," jeers a passerby, "I got your French cuff, right here," meanwhile exposing himself in the grossest possible way and manipulating his foreskin in a manner your correspondent cannot set upon his page.

Manager Zhlubb winces slightly. "That's one of the ringleaders, definitely," he confides. "I've had a lot of trouble with him. Him and that Steve Edelman." He pronounces it "Edelbid." "I'b dot afraid to dabe dabes."

The case he refers to is still pending. Steve Edelman, a Hollywood businessman, accused last year of an 11569 (Attempted Mopery with a Subversive Instrument), is currently in Atascadero under indefinite observation. It is alleged that Edelman, in an unauthorized state of mind, attempted to play a chord progression on the Department of Justice list, out in the street and in the presence of a whole movie-queue of witnesses.

"A-and now they're all doing it. Well, not 'all,' let me just clarify that, of course the actual lawbreakers are only a small but loud minority, what I meant to say was, all those like Edelman. Certainly not all those good folks in the queue. A-ha-ha. Here, let me show you something."

He ushers you into the black Managerial Volkswagen, and before you know it, you're on the freeways. Near the interchange of the San Diego and the Santa Monica, Zhlubb points to a stretch of pavement: "Here's where I got my first glimpse of one. Driving a VW, just like mine. Imagine. I couldn't believe my eyes." But it is difficult to keep one's whole attention centered on Manager Zhlubb. The Santa Monica Freeway is traditionally the scene of every form of automotive folly known to man. It is not white and well-bred like the San Diego, nor as treacherously engineered as the Pasadena, nor quite as ghetto-suicidal as the Harbor. No, one hesitates to say it, but the Santa Monica is a freeway for freaks, and they are all out today, making it difficult for you to follow the Manager's entertaining story. You cannot repress a certain shudder of distaste, almost a reflexive Consciousness of Kind, in their presence. They come gibbering in at you from all sides, swarming in, rolling their eyes through the side windows, playing harmonicas and even kazoos, in full disrespect for the Prohibitions.

"Relax," the Manager's eyes characteristically aglitter. "There'll be a nice secure home for them all, down in Orange County. Right next to Disneyland," pausing then exactly like a nightclub comic, alone in his tar circle, his chalk terror.

Laughter surrounds you. Full, faithful-audience laughter, coming from the four points of the padded interior. You realize, with a vague sense of dismay, that this is some kind of a stereo rig here, and a glance inside the glove compartment reveals an entire library of similar tapes: CHEERING (AFFECTIONATE),

CHEERING (AROUSED), HOSTILE MOB in an assortment of 22 languages, YESES, NOES, NEGRO SUPPORTERS, WOMEN SUPPORTERS, ATHLETIC—oh, come now—FIRE-FIGHT (CONVENTIONAL), FIRE-FIGHT (NUCLEAR), FIRE-FIGHT (URBAN), CATHEDRAL ACOUSTICS....

"We have to talk in *some* kind of code, naturally," continues the Manager. "We always have. But none of the codes is that hard to break. Opponents have accused us, for just that reason, of contempt for the people. But really we do it all in the spirit of fair play. We're not monsters. We know we have to give them *some* chance. We can't take hope away from them, can we?"

The Volkswagen is now over downtown L.A., where the stream of traffic edges aside for a convoy of dark Lincolns, some Fords, even GMCs, but not a Pontiac in the lot. Stuck on each windshield and rear window is a fluorescent orange strip that reads FUNERAL.

The Manager's sniffling now. "He was one of the best. I couldn't go myself, but I did send a high-level assistant. Who'll ever replace him, I wonder," punching a sly button under the dash. The laughter this time is sparse male *oh*-hoho's with an edge of cigar smoke and aged bourbon. Sparse but loud. Phrases like "Dick, you character!" and "Listen to *him*," can also be made out.

"I have a fantasy about how I'll die. I suppose you're on their payroll, but that's all right. Listen to this. It's 3 AM, on the Santa Monica Freeway, a warm night. All my windows are open. I'm doing about 70, 75. The wind blows in, and from the floor in back lifts a thin plastic bag, a common dry-cleaning bag: it comes floating in the air, moving from behind, the mercury lights turning it white as a ghost ... it wraps around my head, so superfine and transparent I don't know it's there really until too late. A plastic shroud, smothering me to my death...."

Heading up the Hollywood Freeway, between a mysteriously-canvased trailer rig and a liquid-hydrogen tanker sleek as a torpedo, we come upon a veritable caravan of harmonica players. "At least it's not those tambourines," Zhlubb mutters. "There aren't as many tambourines as last year, thank God."

Quilted-steel catering trucks crisscross in the afternoon. Their ripples shine like a lake of potable water after hard desert passage. It's a Collection Day, and the garbage trucks are all heading north toward the Ventura Freeway, a catharsis of dumpsters, all hues, shapes and batterings. Returning to the Center, with all the gathered fragments of the Vessels... .

The sound of a siren takes you both unaware. Zhlubb looks up sharply into his mirror. "You're not holding, are you?"

But the sound is greater than police. It wraps the concrete and the smog, it fills the basin and mountains further than any mortal could ever move ... could move in time....

"I don't think that's a police siren." Your guts in a spasm, you reach for the knob of the AM radio. "*I don't think* – "

1273 Leona Dr., Beverly Hills

Jean Renoir (1894–1979)

Jean Renoir was born in 1894, the son of artist Auguste Renoir. He lead an exceptional childhood, surrounded by some of the most famous figures of the day. An early friend was Paul Cézanne, son of the painter, and the two went on long river expeditions on the Sienne, known as the Ource – the same river Renoir's father loved to paint.

After his films brought him much acclaim in France, Renoir boarded the American liner *Siboney* in 1940 bound for New Jersey. From there, he caught a plane to Hollywood, arriving in January 1941. Renoir was another émigré, as Arnold Schoenberg said, "driven into paradise. "

Five days later, Renoir signed a contract at Twentieth Century Fox to make two films. When he was first introduced to some executives at the studio, Renoir mistakenly commented, famously, that he was delighted to be working at Fifteenth Century Fox.

Constant struggles with the formulaic expectations of film executives plagued Renoir throughout his career in Hollywood, and success never materialized.

In early 1946, he bought a plot of land in Benedict Canyon and had a house built there. In the tradition of his father, he held an open house every Sunday. Among his many friends was Bertolt Brecht, who Renoir introduced to the actor Charles Laughton, which lead to their collaboration on Brecht's "Galileo."

In 1973, unable to write himself, Renoir began working with Eva Lothar, a Frenchwoman studying at the American Film Institute in Beverly Hills, hired to take notes for a novel. In between narrating his story, Renoir would reminisce about his life. Lothar suggested that Renoir should write a memoir. His reminiscences were later published as *My Life And My Films.*

from *My Life and My Films* (1974)

The plane was still flying over mountains. The only signs of life in the darkness were occasional specks of light, doubtless indicating the existence of houses. But suddenly we were dazzled by a profusion of light. We had reached the suburbs of the town, and it was as though a river of diamonds were flowing beneath us. In these days nearly every town presents a similar spectacle, but in those days it was still fairly uncommon. It looked like a symbol of triumphant Hollywood. The plane landed. A limousine was awaiting us.

We were wildly anxious to see the centre of the town, and we strained our eyes looking for anything which would give us some idea of the place we were going to live in. What had looked from the air like a river of diamonds turned out to be nothing but an outer boulevard full of petrol pumps and super-markets.

Other streets were like rows of bathing huts. A stand selling orange-juice was shaped like an enormous orange.

Next day we set out to explore. The Chinese Theatre was unexciting; but we continued perseveringly to search for something that would please us in that disappointing town. We were hungry and found a hot-dog stall which sought to attract the public by disguising itself as a huge sandwich, the sausage being a dog of some kind, its head and tail protruding from the cardboard roll of bread.

•

My problem in Hollywood was and will always be the same, arising out of the fact that the calling I seek to practise has nothing to do with the film industry. I have never been able to come to terms with the purely industrial side of films. Hollywood's detractors suppose that the weakness of the industry lies in its anxiety to make money at all costs, and that by catering to the public taste it falls into mediocrity. There is some truth in this, but the desire for gain is not the worst thing about it.

The real danger, in my opinion, lies in a blind love of so-called perfection, to obtain which a multiplicity of talents is called upon. Such and such a film is based on a literary masterpiece, scripted and revised by half-a-dozen leading script-writers and entrusted to a director who is equally celebrated. The actors are all stars, and the editor is the best man in the business. With all these trumps in its hand the studio feels sure that it cannot fail. How can so many talented people possibly produce a flop? And yet this often happens. The warrant for the failures is that by the use of effective publicity they still make money. It can even happen that, by a fortunate chance, by the drawing-power of the cast or the topicality of the subject, some of these productions are genuinely good.

A big Hollywood film is dished up like a melon, in separate slices. This is at the opposite pole from my belief in unity. It is a process of dividing the work and collecting important names.

The term "star" is not confined to actors: there are star writers, star cameramen and star designers, and each works separately, without any real link between them. Isolated in their ivory towers, these stars have to defend themselves against the intrusion of the common enemy, the producer. Each of them, accordingly, plays the prima donna, especially the cameraman. These last are the spoilt children of Hollywood film production. They take advantage of the general ignorance in the matter of framing and lighting. The director is the scapegoat. He is the person held responsible for delays which are really due to the whimsicalities of the cameraman.

This mania for perfection extends to every field. The Industry dishes up perfect cars, perfect shoes, perfect cookery and perfect houses – the whole adding up to perfect monotony. Settings as a rule are so little varied that it is enough to make one scream with boredom. The architects and designers plead not guilty. The things they give us are varied enough, according to their notions. In any American street we can find, so it seems, everything that is needed to gratify our taste for fantasy. One house is in the French provincial style, the one next door is Mexican and the one over the way is New England. Few people realize that the monotony arises out of identity of detail and not out of the general conception. The window-frames are all the same, mass-produced by the same machines. Door-handles are the same, floors are made of the same kind of wood. The nails and screws that hold the building together are all exactly the same size, all perfect.

•

The Americans invented that unreal creature, the cover-girl. They have developed the art of make-up to the utmost of unreality. Every human being is something of an actor. We all like to display to the world an improved version of ourselves. But with the Americans this natural impulse is carried to the point where it becomes camouflage. My wife and I, paying a weekend visit to a respectable middle-class hotel in Palm Springs, thought for a moment that we had come to the wrong place: we seemed to be surrounded by sheriffs and outlaws. Those excellent people greatly enjoyed dressing up. They might have been film extras – and we had come there to get away from films! In these days such things are not uncommon in Europe – there is no stopping "progress."

I have talked about the monotony of American streets despite the apparent variety of the buildings. The house looking like a fortress with impressively thick walls is in fact a sort of hollow-walled box, the tarred paper and wire-netting of which the walls are built being hidden beneath a thick coating of plaster. One half expects the inmates of that historic pile to dress up in medieval costume to eat their hamburgers. The removal of a house is an amazing spectacle to any European. The feudal manor or Spanish hacienda is literally sawn into two or three pieces and conveyed along the roads to its new site. It must be added that these huge match-boxes stand up to the treatment remarkably well and are reassembled intact. They shiver harmlessly in an earthquake and are easily modified.

This fondness for disguise causes Americans to incline to the acting profession. They are born actors. Nothing is easier than to direct a crowd of American extras. They are not better than the French but they get into the act with disturbing rapidity. French actors and extras have more difficulty in divesting themselves of their own personality. They want to understand, and compel the director to explain exactly what he wants – which can be fatal, for who knows exactly what he wants?

•

Dido and I bought a house in what had once been a fashionable quarter. It was about fifty years old – prehistoric, in Hollywood terms. The garden was quite large and roses grew in abundance. The back of the house was shaded by a huge mulberry tree, of which the branches drooped like those of a weeping willow. At the far end of the garden there was a giant avocado, which, however, bore no fruit, all its sap being absorbed by its branches. And there was a small, comfortable apartment over the garage which we used as a guest-house.

A star of the silent screen, Agnes Ayres, had had the house built in the old American style, part timber and part stucco, in the days before she became a celebrity. It was an historic place. Rudolph Valentino, the idol of women all over the world, whose mistress she was, had come to visit her there, and their friend Roy d'Arcy occupied the garage apartment. I have these details from the film-director Robert Florey, who has covered the history of Hollywood from its beginnings. Today the memory of those romantic lovers has been almost effaced. A few old ladies come every year on the anniversary of Valentino's death and place flowers on his grave. And that is all. If you ask a fifteen-year-old boy who Valentino was, the chances are that he won't know. But only fifty years ago women by the million were ready to die for him. Screen fame is an ephemeral thing.

Gabrielle and her family came to live next door to us, in a house which made ours look like a futuristic monument. Slade was delighted with it. There were things about it which recalled the homes of his childhood – sash-windows, a shingle roof, a porch, and above all the smell of wood. He considered that the Americans were bad masons but excellent carpenters. The America of his childhood had lived in wooden houses, and this type of building gave the country an archaic style that is not without charm. When I try to define my own feeling for those toy houses, the word that comes to my mind is "touching."

I have a particular fondness for the Victorian houses, with their lacework decoration, their towers, their capitals and their purely ornamental balconies, on which it is unwise to tread lest you find yourself in the street. And belonging to the same period – that is to say, the start of the century – are the houses with Doric pillars, wooden, of course. Those latter come from the South, but whatever the style of traditional American buildings, they are a symphony in wood. I remember a Los Angeles dance-hall which was entirely surrounded by Greek pillars, like the Church of La Madeleine in Paris. But whereas the Madeleine is heavy and blocks the horizon, American buildings in the same style look as though they were made of paper. Only one other country has done so much honour to wood, and that is Russia.

The back-gardens of our two houses were only separated by a light fence. We removed part of this, so that we shared a single very large garden. Gabrielle and Dido were constantly crossing that national frontier, which made us think of the frontier between France and Germany in the last act of Giraudoux's *Siegfried*. I shall never forget Michel Simon in the role of the customs official.

The life of émigrés was organized around small national centres, the French around Charles Boyer and his wife, the Germans around Lion Feuchtwanger. The brothers Hakim were another centre round which the best elements in the European cinema clustered. I knew them well, having directed *La Bête Humaine* for them. They kept open house: one had only to ring the bell to be sure of a smiling welcome. René Clair and Julien Duvivier were often there, as was Jacques Deval, the author of *Tovarich*, and even Pierre Lazareff, when he happened to be in Hollywood. The producer Lukachevich and his wife Zita also went there when they were being unfaithful to their Russian circle. We drank French apéritifs and played French records, and games of *pelote* went on in the garden.

•

Metro-Goldwyn-Mayer was a separate kingdom. People in the know asserted that its annual turnover was three times that of Portugal. But today the Metro-Goldwyn corridors are empty and its rotting sets scattered by the winds. Everything that could be carried away was disposed of at a fabulous auction sale. In its great days people joined at what would have been their age of military service in France and stayed with the corporation, passing through various stages of promotion, until they retired. They married and died with the corporation, and lived their lives in the comfortable certainty of belonging to an unshakable empire. The great conglomerate was one huge family, its members recruited from among the relatives, legitimate or otherwise, of the executives. I have nothing against keeping things in the family; on the contrary, that is what gives style to an enterprise. The Metro-Goldwyn style was due partly to the fact that they lived, as it were, in an ivory tower. Of course, there were exceptions, but the power of the organization was such that most people were quickly absorbed into it. That small world was the scene of numberless tragedies; suicide, nervous depression and death by alcoholism were of frequent occurrence.

Close by the entrance to the Metro-Goldwyn lot, its door on the same sidewalk, was a funeral parlor. In America these establishments take charge of the dead from the moment of their last breath, and this particular one brought a steady flow of black-clad mourners having little in common with the dream-factory next door. The Metro-Goldwyn management found this exasperating, and vainly offered increasing sums to buy them out. The situation seems to me admirably symbolic of the world's greatest film organization. Fortunately or unfortunately for me, I never penetrated beyond its walls except as a visitor.

•

The Woman on the Beach was a perfect theme for the treatment of this drama of isolation. Its simplicity made all kinds of development possible. The actions of the three principal characters were wholly without glamour; they occurred against empty backgrounds and in a perfectly abstract style. It was a story quite opposed to everything I had hitherto attempted. In all my previous films I had tried to depict the bonds uniting the individual to his background. The older I grew, the more I had proclaimed the consoling truth that the world is one; and now I was embarked on a study of persons whose sole idea was to close the door on the absolutely concrete phenomenon which we call life. It was a mistake on my part which I can explain only by the relative isolation enforced upon me by my limited knowledge of the language of the world in which I now lived.

The drama for me was that the elements which had hitherto constituted my life were changing, so that I was in danger of becoming as much of an outsider on the Place Pigalle as on Sunset Boulevard. I had discovered on my first trip to France after the war that the traditional French mistrust of all things foreign had been doubled by the German Occupation. I remember a typical episode. I had brought an English make of car over from England. Customs formalities had delayed me, so that I drove from Boulogne to Paris at night. French cars are fitted with amber headlights, whereas my own were white. Abuse was hurled at me at every crossing, and at one intersection three or four men got out of their cars and crowded round me in threatening attitudes. My wife tried to reason with them, but her Brazilian accent only made things worse. I finally gathered that the trouble was due to my white headlights, and I tried to explain that I had only just bought the car and would have the headlights changed directly I got to Paris. But what saved us was that I replied to a piece of particularly gross abuse from a lorry-driver with an even coarser bit of French army slang. This at once placated my assailants, and they went away.

But it was among my close friends that I found the greatest change. Many of my film colleagues had worked under German supervision. Rightly or wrongly? They felt the need to justify themselves to me. But I don't like to pass judgment on other men or to have them pass judgment on me. Freedom of speech is an essential of any true dialogue. The French were still unaccustomed to not having their every word and gesture overseen. This surveillance had caused them to live in an atmosphere of constant mistrust. Although the outward appearance had not changed (laughter was perhaps a little more noisy), things were no longer the same. France was different and I myself was different. We were like an old married couple coming together after a long separation, still loving but each seeing faults in the other which at the start we had not seen.

It was natural that I should look for themes having nothing to do with a motherland who was no longer herself. I had a horror of sentimental images of pre-war France. Better a void than the pointed beard of the film Frenchman. But a void offers no solid foothold. Realizing the fragility of the thing I was making, I tried to change the story while the film was being shot. The result was a confused scenario leading to a final work which I consider interesting but which is too obscure for the general public. Nevertheless Joan Bennett is more beautiful than ever in her ghostlike part, Charles Bickford is moving in his efforts to conquer the void, and the admirable Robert Ryan subtly enabled us to share in his suffering. Hanns Eisler had written a musical score stressing the theme of solitude in which he played counterpoint with his customary talent. To conclude, *The Woman on the Beach* was the sort of avant-garde film which would have found its niche a quarter of a century earlier, between *Nosferatu the Vampire* and *Caligari*, but it had no success with American audiences. Worse still, it thoroughly displeased the RKO bosses.

I was under contract to make two films for that company. A few days after the premiere I had a visit from my agent, Ralph Blum, who reported that they were ready to buy me out for a fixed sum. I am no fighter; I accepted, and that was the end of it. But it was the end in the widest sense. The failure of *The Woman on the Beach* marked the finish of my Hollywood adventure. I never made another film in an American studio. It was not only that particular failure that was held against me. Darryl Zanuck, who knew something about directors, summed up my case to a group of film-people. "Renoir," he said, "has a lot of talent, but he's not one of us."

2060 Escarpa Dr. (Eagle Rock)

Martha Ronk (1940–)

Born in Ohio and educated at Wellesley College and Yale University, Martha Ronk came to Los Angeles in 1971. Since 1982 she has taught English Literature, specializing in Shakespeare and the early 17th century, at Occidental College. Her books include: *Desire in L.A.* (1990), *Desert Geometries* (1992), *State of Mind* (1996), *Eyetrouble* (1998) and *Allegories* (1998).

As the former poet laureate Robert Haas wrote of her collection *State of Mind*, citing in particular the poem "The Moon over L.A.": "I like the way that the only metaphor for the moon is the moon. That seems to be what happens in the fifth line. 'Blank as the face of,' she writes, and then, seeing that she was about to say that the face of the moon was as blank as the face of the moon, she stops, lets the silence do its work.... If you put Sidney's 'With how sad steps, O moon, thou climb'st the skies' next to Ronk's 'She is no more than any other except her shoulders forever' you will have your fractured, postmodern Renaissance summer moon for this week. And it seems right for Southern

California. You can almost imagine one of Raymond Chandler's tough guy detectives going his lonely way under those shoulders."

from DOMESTIC SURREALISM

6

If the chair doesn't move across polished floors
and tables aren't burning with electric pulse,
if I can't glide in patent shoes over turquoise tile.
why have you brought me here?
What reason for such straight lines,
such an ill-drawn moon?
When the cactus glows at night I'll swim the length
and hold my breath until the edge of the sea.
Once, in between one belief and another, I thought
this town's at the end of all waters.
Nobody lives here who isn't already taking notes.
Across from her at the counter a cowboy reads a script
and she responds with coy laughter.
Nothing happens. We take walks. Suddenly the slide.

PICO BOULEVARD

From behind the glass they are unmitigatedly still
or passed over. Pico is another.
Driving is to driving as from one end to the other
over bridge and vale. Their eyes unnervingly swerved.
Celan says *over wine and lostness, over*
the running out of both.
I don't find you behind any eyes you open.

L.A. EXILE

After the earthquake it was closed to traffic.
I look at the eyes, the sex, the eyes.
We lap at it fearful of running out,
gulps of red wine. He says
what can the translator mean by *over*?

NEUTRA'S WINDOW

Behind the glass barrier by moving her lips
a woman forms exhortations. Her mind is made up.
What shadows of silence under eucalyptus
where the absence of mirrors protects children
and breaks relentless cycles of words.
Fingers over lips in early portraits marks the mastery
of silent reading, a conclusion of mouth begun by all
who suck out conclusion from the ragged spill
of palm and encumbent dust. The child reads her mind.
Silently and with the stealth of figures pilfered from story
one escapes dominion.

DRIVING

The film breaks into dialogue after long stretches
of the sort of silence associated with wet roads
and the sounds of tires hissing in the trees as
the wind's an artificial product of moving toward the horizon
as enclosure's only a category of mind.
And then the final exchanges about the weather first
and tentative efforts to snare the other's litany of complaints
the very act of driving was designed to eliminate any sense of.

Martha Ronk

THE MOON OVER LA

The moon moreover spills onto
the paving stone once under foot.
Plants it there one in front.
She is no more than any other except her shoulders forever.
Keep riding she says vacant as the face of.
Pull over and give us a kiss.
When it hangs over the interchange
she and she and she. A monument to going nowhere,
a piece of work unmade by man. O moon,
rise up and give us ourselves awash and weary –
we've seen it all and don't mind.

708 N. Rodeo Dr., Beverly Hills

William Saroyan (1908–1981)

In 1941, William Saroyan spent several months in Fresno, visiting family and friends while his play *The Beautiful People* folded under the summer heat on Broadway. Rather than return to New York to try to stage a new play, Saroyan headed for Los Angeles.

Saroyan had worked as a dialogue doctor for B. P. Schulberg in 1936, and Hollywood was eager to hire him. Saroyan met with Louis B. Mayer, who immediately offered him a job which Saroyan, then financially stable, turned down. But after a rough night in Las Vegas, Saroyan began to reconsider: "Very often, more often than not, whenever I gambled I lost all the money I had ... The reason I wrote *The Human Comedy* in eleven days, for instance, was that I had gone to Las Vegas and in one night had lost three thousand dollars, which at that time was a lot of money."

Mayer purportedly wept when the outline of *The Human Comedy* was read to him, and tried to reach the writer to offer congratulations, but Saroyan was nowhere to be found. The studio finally tracked him down in San Francisco. Saroyan would tell a friend years later: "They gave me a crib of a room, a typewriter, a cell of a window, and told me to bang away. Finally, I saw that I wouldn't get anywhere at all if I were to remain in that city and that dungeon, and that I ought to return to civilization as soon as possible. So I just got up and left, not a word to anyone, and went directly to San Francisco, where I hired a room in a hotel on Powell Street and went to work."

Saroyan wrote the script of *The Human Comedy* and returned to Hollywood, where he sold the script for $60,000, with an additional $1,000 a week for the time Saroyan stayed on as a production and directorial consultant. Expecting to direct the picture, Saroyan left MGM after hearing directly from Mayer that the writer did not have enough directing experience. Saroyan was outraged and fired off a letter attacking Mayer, which, as Budd Schulberg later recalled, "was like writing your own exit, your pass out of there."

MGM's advertising for the movie read: "based on the novel by William Saroyan." Saroyan's script was duly released and the book proved more successful than his first, *My Name Is Aram*.

Ten years later, in March 1951, Saroyan and his ex-wife Carol were remarried in Los Angeles and moved into the house on Rodeo Drive to start anew. By October they were divorced again.

from *The Bicycle Rider in Beverly Hills* (1952)

In my time I have seen with my own eyes perhaps more than a million people. I have spoken to surely fifty thousand of them, perhaps twice that many. Most of them I never knew by name. I saw them once and never saw them again. A great many I saw again and again but still did not know by name. What is a name anyway? A nuisance, in a way. Many I saw and spoke to are now dead.

One of these was an uncle by marriage who when he died said, "Too bad."

I sit at a fine new desk early in the forty-fourth year of my life and write.

Why ?

I have the time.

The new desk is in a new office in a new building in a city named Los Angeles, which is Spanish for *The Angels*, I believe.

Los Angeles? What am I doing here? As always, my best.

•

Here I am at daybreak somewhere in the street-and-house sprawl of an unlikely city. Farewell, my friends. Farewell to the feast, the talk, the drink, the smoke, the eyes and mouths of busy despair. I ate, I drank, I spoke, I listened, I looked, I saw. The eyes of anxiety I saw, and the mouths of misery. I heard the false voices, farewell, I wish you well. No more, I want nothing better than bread and water, air and light, my own poor body making a place for my own poor soul.

Yesterday evening my daughter said, "Why do you walk around the house barefooted?"

"I pay the rent."

"He pays the rent," my son said.

"How much?" my daughter said.

"Four hundred and forty-five dollars a month."

"Why are we poor?" my son said.

To the house on North Rodeo have come a number of millionaires. One inherited his money from his father, another earned his. The poorest man who ever came to the house was a writer who had just sold a story to a film producer for fifty thousand dollars. My children felt sorry for him.

"We are not poor," I said. "We are living over our heads."

•

My son wanted a bicycle, I bought him one, he rode it a month, and then he wanted a bigger one. His own bicycle was too big for him, but it was not the biggest bicycle built, and he wanted the biggest. I told him he would not be able to ride the big bicycle. He said he would. I knew he wouldn't, but I also knew it was necessary and important for him to believe that he would. I spoke to the bicycle man about the matter while my son listened. The man said my son would not be able to ride the bicycle. It was altogether too big for him. My son told the bicycle man that he would be able to ride it. I asked the man how much of the sixty dollars I had paid for my son's bicycle he would be able to allow me in a trade-in for the big bicycle. He said he would not be able to allow me anything for it, but that he would try to sell the bicycle for me. He believed he might be able to get thirty dollars for it. I took my boy and his bike home. I told him his bike was a fine one. I told him he rode it well, which was the truth. These things meant nothing to him. He wanted the big bike. I discussed the matter with his mother and we had an argument, and I became angry at my son, at his mother, and at myself. The boy wept. I went out of the house to a small bar and sat there an hour, drinking and thinking. I had shouted at my son that I would not buy him the big bike, I would never again buy him anything, because he did not appreciate anything I bought him. Early the next morning I went to the bicycle shop and bought the big bike, a Raleigh, manufactured in England. I took it home and showed it to my son. I let him get up on the seat and try to ride, and sure enough, my son rode the bike, just as he had said he would, but he did not ride it well. I told him it was my bike but that it was also his bike, and that he and I would go for rides in Beverly Hills together, beginning that May evening when I got home after work. I put the bike in the garage of the house on North Rodeo and locked it. That evening after work my son and I got on our bikes and rode up Benedict Canyon until we came to the top of a hill there. Then we rode down the hill together.

Riding a bicycle in Beverly Hills with my son made me remember the bicycle-rider I was years ago in Fresno, and it made me want to keep a record of what I remember, which is this book.

1407 Sunset Ave., (Pasadena)

Upton Sinclair (1878–1968)

Upton Sinclair moved to California from Mississippi in 1915. After a breif stay in Coronado, Sinclair and his family settled in Pasadena. A devoted muckraker, Sinclair began writing his series of Dead Hand books – each describing the strangling effect of a different institution on American liberties.

In 1923, he was kidnaped by the Los Angeles police. Transport workers were on strike in San Pedro and being brutally repressed by the police. Sinclair had arranged to address the strikers and their families on private property with the owner's written permission. No sooner had he begun reading the First Amendment to the crowd than he was arrested. The police drove Sinclair around for hours, shuttling him from one station house to another, refusing to book him and holding him overnight. The plan of the Police Chief, Louis D. Oaks, was to bring Sinclair into court moments before it closed, have the judge commit Sinclair to jail without bail, and then hide him again. One of Oaks' subordinates tipped off Sinclair's wife to the plan, and attorneys ambushed the party as they entered the court. This incident was the making of the Southern California branch of the American Civil Liberties Union, which Sinclair had recently founded.

Sinclair ran for Governor of California in 1934. An extravagant, ten-million-dollar slander campaign was mounted against Sinclair, led by Louis B. Mayer of MGM.Mayer's bullying tactics represented all the other movie magnates fearful of losing their fortunes and stranglehold over the film industry and its workers. As noted director Billy Wilder said, Sinclair "scared the hell out of the community. They all thought him to be a most dangerous Bolshevik beast."Sinclair eventually lost the election by a slim margin, but not without making his platform heard – the re-elected governor embraced a number of Sinclair's proposals, and no one doubted that President Roosevelt was paying attention to the race. Sinclair took the defeat in stride. Within a matter of weeks he'd fired off another book, *I, Candidate for Governor – and How I Got Licked.*

from *American Outpost* (1932)

From this point the story becomes Craig's story, and the time for telling it is not yet. It is a story of true love, which sometimes has "run smooth," and sometimes less so. Craig and her husband are two very different persons, and the story of their differences, and how they have been reconciled, would make a curious record for the archives of Hymen. But you who want to read it will have the task of changing Craig's nature. When she was a golden-haired child, they used to set her up on a chair to recite poetry for company; and therefore when she saw company coming, she would run upstairs and hide under the bed. Now, at the age of forty-eight, she has the same attitude toward publicity; and fate has given her for husband a man who wants to record all his blunders, in the hope that the next generation may know what not to do. Her new feminism wars with her old instincts – those traditions of the old South, where a lady's name was supposed never to be seen in print.

Suffice it for the present to say that in the course of nineteen years Craig has shepherded the production of fourteen novels, seven plays, an anthology, a guide to the problems of life, and six volumes of muckraking, containing – so the lawyers said – fifty criminal libels and a thousand civil suits per volume. She has taken part in half a dozen crusades, including three arrests of her husband; a monthly magazine in war-time; the financing of a motion picture, and the publishing and marketing of half a million books, at an average net loss of ten cents per copy. Also there have been various undertakings of her own: writing sonnets in a vain attempt to stop a war; buying five old houses and making them into one house for an author and his books; the planting of gardens; and the remodeling of several other old houses, and buying and selling of lots, to make money to pay debts.

Three years ago nature ordered a sudden halt, and Craig went into retirement, and joined Doctor Faustus and Mother Eddy in a search for God. If she hasn't found Him, she has discovered powers of her own mind that she didn't know about, and has demonstrated telepathy and clairvoyance in such a way as to convince her husband, and make him into one more kind of a "crank."

While I am revising this book there is one more adventure going on, and in strict secrecy I will tell you about it. Two years ago Sergei Eisenstein, Russian film director, came to Hollywood to make a picture. Because he would not do what our screen masters wanted, his plans fell through, and in the last hour of his stay in America he came to us with a wonderful idea: if only some one would raise the money, he would go to Mexico and make an independent picture of the primitive Indians, about whom Diego Rivera had told him. We hated to see a Soviet director and great artist humiliated by the forces which had assailed Eisenstein in California; so we undertook to raise the money.

Now, the way in which independent pictures are made is as follows: the director gets a certain sum of money, and shoots a certain number of miles of films; then he telegraphs back to the investors that the picture is, unfortunately, not completed, and that he must have more money, and more miles of film, or else, unfortunately, the investors will have no picture. Thereupon the investors put up more money, and the director shoots more miles of film, and then telegraphs that the picture is, unfortunately, not completed, and that he must have more money, and more miles of film, or else, unfortunately, the investors will have no picture. There may have been some case in the history of movie expeditions where that did not happen, but I have not been able to come upon any record of it in Hollywood.

Eisenstein and his staff went to the tropical land of Tehuantepec, and made pictures of Tehuana maidens with great starched ruffles over their heads, and bare feet that gripped the rough hillsides like hands, and baskets made of gourds painted with roses. He went to Oaxaca and made pictures of masonry tumbling into ruins during an earthquake. He went to Chichen-Itza and made pictures of Mayan temples with plumed serpents, and stone-faced men, and their living descendants, unchanged in three thousand years. He climbed Popocatepetl and made pictures of Indian villages lost in forgotten valleys. Miles and miles of film were exposed, and packing-cases full of negatives in tin-cans came back to Hollywood.

Meanwhile, my wife and I found ourselves turned into company promoters, addressing persuasive letters, many pages long, to friends of Soviet Russia, and devotees of Mexican art, and playboys of the film colony – any one who might be tempted by a masterpiece of camera work and montage. We interviewed lawyers and bankers, and signed trust agreements and certificates of participating interest. We visited Mexican Consuls and United States customs inspectors, and arranged for censorship exhibitions. We mailed bank-drafts, and took out insurance policies, and telephoned brokers, and performed a host of other duties far out of our line

And Eisenstein went to the Hacienda Tetlapayac, and made endless miles of film of maguey plantations, with peons wearing gorgeous striped serapes, singing work-hymns at dawn by old monastery walls, driven to revolt by cruel task-masters, and hunted to their death by wild-riding vaqueros. He went to Merida and "shot" senoritas with high-piled head-dresses and embroidered mantillas. He made the life story of a bullfighter, his training and technique, his foot-work and capework, his intrigue with the ladies of fashion, and his escape from the vengeful husbands, fiercer than any bull from Piedras Negras. The most marvelous material: pictures of golden sunlight and black shadows; dream-scenes of primitive splendor; gorgeous pageants, like old tapestries come to life; compositions in which the very clouds in the sky were trained to perform!

But, oh, the tens of miles of film and the tens of thousands of dollars! The months and months – until at last Craig began to cry out in protest, and to demand an end. Mexico is a land of difficulties and dangers, and her younger brother was managing the expedition, and her affection multiplied the troubles many fold in her mind. "Bring them home!" became her cry.

And meanwhile Eisenstein was in Chapala, "shooting" white pelicans, and grey pumas, and Nayarita damsels paddling dugouts in mangrove swamps. He was in Cholulu, "shooting" Catholic churches with carven skulls, and images of Jesus with real hair and teeth. He was in Guadalupe, photographing miraculous healings, and penitents carrying crosses made of spiny cactus, crawling by hundreds up rocky hillsides on bare knees.

"Bring them home!" demanded Craig; and she and her husband came to a deadlock over the issue. The husband was infatuated, she declared; he was as complete a madman as a Soviet director. They argued for days and nights; and meanwhile Eisenstein tore off the roof of a Tehuantepec mansion, to photograph a dance inside, and gave a bull-fight to keep an actor from going to Spain, and made arrangements to hire the whole Mexican army. Again Craig clamored, "Bring them home!" And again husband and wife took up the issue, and this time the husband was seized by a deadly chill, and had to be taken to the hospital in an ambulance, and lay on his back for two weeks.

The raising of money went on, and freight-trains groaned under the loads of raw film going into Mexico, and exposed film coming out. Eisenstein "shot" the standing mummies of Michoacan, and the flower festivals of Xochimilco, and the "dead peoples' day" celebrations of Amecameca, and ordered the Mexican army to march out into the desert, to fight a battle with a background of organ-cactuses thirty feet high. It was the beginning of the fifteenth month of this Sisyphean labor when Craig assembled the cohorts of her relatives and lawyers, and closed in for the final grapple with her infatuated spouse. "Bring them home!" she commanded; and for eight days and nights the debate continued. To avoid going to the hospital, the husband went to the beach for three days; then he came back, and there were more days and nights of conferences with the assembled cohorts. At times such as this, husbands and wives discover whether they really love each other!

Some day this colossal work will be completed. At any rate, I, the optimist, believe that; Craig, the pessimist, insists that when Gabriel blows his trumpet in the morning, Sergei Eisenstein and his staff will be found on the top of the volcano of Orizaba, photographing snow and fire effects under the shadow of the clouds of doom. But, assuming that the work is ever finished, you will have a chance to see it, and judge whether it is worth the anguish it has cost the Sinclair family.

Some day I may make some money out of it; and being of an imaginative temperament, I already have that money burning holes in my pocket. To invest it under the profit system is contrary to my life convictions; so I have established, under the laws of the State of California, the Sinclair Foundation, a charitable trust, following in the text of its charter another foundation, which has already been validated by our State Supreme Court. I am proceeding to deed my interest in the profits of the picture to the Foundation, and before this book appears the deed will be recorded in the archives of Los Angeles County. If the profits should be large, the Foundation will place a set of my books in every public library in the world; and I will be able to comply with the requests for books which come to me in every mail – from a YMCA secretary in Shanghai, a political prisoner in Finland, a prison chaplain in Ohio, a miners' union in West Virginia, a translator in Ceylon, an editor in Iceland, a college librarian in South Africa. I spend several thousand dollars of my hardearned money every year complying with such requests; and if I had real money – such as people make in the movies – how many millions I could educate!

But I started out to tell about Craig. She is with me in this dream of books; she was even with me in the dream of a picture – until she decided that Eisenstein meant to grind her husband up in a pulp machine, and spin him out into celluloid film. She thinks that thirty-five miles is enough for any picture. And now she stands and looks at her husband, and her hands tremble and her lips quiver; because she licked him in that last desperate duel, and she wonders if in his heart he can ever forgive her. My way of proving it to her is to put it into a book, and bring it to her some day and lay it in her lap – and then run away and hide!

Twenty-three years have passed since Mary Craig Kimbrough walked up and down the veranda of a sanitarium in Battle Creek and questioned her future husband about his ideas. Now the husband looks at his wife and says, "Why should I have the funniest one?" She answers, "I am not as funny as you are." Says he, "I'll write all the funny things I know about you, and you write all the funny things you know about me, and we'll let our readers decide!" But Craig will never accept that challenge.

During the war she wrote twenty-five sonnets, and after five years of pleading, her husband obtained permission to publish them in a little pamphlet. The first of these sonnets has been reprinted in several anthologies; Luther Burbank wrote of it: "The finest thing of the sort ever born of the human mind." I don't claim that much for it, but I call it one of the great English sonnets. And now, when I ask Craig how to bring this story to a close, she bids me publish it as her contribution.

LOVE

You are so good, so bountiful, and kind;
    You are the throb and sweep of music's wings;
The heart of charity you are, and blind
    To all my weaknesses; your presence brings
The ointment and the myrrh to salve the thorn
    Of daily fret of concourse. That you live
Is like to bugles trumping judgment-morn,
    And stranger than the cry the new-born give.

And yet, some day you will go hence. And I
    Shall wander lonely here awhile, and then –
Then I, like you, shall lay me down and die.
    Oh, sweetheart, kiss me, kiss me once again!
Oh, kiss me many times, and hold me near;
    For what of us, when we no more are here?

2741 El Roble Dr. (Eagle Rock)

John Steinbeck (1902–1969)

John Steinbeck and Carol Henning, recently engaged, initially moved to Los Angeles in January of 1930, staying temporarily with Steinbeck's long-time friend and former roommate at Stanford, Carlton "Dook" Sheffield. Sheffield had recently taken a teaching appointment at nearby Occidental College. Steinbeck and Sheffield talked about the possibility of Steinbeck being hired as well, having recently published his first novel, but the job never materialized. Steinbeck refused to even step foot on the campus to meet Sheffield's colleagues.

John and Carol soon found a place of their own: a rundown shack near the Sheffields' residence, with rent going for fifteen dollars a month. The shack was in poor shape, having been vacated for some time, and badly vandalized. It took a month of hard work on the part of John and Carol, along with some help from the Sheffields, to make the shack liveable. They replaced the electrical wiring, fixed the plumbing, re-plumbed the gas line, installed new windows, patched the roof, sanded the planks of the living room floor by hand (and attempted to stain and finish them with crankcase oil, which merely sat there on the surface. Holes had to be bored in the floor to get the oil out). In short, they turned a dump into a house.

John and Carol were surviving at this point on a monthly allowance of fifty dollars from John's father, who'd agreed to help support them until they got established. Money was scarce, and life was somewhat difficult, but Steinbeck looked back on this time fondly: "Remember the days when we were all living in Eagle Rock? As starved and as happy a group as ever robbed an orange grove. I can still remember the dinners of hamburger and stolen avocados."

Sheffield's wife, Maryon, pushed the issue of marriage on Steinbeck, fearing he would stall and never marry Carol. The Sheffields dragged John and Carol to the courthouse in Glendale, where they were married in a ten-minute ceremony. Dook decided to take the wedding party (John, Carol, Maryon and himself) out for a wedding meal – fifteen-cent hamburgers at a nearby eatery.) Many of the Sheffields' friends would come over to their secluded house to sunbathe nude. One day, a friend recounts, Steinbeck awoke from a sunbathing nap to find bows of ribbon tied in his pubic hairs, courtesy of Carol and Maryon. He wore the ribbons all afternoon.

While living in Eagle Rock, Steinbeck worked on revising a story called "The Green Lady," which he'd based on an unfinished play of the same name by friend Webster "Toby" Street (with Street's permission). This revision became "To an Unknown God"; the final revision, and published novel, would be known as *To A God Unknown*. It appeared in 1933 to unenthusiastic reviews and lackluster sales.

John Steinbeck

from *To a God Unknown* (1933)

Joseph could hear the creaking wheels after the teams disappeared. He strolled to the house that had been Juanito's, where the drovers were finishing their coffee and fried meat. As the first dawn appeared, they emptied their cups and rose heavily to their feet. Romas walked out to the corral with Joseph.

"Take them slowly," Joseph said.

"Sure, I will. It's a good bunch of riders, Mr. Wayne. I know all of them."

The men were wearily saddling their horses. A pack of six long-haired ranch dogs got up out of the dust and walked tiredly out to go to work, serious dogs. The red dawn broke. The dogs lined out. Then the corral gate swung open and the herd started, three dogs on each side to keep them in the road, and the riders fanned out behind. With the first steps the dust billowed into the air. The riders raised their handkerchiefs and tied them over the bridges of their noses. In a hundred yards the herd had almost disappeared in the dust cloud. Then the sun started up and turned the cloud to red. Joseph stood by the corral and watched the line of dust that crawled like a worm over the land, spreading in the rear like a yellow mist.

The thick cloud moved over the hill at last, but the dust hung in the air for hours.

Joseph felt the weariness of the long journey. The heat of the early sun burned him and the dust stung his nose. For a long time he did not move away from his place, but stood and watched the dust-laden air where the herd had passed. He was filled with sorrow. "The cattle are gone for good," he thought. "Most of them were born here, and now they're gone." He thought how they had been fresh coated calves, sleek and shiny with the licking of their mothers; how they had flattened little beds in the grass at night. He remembered the mournful bellowing of the cows when the calves got lost; and now there were no cows left.

He turned away at last to the dead houses, the dead barn and the great dead tree. It was quieter than anything should be. The barn door swung open on its hinges. Rama's house was open, too. He could see the chairs inside, and the polished stove. He picked up a piece of loose baling wire from the ground, rolled it up and hung it on the fence. He walked into the barn, empty of hay. Hard black clods were on the floor, on the packed straw. Only one horse was left. Joseph walked down the long line of empty stalls, and his mind made history of his memories. "This is the stall where Thomas sat when the loft was full of hay." He looked up and tried to imagine how it had been. The air was laced with flashing yellow streaks of sun. The three barn-owls sat, faces inward, in their dark corners under the eaves. Joseph walked to the feed-room and brought an extra measure of rolled barley and poured it in the horse's barley box, and he carried out another measure and scattered it on the ground outside the door. He sauntered slowly across the yard.

It would be about now that Rama came out with a basket of washed clothes and hung them on the lines, red aprons and jeans, pale blue with so much soaking, and the little blue frocks and red knitted petticoats of the girls. And it would be about now that the horses were turned out of the barn to stretch their necks over the watering trough and to snort bubbles into the water. Joseph had never felt the need for work as he did now. He went through all the houses and locked the doors and windows and nailed up the doors of the sheds. In Rama's house he picked up a damp drying cloth from the floor and hung it over the back of a chair. Rama was a neat woman; the bureau drawers were closed and the floor was swept, the broom and dustpan stood in their corner, and the turkey wing had been used on the stove that morning. Joseph lifted the stove lid and saw the last coals darkening. When he locked the door of Rama's house he felt a guilt such as one feels when the lid of a coffin is closed for the last time, and the body is deserted and left alone.

He went back to his own house, spread up his bed, and carried in wood for the night's cooking. He swept his house and polished the stove and wound the clock. And everything was done before noon. When he had finished everything he went to sit on the front porch. The sun beat down on the yard and glittered on bits of broken glass. The air was still and hot, but a few birds hopped about, picking up the grain Joseph had scattered. And, led on by the news that the ranch was deserted, a squirrel trotted fearlessly across the yard, and a brown weasel ran at him and missed, and the two rolled about in the dust. A horned toad came out of the dust and waddled to the bottom step of the porch, and settled to catch flies. Joseph heard his horse stamping the floor, and he felt friendly toward the horse for making a sound. He was rendered stupid by the quiet. Time had slowed down and every thought waddled as slowly through his brain as the horned toad had when he came out of the fine dust. Joseph looked up at the dry white hills and squinted his eyes against their reflection of the glaring sun. His eyes followed the water scars up the hill to the dry springs and over the unfleshed mountains. And, as always, his eyes came at last to the pine grove on the ridge. For a long time he stared at it, and then he stood up and walked down the steps. And he walked toward the pine grove – walked slowly up on the gentle slope. Once, from the foothills, he looked back on the dry houses, huddled together under the sun. His shirt turned dark with perspiration. His own little dust cloud followed him, and he walked on and on toward the black trees.

At last he came to the gulch where the grove stream flowed. There was a trickle of water in it, and the green grass grew on the edges. A little watercress still floated on the water. Joseph dug a hole in the bed under the tiny stream, and when the water had cleared, he knelt and drank from it, and he felt the cool water on his face. Then he walked on, and the stream grew a little wider and the streak of green grass broadened. Where it ran close under the bank of the gully, a few ferns grew in the black and mossy earth, out of reach of the sun. Some of the desolation left Joseph then. "I knew it would still be here," he said. "It couldn't fail. Not from that place." He took off his hat and walked quickly on. He entered the glade bareheaded and stood looking at the rock.

The thick moss was turning yellow and brittle, and the ferns around the cave had wilted. The stream still stole out of the hole in the rock but it was not a quarter as large as it had been. Joseph walked to the rock apprehensively and pulled out some of the moss. It was not dead. He dug a hole in the stream bed, a deep hole, and when it was full he took up water in his hat and threw it over the rock and saw it go sucking into the dying moss. The hole filled slowly. It took a great many hatfuls of water to dampen the moss, and the moss drank thirstily, and showed no sign that it had been dampened. He threw water on the scars where Elizabeth's feet had slipped. He said, "Tomorrow I'll bring a bucket and a shovel. Then it will be easier." As he worked, he knew the rock no longer as a thing separated from him. He had no more feeling of affection for it than he had for his own body. He protected it against death as he would have saved his own life.

When he had finished throwing water, he sat down beside the pool and washed his face and neck in the cold water and drank from his hat. After a while he leaned back against the rock and looked across at the protecting ring of black trees. He thought of the country outside the ring, the hard burned hills, the grey and dusty sage. "Here it is safe," he thought. "Here is the seed that will stay alive until the rain comes again. This is the heart of the land, and the heart is still beating." He felt the dampness of the watered moss soaking through his shirt, and his thought went on, "I wonder why the land seems vindictive, now it is dead." He thought of the hills, like blind snakes with frayed and peeling skins, lying in wait about this stronghold where the water still flowed. He remembered how the land sucked down his little stream before it had run a hundred yards. "The land is savage," he thought, "like a dog far gone in hunger." And he smiled at the thought because he nearly believed it. "The land would come in and blot this stream and drink my blood if it could. It is crazy with thirst." He looked down at the little stream stealing across the glade. "Here is the seed of the land's life. We must guard against the land gone crazy. We must use the water to protect the heart, else the little taste of water may drive the land to attack us."

The afternoon was waning now; the shadow of the tree-line crossed the rock and closed on the other side of the circle. It was peaceful in the glade. "I came in time," Joseph said to the rock and to himself. "We will wait here, barricaded against the drought." His head nodded forward after a while, and he slept.

The sun slipped behind the hills and the dust withdrew, and the night came before he awakened. The hunting owls were coasting in front of the stars and the breeze that always followed the night was slipping along the hills. Joseph awakened and looked into the black sky. In a moment his brain reeled up from sleep and he knew the place. "But some strange thing has happened,"he thought. "I live here now." The farmhouses down in the valley were not his home any more. He would go creeping down the hill and hurry back to the protection of the glade. He stood up and kicked his sleeping muscles awake, and then he walked quietly away from the rock, and when he reached the outside he walked secretly, as though he feared to awaken the land.

There were no lights in the houses to guide him this time. He walked in the direction of his memory. The houses were close before he saw them. And then he saddled his horse and tied blankets and a sack of grain and bacons and three hams and a great bag of coffee to the saddle. At last he crept away again, leading the packed horse. The houses were sleeping, the land rustled in the night wind. Once he heard some heavy animal walking in the brush and his hair pricked with fear, and he waited until the steps had died away before he went on.

He arrived back at the glade in the false dawn. This time the horse did not refuse the path. Joseph tied it to a tree and fed it from the bag of rolled barley; then he went back to the rock and spread his blankets beside the little pool he had built. The light was coming when he lay down to sleep in safety beside the rock. A little tattered fragment of cloud, high in the air, caught fire from the hidden sun, and Joseph fell asleep while he watched it.

2245 Lakeshore Ave. (Echo Park)

John Thomas (1930–)

Born and raised in Baltimore, John Thomas came to Los Angeles in 1959, arriving in Venice, or what was then called Venice West, one of the thriving "Beat" communities. Thomas also lived for some years, in the early 60s, in San Francisco and Northern California, before returning to Los Angeles in 1965. His books of poetry include, *john thomas john thomas* (1972), *Il vecchio Strawinsky prova con orchestra* (1975), *Epopoeia and the Decay of Satire* (1976) and *Abandoned Latitudes* (with Robert Crosson & Paul Vangelisti, 1983).

As Thomas describes his "position" in Los Angeles, in his unfinished "In Patagonia": "Most writers would regard Southern California as banishment enough. To live in Los Angeles, a minor poet of some local repute: surely this satisfies any interpretation of the Doctrine of Sufficient Disgrace. Well, for me, nothing has ever proved Sufficient. The Fatal Flaw, amigo."

OLD MAN STRAVINSKY REHEARSING WITH ORCHESTRA

(in *memory of John Gifford*)

I

this
voice
so po
lite bene
volent & such
pa
tience
with these Los
Angeles mu
                    si
                        cians – be
comes (this
voice) the
archetype of sweet old
                    genius everyone's
                    papa Jungian wise old
                    man all of
                    that &

I can cite many who have acquired it (that
voice): Robt Frost Carl Sandburg Wm Williams Black
Jack Pershing Einstein even old Ez Pound &
hearing Stravinsky now so sweetly patient
working with his orchestra
No I sd No I
remember certain things / he is not
like that

& my mind held such very specific
matters as: Stravinsky the Evil Unscrupulous
Mephistophelian Mastermind who
every time Nijinsky tried to break with Diaghilev
somehow got the poor sod to climb back gloomily
into D's socratical bed / poor
Nijinsky he really wasn't that way didn't
dig all that suave & Arty cornholing he was getting
from the prick of that prick of a
secondrate impresario
Stravinsky-Svengali his schemes ruining Nijinsky's
married life just to suit his own devious
purposes heh! heh! heh! he sniggers like the
villain in some old villain flick
Stravinsky yes one of that bunch – mad
evil silly cloak-&-dagger Tsarist emigres of
fifty years ago &
now sounding for all
the world like good old Papa Haydn
rehearsing his toy symphony
somewhere in lollypop land

2

!! does it truly happen that way
that you can be the cruelest sonofa
bitch in the world then
lose it all with age?
lose yr
nuts lose all yr
evil all yr
badass potential
lose that fine buccaneer swagger
that One False Move & I'll Blow Yr Brains Out

lose it? & git old? lose all yr taste for

    raping teenagers insulting
    princes of the blood royal & just generally
    fucking with people
    out of pure evil joy

?? watching your diet instead
carrying that silverheaded ebony stick now
because you fucking well need it
to hold you upright on yr feeble & arthritic pins
& oh sweet Christ suffering
those horrible disciples they all
sit around yr gouty feet
so industriously copying down
those brainless afterdinner ruminations
yr Tabletalk they call it

do you really have to
run out your string in toytown
sooo po
lite you
droll & foxy grampaw you!

                Papa Haydn rehearsing toy
                symphonies in disneyland!
                "Now chentlemen if you would chust
                hold that B-
                flat pleass a bit longer &
                mek an old man happy oh thank
                you sooo much chentlemen perfect!"

is that how it will be?
that phony mellowness like a
rotten old cantelope?

3

I hope it needn't always be that way / let me
suggest a certain developmental
path which only seems to leave you so
utterly nutless

getting old means getting lucky sometimes
means sometimes you *learn*
& along with other sweeter acquisitions
you learn that nine
tenths of what goes down is
bullshit
that there's just no way to be with people & not
smear yr tongue with bullshit lies
that it doesn't help to fuck with people & anyway
once you know how it's no fun any more

& when you've learned
these things & like *really*
know them every minute
oh then its like a gear shifts inside
so that now you can

just git on with it, yr
work
you can be God all day now
spinning out new suns & feathery nebulae
doing yr
own

L.A. EXILE

proper
work
thank goodness finally
just stand there smiling
another old Haydn
polite & patient
patiently rehearsing yr
toys yr
symphonies
in disneyland

3132 Berkeley Circle (Silverlake)

Paul Vangelisti (1945–)

Vangelisti was born in San Francisco in 1945 and has lived in Los Angeles since 1968, where he has worked principally as a journalist and teacher. He is the author of some twenty books of poetry, as well as being a noted translator from the Italian. From 1971–1982 he was co-editor of the award-winning literary magazine *Invisible City* and, since 1993, has been the editor of the visual and literary arts annual, *Ribot*. With Charles Bukowski and Neeli Cherkovski, Vangelisti edited the seminal *Anthology of L.A. Poets* in 1972, and in 1973 he curated the year-long, groundbreaking exhibition of Southern California poetry, *Specimen 73* (along with an anthology of the same name) for the Pasadena Museum of Art. He has twice been a recipient, in 1981 and 1988, of National Endowment for the Arts Writing Fellowships.

In his career as a journalist, Vangelisti worked as assignment editor for *The Hollywood Reporter* (1972–1974) and as Cultural Affairs Director at KPFK Radio, Los Angeles (1974–1983). As a freelance writer, he has published articles on literature, art and music for various magazines and newspapers, including the *L.A. Times, L.A. Herald-Examiner, L.A. Weekly, L.A. Free Press, Artweek, Downbeat* and *Abitare.*

Since 1984, Vangelisti has taught literature and writing at Otis College of Art & Design, where he is Chair of the Graduate Writing Program.

from *Rime* (1983)

4
who can deny a city that gives nothing back
where the rain always leaves at night
and only leprechauns and gaffers
whistle at the end of a rainbow
who can deny the sincerity of
hot dog stands envisioned as hot dogs
checks emblazoned with skiers and
snow-capped Sierras who can deny
a communion of lovers at eighty
miles per hour shot once through the head
a replay of roses of ten million
sincere words still missing still arriving
to die among strangers once and for all

5
dry and redundant
as cold November
sky are skin
light and french

window are
feathers I deny
your fervent neck
this beak that
won't give or
spend the heat
of the little there
is to write of
skin light and
french window

8
fickle cypresses Juno is in heat
as arid now a season as any
more or less comfortable with clouds
and nobody's to redeem the dead kittens
vomit demons on your rocking chair
someday of course German may again
become the esperanto of the streets
you read me Jack the boys are off to college
mother's on retreat it's just us and them and
cartoons on the windshield of a '62 Dodge
to steer the tongue westerly decode ashes
of remorse arouse the insurrection
of innocence after all who ever said
we could take the heat of inspiration

9
flagrant periscope Pluto in retreat
as tepid a wind as the whimsy
of a feather that unframes the story crowds
attention if only because what's written
doesn't snare what's seen so to speak is air
heavier than matter or any terrain

of rhyme even the agile sweetmeats
the fragrant passages of pleasure knowledge
stands isolate hence useless to memorize
a list of survivors to lodge
protest with the sublime when its lashes
envisioned on the lens of time nations
of whispers lies that demand not to be read
silences that arc no less incrimination

10

are the cumulus so heavy the stew
doesn't boil Persephone just belches
the shrews won't rut I incite a face
with windows and dictionary satisfied
to outscribble buses read the lisp
of a pen indite what could have been
on the back of an envelope beset
a memory or two catch myself
rewriting 'clearly' less like 'dearly'
wipe sweat off the scalp as it glistens
December late afternoon a yearning
sudden and liquid as if I'd paused to step
off the boulevard into an alley and
begun to talk to you in my sleep

11

as this syllabus of remorse dares
the season as this late Arcadia
forges memory tries even the umbra
of desire each day unlike the heart captures
more light grows warmer pajama and shirt flap
on the clothesline any previous intent
purely temperamental not bemoaning
as some would have it all that artifice

Buscas en Roma a Roma, oh peregrino!
y en Roma misma a Roma no la hallas
what splendor remains antipasto for
senator or semiologist in that face
of a busboy big dusky eyes the slight grin
wavers a shadow of this mausoleum

12

nothing incumbent after the rain
least not the caliber
of dreams a skin
of adjectives the hunch
of barking sleep are
tabled this dry
morning this lingering wreck
of a passage that
vanishes at the door
rings like fresh meat
spills the busy air
swells the coloratura of
the refrigerator and
dwells in the cruelty of a rainbow

2562 Outpost Dr. (Hollywood Hills)

Gore Vidal (1925–)

Two framed documents hang on a wall among various photos in Gore Vidal's home in Ravello, Italy: an honorary citizenship of Ravello and an honorary citizenship of Los Angeles, the two places he has split his time for years.

Born in 1925 at the United States Military Academy, Vidal spent his childhood shuttling between Washington D.C., the household of his grandfather T.P. Gore, the blind senator from Oklahoma, and various domestic situations with his exasperating mother, Nina. He attended posh prep schools St. Albans and Exeter before enlisting in the army at seventeen. While on night watch on a ship he wrote his first novel, *Williwaw* (1946). Over twenty novels have followed, as well as Broadway plays, plays for television's "golden age," screenplays, several volumes of essays, and a memoir.

Vidal took a contract at MGM in the mid-fifties. Having just adapted two short stories of William Faulkner's for the stage, Vidal ran into the author in New York. Vidal writes: "When I said I was going out to Hollywood, under contract to MGM, he frowned. 'Well of course, the money is very good and we have to live, but I would advise you never to take the movies seriously. It's not worth it. Scott Fitzgerald made that mistake, and it did him a lot of harm. Just go. Do the work. And then go home and write what you should be writing.' ... Unfortunately," Vidal continues, "I did take the movies seriously, and if it did me no harm, it certainly tested my temper."

from *Screening History* (1994)

Screen-writing has been my second career for close to forty years. By and large, my generation of writers did not become schoolteachers; if we needed money, we took a job at Columbia – the studio, *not* the university. What I began out of financial need I have persisted in out of fascination. In a sense, the movies lost their singular power when television was invented. The screen was literally shrunk, and what had once been a rare exciting vast spectacle screened in the dark of an exotic palace became a small, prosaic moving picture made up of a thousand lights behind the glass of a household appliance. Thus history is daily screened for us by network and cable news programs.

I suspect that even our pre-Japanese view of the world was more controlled and limited than that of Oblomov and his coffeehouse friends. Also, where he could always tell when government censors had been at work on the text of a newspaper, we have no idea at all what happened or did not happen in, say, the Persian Gulf. We also have no idea, as I write, which of our grateful allies has paid us compensation for that war – compensation is, of course, a euphemism for extortion.

As for the screening of our past, it has rarely been done.

When it *is* attempted, the aim of the exercise is to teach simple patriotism to a people become so heterogeneous that many of them have little or nothing in common with one another, including, often, the English language. Plainly, it is not easy to inculcate patriotism when there is no agreed-on patria.

From the beginning of my not-so-happy career as a dramatist, I was drawn to politics and to religion, the only two subjects that Bernard Shaw thought worth our attention and, of course, the two subjects absolutely forbidden us not only in the popular arts but in the public schools as well. Public schools do not give us our history; instead, they try, nobly but futilely, to indoctrinate their charges in good citizenship. As each minority gains economic power, it is discussed in admiring terms. This is very good civics, but it is hardly history or even politics, since a text with no context is meaningless. Periodically, effort is made to present our founders as gods; these efforts fail.

Lately, ordinary families have taken to tracing their roots as far back into history as they can go; and they also hold annual get-togethers to discuss their findings. Recently, I attended Gore Day in Mississippi, where I gazed with some anguish upon two hundred variations of my own nose. It is humbling to realize that one's nose – persona, too – is just a bit of genetic encodement temporarily housed in a somewhat haywire molecular envelope, soon to be dispersed, with relief, if I may strike the plangent personal note.

My seventh or so cousin, Albert Gore, the future president, stayed away on my account. But then I disapprove of his fearsome wife, "Tipper," the scourge of the First Amendment. Last year there was a reunion of my grandmother's family, the Kays, which neither I nor my fifth cousin Jimmy Carter attended. So what the tribes cannot get in the schools, they now seek through genealogy and through the web of kinship. There is something not only touching but primal in this coming-together of blood kin. But, touching or not, this Homeric reversion to tribal life is no way to inspire a country, or, perhaps, the better verb would be to "invent" a country.

When I wrote for television I was able, every now and then, to comment on power as exercised in the great republic. Then I moved to Hollywood, where I wrote movies for MGM. As one always had more freedom in writing of the past than of the present – that is, if the past was not American – I took to writing such gorgeous junk as *Ben Hur*. Here I was at least able to present the serious Tiberius of Tacitus rather than the scurrilous caricature of Suetonius. My Tiberius resembled a hardworking but totally ineffectual chief executive of a lousy company like Chrysler.

In due course, I wrote plays that were staged on Broadway. One of them was called *The Best Man*, about a contest for the presidency between a man with a virtuous public life and a messy private life, and a man with a vicious public life and a private life beyond reproach. A former president acts as chorus and referee. The play was a success. The studios began to bid for the screen rights. At last I would be able to make my own movie. What follows is a paradigm of how rigidly our history and our politics are screened for us and how seldom anyone is allowed to reveal anything as it is.

United Artists bought the film rights. I would be a sort of producer as well as the writer of the screenplay. Then it was announced that the great Frank Capra would produce and direct. As I have noted, I never liked his political films. Even at twelve, I knew too much about politics to be taken in by his corny Mr. Smith coming to my town. Capra's movies usually pitted the good guy, Jimmy Stewart, to be admired because he has been elected to the Senate without any understanding of politics, against the bad guys who want to build a dam when what the folks really need is a new river, or the other way around.

What was I to do with Mr. Capra? My play was unusual; it was not only political but it was accurate, though Jack Kennedy did say to me, "When you're running for president, you don't have all that time to sit around and discuss the meaning of it all." Plainly, the vision thing is a hang-up of writers.

Frank Capra was an engaging and lively Sicilian-American. But age had made Capra, if possible, more sentimental than he had been in his youth. I had already lost two films based on my work, *The Left-Handed Gun* and *Visit to a Small Planet*. In each case, the wrong director had made the wrong film. I was not about to lose a third one. But how to get rid of Capra? The French *auteur* virus had already infected Hollywood, and dozens of brothers-in-law of producers who had spent years locked up on sound stages with actors no one wanted to talk to were now being treated as if they were singular creators, so many Leonardos, sprung, as it were, from the good earth of the San Fernando Valley. Of these auteurs, Capra was an acclaimed master, at least by *Cahiers du Cinéma*.

Capra and I discussed the script a number of times. The realism of the piece did not impress him because, for him, politics was not what it is but what he himself had screened. As William Wyler studied not Roman history but other Roman movies in preparation for *Ben Hur*, so Capra tried to conform my, to him, disagreeable realism with the screened America that he was used to; that he had, in fact, helped invent. Once again the story was to be about the good guy who speaks for all The Little People.

Suddenly, Capra was inspired. "Let's open this up," he said, small bright eyes like black olives. "At the convention, on the first day, our good guy – we'll get Stewart or maybe Fonda – he goes out into the crowd, where all these little people are the – you know, delegates ..." I pointed out that between the Secret Service and the press, this was not only not done by the candidates but not do-able. "We'll find a way." He was confident. "The point is he gets out there among the ordinary people, and he talks straight to them." What, I asked, masking my inner despair with a Mickey Rooney smile left over from Boy Airman days, "does he *say* to them that's going to be so important?" Capra was radiant in his vision. "He quotes Lincoln to them ..."

I pointed out that Lincoln quotations probably wouldn't win anyone any votes. Certainly, they would not amuse the blacks who were in rebellion that year, 1963. But Capra was exalted. He had also visualized the scene. "Now then, get this. *He dresses up as Abraham Lincoln.* Then he gives them the Gettysburg Address, or something."

I said that I thought that this was truly inspired. Then I went to United Artists and got Capra off the movie and put myself in control. Next I picked a pair of bright young producers to produce, and we hired a director who had worked for me in television.

Henry Fonda played the lead without once resorting to the stove-pipe hat that he had worn with such magical effect in *Young Mr. Lincoln.* Those who would like to know Frank Capra's version of all this will find *his* story in his memoirs. In any event, I was able, that once, to screen our politics the way they are or were as of 1963. The picture was also entirely mine until I got to the Cannes Film Festival to receive a prize and saw, on a billboard, a vast advertisement for *The Best Man – un film de Franklin Schaffner*.

•

I often upset professional keepers of the national myths with the phrase "the agreed-upon facts." I would have thought that this was a reasonably careful way of saying that there are not many facts of any kind that we can ever be sure of, and since endless disputes over this or that detail will bring to a halt any description of earlier times, there is almost always a general, often exhausted, consensus that Lincoln, say, appears to be on record as thinking that if slavery is not an evil then nothing is evil, and so he *might* be thought of as an Abolitionist in his heart if not his politics. Naturally, some agreed-upon facts are more agreed-upon than others. But these imprecise consensuses are all that we have. Certainly, the notion that, with sufficient graduate students under a professor's magisterial direction, the actual true story of a life lived long ago can be told is nonsense. Even those lives that occurred entirely in the age of newsprint and television tapes and oral histories can never be more than guessed at. Who tells the truth? Who knows the truth? What is the truth?

The New York Times is always regarded as an authoritative primary source. But the *Times* often presents as facts fantasies that no one in good faith could ever accept unless he shares the narrow sectarian world-view of the editors. Since I have been occasionally fictionalized by that paper, I keep them at a distance. My last encounter was typical. The interviewer's opening words to me were, "You hate the American people, don't you?" I said, "No, I hate the *New York Times* and the two are not the same." I then turned to the photographer and his assistant and I got them to sign a statement to the effect that the interviewer, not I, had said that I hated the American people; all in all, a curious thing to pretend that a populist had said, particularly one who had made those same people the subject of his life's work.

But the *New York Times* is a reckless paper when dealing with those who question its values; hence, it is a primary source to be used with caution. Since I have been written about perhaps a bit more than most historians, I am not as impressed as they are by what I see in print, no matter how old and yellow the cutting. Obviously each of us has his prejudices, and no one can ever claim purity in the interpretation of those facts that he has chosen to agree upon. But this does not mean, as I am said to have said and did not say, that history is fiction. I only suggest that much of what we take to be true is often seriously wrong, and the *way* that it is wrong is often more worthy of investigation than the often trivial disagreed-upon facts of the case.

Why nations choose some myths to live by and not others brings us to the great proposition of Alfred North Whitehead: "When you are criticizing the philosophy of an epoch, do not chiefly direct your attention to those intellectual positions which their exponents feel it necessary explicitly to defend. There will be some fundamental assumptions which adherents of all the variant systems within the epoch unconsciously presuppose." In other words, listen for what is *not* said.

•

The actual world of politics may be cynical and amoral to a school teacher in Gettysburg, but what he takes to be cynicism on my part is simply realism. As for amorality, that word is so relative in its meaning and so random in its application that one should be wary of using it at all. Actually, what our governors want screened for the masses are heroic morality tales that will so inspire and distract them that they will surrender their tax money in order to maintain an empire profitable to the few and ruinous for the many.

I would suggest that our icon-dusters ponder the cynicism and amorality *back* of the entire political system, and investigate that, if they dare. But the true nature of any political arrangement is one of Whitehead's illuminating *non*-subjects and any attempt to deal with it causes distress in a society where what ought not to be is not. Even so, despite my tendentious nature, I think that I have been tactful in not imposing my own views where they do not belong. In the case of Lincoln, I look at him from every possible angle and leave the conclusion – if any – to the reader. This is hardly a-historical, but it is certainly not mythical.

Since George Bush and I were brought up on the same movies and newsreels, I think I can tell what he would *like* to do next, though a country with a collapsing banking system is not exactly the best launching pad for a would-be-Trajan. Bush sees himself as avatar to Roosevelt and Churchill. He sees this tiny little island – well, this fairly large country, comprising but a third of a continent – as the center of a world empire where everyone will do what we tell them to do because we're stronger than they are; it is also a lot of fun to order people around, and there may even be some money in it if we can periodically blackmail countries richer than we are. At the time of the Spanish-American war, Mark Twain proposed that we replace our flag with the Jolly Roger. Now here it is again, old Skull and Bones at twilight's last gleaming, snapping in the breeze.

For George Bush it is always 1939, the year of *The Wizard of Oz*, *Gone with the Wind*, and *Young Mr. Lincoln*. It is the year that Hitler invaded Poland; that Japan was conquering China. It is the year when that magnificent windbag, Churchill, was speaking up for war and that truly amoral and cynical politician, Roosevelt, was trying simultaneously to get us into the war while carefully staying out of the war. This sort of statesmanship deeply puzzles school teachers in Gettysburg, where one is either great and good and always right or not.

Bush sees himself in this heroic line of the great and the good and the right. But the world of the nineties does not resemble, in any way, the thirties. There is no Hitler, no Stalin. There are no regnant ideologies other than our own, which is consumerism. There is no enemy of all that is good in the human race unless it be the United States, or at least that military-industrial-political combine that has locked us all up inside a National Security State and thrown away the key.

Although George Bush does not like to read books, he did say, in the 1988 New Hampshire primary, that the presidency is a lot harder job than any Gore Vidal novel might lead you to believe. I wish it were so in his case. As it is, he will try for further military victories. But if the Germans and the Japanese don't pay our bills, then the last best hope of earth will be obliged, under a new president and perhaps political system, to repair our broken state and forego international piracy of the sort that we are lately prone to. He himself is of no account, and unlucky in his epoch. He may dream of himself as a new Lincoln, standing in the wings, but he is no more than another dim Hoover, presiding over what looks to be a pre-revolutionary time. I suspect that even as I write, there is already a great somber figure, ready to play Lincoln when history gives the cue. I hope we survive him.

•

Since future classrooms are bound to show more and more history on film, I think it a good idea to make sure that the greatest art is employed in screening not only Lincoln but Confucius and the Buddha. Yes, I would encourage reading and writing for those so disposed, but the generality will get *their* world-view on screen as they now get everything else. Let us face the shift from linear type to audiovisual the way that our fifth-century BC ancestors were obliged to do in China, India, Persia, Greece, as each culture, simultaneously, shifted from the oral tradition to the written text. Where do I stand in all this? Well, I am a creature of the written word, and I only go to the movies for fun.

Where was *I,* when last referred to in these pages? Oh, yes. Alaska. In an army hospital at Fort Richardson, having been frozen in the Bering Sea, a misadventure which Anaïs Nin was to find hugely symbolic: every writer gets the Louise Colet he deserves.

I had, by then, started a novel, about a ship in a storm in the Bering Sea. After the hospital, I was transferred to the Gulf of Mexico. I was unable to finish this novel until I went to see *Isle of the Dead,* with Boris Karloff. As Boris Karloff first haunted my imagination in *The Mummy,* so Boris Karloff, as a Greek officer on an island at a time of plague, broke, as it were, the ice and I completed my first novel right then and there in Apalachicola, Florida.

I have no idea what it was in the movie that did the trick. But then some things are best left to what the surrealists called the night mind, where it is always noon, beneath the languorous palm trees of my *un*screenable Alaska.

415 S. Ogden (Park LaBrea)

Diane Ward (1956–)

Diane Ward was born in Washington, D.C. in 1956 and studied for a time at the Corcoran School of Art before moving to New York City in 1979. Since 1987 she has lived in Los Angeles. Her books of poetry include *On Duke Ellington's Birthday* (1977), *Trop-i-dom* (1977), *The Light American* (1979), *Theory of Emotion* (1979), *Never Without One* (1984), *Relation* (1989), *Imaginary Movie* (1992) and *Human Feeling* (1994).

As Paul Hoover noted in his anthology, *Postmodern American Poetry*, "Like Virginia Woolf, Ward gives precedence to the state of 'mood' of a work over its story.... Rejecting, however, the 'automatic connection between women and a preoccupation with emotion,' Ward sees emotion as the result of a deliberate use of form." As Ward herself has written, "I believe mood can convey a thought as it moves in and out, around, as if on a string.... I can put things side by side that wouldn't make sense in another context, or I can contrast two disparate objects or events thereby creating a third feeling (state) of perception."

RE-VERSE

sensing the next
latitude grown heavy
through heavy metals
fuschia sunsets
extremities to the elegy

indifference to difference
bent on flowing toward
as an indescribable other
digital interloper
the blue hour's
birth of commerce

its surface passes
indentation corresponds
to the background
the head-like in our town
deviate and focus

given it's market-driven
within ditties
protuberance heightens the jinx
chairman: doorman(person)
curl up! We'll change the nets
the vertebral column it takes
to act back

the profile confirms your face
in skeptical spaces
create a California
no succor toward below
suction off

a half face of 3 seconds
assenting hierarchy
shut down in slender town
bedlam communities
the incentive to

broad pink hairy hands
hold the waxy face
the cloth away
from the neck

accelerate to penciled stops
cry out specific sites
sleep in altogether primer
the commotion's distance in me

survive as if in two
as windows in the desert
air waves
water from the moldy jar
sidelong and living

melt away to a singular fence
no uprights, apertures, no placement
I, willing to oscillate
arid and unlike the body's
loamier life

L.A. EXILE

one bell left in the phone
my own atmosphere
is more like a cylinder
shoulders flow up in turn
we don't meet community hours
we know you're keeping track

noxious clouds on the horizon
same blue gray everyday
now war *is* like tv:
inversion presses down
the hills' perspective disappears
until you forget they were
what was ever there

1817 Ivar Ave. (Hollywood)

Nathanael West (1903–1940)

Nathanael West arrived in Hollywood in July of 1933 to work for the Junior Writing Department at Columbia Pictures. Shortly after arriving, West wrote Josephine Herbst, "This place is just like Asbury Park, New Jersey. The same stucco houses, women in pajamas, delicatessen stores, etc. There is nothing to do, except tennis, golf or the movies.... In other words, phooey on Cal."

West returned to New York in December of 1933, then came back to Hollywood in 1935.Unemployed and impoverished, West lived at the seedy Pa-Va-Sed apartment hotel, which would later be the model for Tod's hotel in *The Day of the Locust.* A friend relates West's telling of a scene he witnessed at the Pa-Va-Sed: "He said he was coming home about three or four in the morning, walking down a dim corridor to his apartment, when he heard screaming and yelling and cursing in a woman's voice. Suddenly the door opposite opened and one of the prostitutes whom he happened to know, and knew was a prostitute, said something like, 'You goddam son of a bitch, get out of here,' and kicked something out of the door that looked like a dirty bundle of laundry. It started rolling down the hall and suddenly it got up and walked off." A similar incident introduces the character Abe in *The Day of the Locust.*

According to one of West's producer friends, West "knew a lot of tarts and madams around town in a nice way – I think he liked to listen to them. They used to talk to him...they trusted him. I knew the same people – not in a 'nice' way – but [West] was an intimate of theirs. I'm certain they must have told him all kinds of things that they would tell to no one else." West began *The Day of the Locust* in 1935, and finished it in 1938. According to Philip Durham, Raymond Chandler referred to *The Day of the Locust* as excellent in many ways, although hardly more than a suicide note: "not tragic, not bitter, not even pessimistic. It simply washes its hands of life."

In December of 1938, anxious over the ensuing publication of his book and wearied of Los Angeles, West wrote Random House editor Saxe Commins: "I got back to this sun-drenched desert with everything intact except my spirits, which are lower than (name omitted) of Liveright Inc.'s moral standards. During the four months I was away I think the sand has encroached at least a few feet on this town and if I can get a group of people together to hide the brooms of the Japanese gardeners for a few weeks, maybe the surrounding desert will overwhelm it."

A few weeks later, he wrote Commins again: "I would be very much obliged to receive a list of worse places at this moment than Hollywood. I suppose you mean Hitler's Munich as one of them. However, if like me and St. Thomas Aquinas, you believe that man is duplex, body and soul being separate entities, then you would also know that there is very little to choose since in Munich they murder your flesh, but here it is the soul which is put under the executioner's axe."

Nathanael West

from *The Day of the Locust* (1950)

I

Around quitting time, Tod Hackett heard a great din on the road outside his oflfice. The groan of leather mingled with the jangle of iron and over all beat the tattoo of a thousand hooves. He hurried to the window.

An army of cavalry and foot was passing. It moved like a mob; its lines broken, as though fleeing from some terrible defeat. The dolmans of the hussars, the heavy shakos of the guards, Hanoverian light horse, with their flat leather caps and flowing red plumes, were all jumbled together in bobbing disorder. Behind the cavalry came the infantry, a wild sea of waving sabretaches, sloped muskets, crossed shoulder belts and swinging cartridge boxes. Tod recognized the scarlet infantry of England with their white shoulder pads, the black infantry of the Duke of Brunswick, the French grenadiers with their enormous white gaiters, the Scotch with bare knees under plaid skirts.

While he watched, a little fat man, wearing a cork sun-helmet, polo shirt and knickers, darted around the corner of the building in pursuit of the army.

"Stage Nine – you bastards – Stage Nine!" he screamed through a small megaphone.

The cavalry put spur to their horses and the infantry broke into a dogtrot. The little man in the cork hat ran after them, shaking his fist and cursing.

Tod watched until they had disappeared, behind half a Mississippi steamboat, then put away his pencils and drawing board, and left the office. On the sidewalk outside the studio he stood for a moment trying to decide whether to walk home or take a streetcar. He had been in Hollywood less than three months and still found it a very exciting place, but he was lazy and didn't like to walk. He decided to take the streetcar as far as Vine Street and walk the rest of the way.

A talent scout for National Films had brought Tod to the Coast after seeing some of his drawings in an exhibit of undergraduate work at the Yale School of Fine Arts. He had been hired by telegram. If the scout had met Tod, he probably wouldn't have sent him to Hollywood to learn set and costume designing. His large sprawling body, his slow blue eyes and sloppy grin made him seem completely without talent, almost doltish in fact.

Yes, despite his appearance, he was really a very complicated young man with a whole set of personalities, one inside the other like a nest of Chinese boxes. And "The Burning of Los Angeles," a picture he was soon to paint, definitely proved he had talent.

He left the car at Vine Street. As he walked along, he examined the evening crowd. A great many of the people wore sports clothes which were not really sports clothes. Their sweaters, knickers, slacks, blue flannel jackets with brass buttons were fancy dress. The fat lady in the yachting cap was going shopping, not boating; the man in the Norfolk jacket and Tyrolean hat was returning, not from a mountain, but an insurance office; and the girl in slacks and sneaks with a bandanna around her head had just left a switchboard, not a tennis court.

Scattered among these masquerades were people of a different type. Their clothing was somber and badly cut, brought from mail-order houses. While the others moved rapidly, darting into stores and cocktail bars, they loitered on the corners or stood with their backs to the shop windows and stared at everyone who passed. When their stare was returned, their eyes filled with hatred. At this time Tod knew very little about them except that they had come to California to die.

He was determined to learn much more. They were the people he felt he must paint. He would never again do a fat red barn old stone wall or sturdy Nantucket fisherman. From the moment he had seen them, he had known that, despite his race, training and heritage, neither Winslow Homer nor Thomas Ryder could be his masters and he turned to Goya and Daumier.

He had learned this just in time. During his last year in art school, he had begun to think that he might give up painting completely. The pleasures he received from the problems of composition and color had decreased as his facility had increased and he had realized that he was going the way of all his classmates, toward illustration or mere handsomeness. When the Hollywood job had come along, he had grabbed it despite the arguments of his friends who were certain that he was selling out and would never paint again.

He reached the end of Vine Street and began the climb into Pinyon Canyon. Night had started to fall.

The edges of the trees burned with a pale violet light and their centers gradually turned from deep purple to black. The same violet piping, like a Neon tube, outlined the tops of the ugly, hump-backed hills and they were almost beautiful.

But not even the soft wash of dusk could help the houses. Only dynamite would be of any use against the Mexican ranch houses, Samoan huts, Mediterranean villas, Egyptian and Japanese temples, Swiss chalets, Tudor cottages, and every possible combination of these styles that lined the slopes of the canyon.

When he noticed that they were all of plaster, lath and paper, he was charitable and blamed their shape on the materials used. Steel, stone and brick curb a builder's fancy a little, forcing him to distribute his stresses and weights and to keep his corners plumb, but plaster and paper know no law, not even that of gravity.

On the comer of La Huerta Road was a miniature Rhine castle with tarpaper turrets pierced for archers. Next to it was a highly colored shack with domes and minarets out of the *Arabian Nights.* Again he was charitable. Both houses were comic, but he didn't laugh. Their desire to startle was so eager and guileless.

It is hard to laugh at the need for beauty and romance, no

matter how tasteless, even horrible, the results of that are. But it is easy to sigh. Few things are sadder than the truly monstrous.

4

Claude was a successful screen writer who lived in a big house that was an exact reproduction of the old Dupuy mansion near Biloxi, Mississippi. When Tod came up the walk between the boxwood hedges, he greeted him from the enormous, two-story porch by doing the impersonation that went with the Southern colonial architecture. He teetered back and forth on his heels like a Civil War colonel and made believe he had a large belly.

He had no belly at all. He was a dried-up little man with the rubbed features and stooped shoulders of a postal clerk. The shiny mohair coat and nondescript trousers of that official would have become him, but he was dressed, as always, elaborately. In the buttonhole of his brown jacket was a lemon flower. His trousers were of reddish Harris tweed with a hound tooth check and on his feet were a pair of magnificent, rust-colored blüchers. His shirt was ivory flannel and his knitted tie a red that was almost black.

While Tod mounted the steps to reach his outstretched hand, he shouted to the butler.

"Here, you black rascal! A mint julep."

A Chinese servant came running with a Scotch and soda.

After talking to Tod for a moment, Claude started him in the direction of Alice, his wife, who was at the other end of the porch.

"Don't run off," he whispered. "We're going to a sporting house."

Alice was sitting in a wicker swing with a woman named Mrs. Joan Schwartzen. When she asked him if he was playing any tennis, Mrs. Schwartzen interrupted her.

"How silly, batting an inoffensive ball across something that ought to be used to catch fish on account of millions are starving for a bite of herring."

"Joan's a female tennis champ," Alice explained.

Mrs. Schwartzen was a big girl with large hands and feet and square, bony shoulders. She had a pretty, eighteen-year-old face and a thirty-five-year-old neck that was veined and sinewy. Her deep sunburn, ruby colored with a slight blue tint, kept the contrast between her face and neck from being too startling.

"Well, I wish we were going to a brothel this minute," she said. "I adore them."

She turned to Tod and fluttered her eyelids.

"Don't you, Mr. Hackett?"

"That's right, Joan darling," Alice answered for him. "Nothing like a bagnio to set a fellow up. Hair of the dog that bit you."

"How dare you insult me!"

She stood up and took Tod's arm.

"Convoy me over there."

She pointed to the group of men with whom Claude was standing.

"For God's sake, convoy her," Alice said. "She thinks they're telling dirty stories."

Mrs. Schwartzen pushed right among them, dragging Tod after her.

"Are you talking smut?" she asked. "I adore smut."

They all laughed politely.

"No, shop," said someone.

"I don't believe it. I can tell from the beast in your voices. Go ahead, do say something obscene."

This time no one laughed.

Tod tried to disengage her arm, but she kept a firm grip on it. There was a moment of awkward silence, then the man she had interrupted tried to make a fresh start.

"The picture business is too humble," he said. "We ought to resent people like Coombes."

"That's right," said another man. "Guys like that come out here, make a lot of money, grouse all the time about the place, flop on their assignments, then go back East and tell dialect stories about producers they've never met."

"My God," Mrs. Schwartzen said to Tod in a loud, stagey whisper, "they *are* talking shop."

"Let's look for the man with the drinks," Tod said.

"No. Take me into the garden. Have you seen what's in the swimming pool?"

She pulled him along.

The air of the garden was heavy with the odor of mimosa and honeysuckle. Through a slit in the blue serge sky poked a grained moon that looked like an enormous bone button. A little flagstone path, made narrow by its border of oleander, led to the edge of the sunken pool. On the bottom near the deep end, he could see a heavy, black mass of some kind.

"What is it?" he asked.

She kicked a switch that was hidden at the base of a shrub and a row of submerged floodlights illuminated the green water. The thing was a dead horse, or, rather, a life-size, realistic reproduction of one. Its legs stuck up stiff and straight and it had an enormous, distended belly. Its hammerhead lay twisted to one side and from its mouth, which was set in an agonized grin, hung a heavy, black tongue.

"Isn't it marvelous!" exclaimed Mrs. Schwartzen, clapping her hands and jumping up and down excitedly like a little girl.

"What's it made of?"

"Then you weren't fooled? How impolite! It's rubber, of course. It cost lots of money."

"But why?"

"To amuse. We were looking at the pool one day and somebody, Jerry Appis, I think, said that it needed a dead horse on the bottom, so Alice got one. Don't you think it looks cute?"

"Very."

"You're just an old meanie. Think how happy the Estees must feel, showing it to people and listening to their merriment and their oh's and ah's of unconfined delight."

She stood on the edge of the pool and "ohed and ahed" rapidly several times in succession.

"Is it still there?" someone called.

Tod turned and saw two women and a man coming down the path.

"I think its belly's going to burst," Mrs. Schwartzen shouted to them gleefully.

"Goody," said the man, hurrying to look.

"But it's only full of air," said one of the women.

Mrs. Schwartzen made believe she was going to cry.

"You're just like that mean Mr. Hackett. You just won't let me cherish my illusions."

Tod was half way to the house when she called after him. He waved but kept going.

The men with Claude were still talking shop.

"But how are you going to get rid of the illiterate mockies that run it? They've got a strangle hold on the industry. Maybe they're intellectual stumblebums, but they're damn good business men. Or at least they know how to go into receivership and come up with a gold watch in their teeth."

"They ought to put some of the millions they make back into the business again. Like Rockefeller does with his Foundation. People used to hate the Rockefellers, but now instead of hollering about their ill-gotten oil dough, everybody praises them for what the Foundation does. It's a swell stunt and pictures could do the same thing. Have a Cinema Foundation and make contributions to Science and Art. You know, give the racket a front."

Tod took Claude to one side to say good night, but he wouldn't let him go. He led him into the library and mixed two double Scotches. They sat down on the couch facing the fireplace.

"You haven't been to Audrey Jenning's place?" Claude asked.

"No, but I've heard tell of it."

"Then you've got to come along."

"I don t like pro-sport."

"We won't indulge in any. We're just going to see a movie."

"I get depressed."

"Not at Jenning's you won't. She makes a vice attractive by skillful packaging. Her dive's a triumph of industrial design."

Tod liked to hear him talk. He was master of an involved comic rhetoric that permitted him to express his moral indignation and still keep his reputation for worldliness and wit.

Tod fed him another lead. "I don't care how much cellophane she wraps it in," he said – "nautch joints are depressing, like all places for deposit, banks, mail boxes, tombs, vending machines."

"Love is like a vending machine, eh? Not bad. You insert a coin and press home the lever. There's some mechanical activity inside the bowels of the device. You receive a small sweet, frown at yourself in the dirty mirror, adjust your hat, take a firm grip on your umbrella and walk away, trying to look as though nothing had happened, It's good, but it's not for pictures."

Tod played straight again.

"That's not it. I've been chasing a girl and it's like carrying something a little too large to conceal in your pocket, like a briefcase or a small valise. It's uncomfortable."

"I know, I know. It's always uncomfortable. First your right hand gets tired, then your left. You put the valise down and sit on it, but people are surprised and stop to stare at you, so you move on. You hide it behind a tree and hurry away, but someone finds it and runs after you to return it. It's a small valise when you leave home in the morning, cheap and with a bad handle, but by evening it's a trunk with brass corners and many foreign labels. I know. It's good, but it won't film. You've got to remember your audience. What about the barber in Purdue? He's been cutting hair all day and he's tired. He doesn't want to see some dope carrying a valise or fooling with a nickel machine. What the barber wants is amour and glamor."

The last part was for himself and he sighed heavily. He was about to begin again when the Chinese servant came in and said that the others were ready to leave for Mrs. Jenning's.

1647 Ocean Ave., Santa Monica (demolished & "redeveloped")

Tennessee Williams (1911–1983)

In 1939, Tennessee Williams left New Orleans with a friend and drove to Los Angeles in a Ford v-8 clunker. He worked for a time at Clark's Bootery, a shoe store in Culver City, where he would ride his bicycle to work past the sprawling MGM Studios.

Williams was back in Culver City in 1943, this time with a contract to work at MGM. "Isn't money beautiful?" he wrote to his agent Audrey Wood. His first assignment was to fashion what he called a "celluloid brassiere" for Lana Turner. After working half-heartedly on the project, Williams was removed from the film, suspended from the studio for six weeks, and finally dismissed. He used his savings to complete a play he was writing, *The Gentleman Caller*, which was later renamed *The Glass Menagerie.*

Williams found, as he wrote in his *Memoirs*, "what were to be ideal living-quarters in Santa Monica. It was a two-room apartment on Ocean Boulevard in a large frame building called The Pallisades. It was managed by a fantastic woman, half gypsy, matrimonially shackled by an unpleasant little man who was withering with cancer... and as for that summer, it was as golden as the later summers in Rome... full of young servicemen, positively infested with them I'd say, and when I had driven by one who appealed to my lascivious glance, I would turn the bike about and draw up alongside him to join him in his spurious enchantment with the view."

Williams recalled of his Hollywood work, "There is a curious sort of spiritual death-ray that is projected about the halls of Hollywood. I sensed it first in the writers I met out here. All spiritual zombies it seemed to me." He would add: "I was frightened by the emotional deadness of these people, all superior craftsmen and many with really fine talents, but seeming all withered inside – the kiss of Lana Turner?" By the end of 1943 he was gone.

"The Mattress by the Tomato Patch"

My landlady, Olga Kedrova, has given me a bowl of ripe tomatoes from the patch that she lies next to, sunning herself in the great white and blue afternoons of California. These tomatoes are big as my fist, bloody red of color, and firm to the touch as a young swimmer's pectoral muscles.

I said, Why, Olga, my God, it would take me a month to eat that many tomatoes, but she said, Don't be a fool, you'll eat them like grapes, and that was almost how I ate them. It is now five o'clock of this resurrected day in the summer of 1943, a day which I am recording in the present tense although it is ten years past. Now there are only a couple of the big ripe tomatoes left in the paleblue china bowl, but their sweetness and pride are undimmed, for their heart is not in the bowl which is their graveyard but in the patch that Olga lies next to, and the patch seems to be inexhaustible. It remains out there in the sun and the loam and in the consanguine presence of big Olga Kedrova. She rests beside the patch all afternoon on a raggedy mattress retired from service in one of her hotel bedrooms.

This resurrected day is a Saturday and all afternoon pairs of young lovers have wandered the streets of Santa Monica, searching for rooms to make love in. Each uniformed boy holds a small zipper bag and the sunpinked-or-gilded arm of a pretty girl, and they seem to be moving in pools of translucent water. The girl waits at the foot of steps which the boy bounds up, at first eagerly, then anxiously, then with desperation, for Santa Monica is literally flooded with licensed and unlicensed couples in this summer of 1943. The couples are endless and their search is unflagging. By sundown and long after, even as late as two or three in the morning, the boy will bound up steps and the girl wait below, sometimes primly pretending not to hear the four-letter word he mutters after each disappointment, sometimes saying it for him when he resumes his dogged hold on her arm. Even as daybreak comes they'll still be searching and praying and cursing with bodies that ache from pent-up longing more than fatigue.

Terrible separations occur at daybreak. The docile girl finally loses faith or patience; she twists violently free of the hand that bruises her arm and dashes sobbing into an all-night cafe to phone for a cab. The boy hovers outside, gazing fiercely through fog and window, his now empty fist opening and closing on itself. She sits between two strangers, crouches over coffee, sobbing, sniffing, and maybe after a minute she goes back out to forgive him and rests in his arms without hope of anything private, or maybe she is relentless and waits for the cab to remove her from him forever, pretending not to see him outside the fogged window until he wanders away, drunk now, to look for more liquor, turning back now and then to glare at the hot yellow pane that shielded her from his fury. Son of a bitch of a four-letter word for a part of her woman's body is muttered again and again as he stumbles across the car tracks into Palisades Park, under royal palm trees as tall as five-story buildings and over the boom of white breakers and into mist. Long pencils of light still weave back and forth through the sky in search of enemy planes that never come over and nothing else seems to move. But you never can tell. Even at this white hour he might run into something that's better than nothing before the paddy-wagon picks him up or he falls onto one of those cots for service men only at some place like the Elks' Lodge.

Olga knows all this, but what can she do about it? Build more rooms single-handed ? To look at Olga you'd almost believe that she could. She is the kind of woman whose weight should be computed not in pounds but in stones, for she has the look of a massive primitive sculpture. Her origin is the Middle East of Europe. She subscribes to the *Daily Worker*, copies of which she sometimes thrusts under my door with paragraphs boxed in red pencil, and she keeps hopefully handing me works by Engels and Veblen and Marx which I hold for a respectful interval and then hand back to her with the sort of vague comment that doesn't fool her a bit. She has now set me down as a hopelessly unregenerate prostitute of the capitalist class, but she calls me "Tennie" or "Villyums" with undiminished good humor and there is nothing at all that she doesn't tell me about herself and nothing about myself that she doesn't expect me to tell ... When I first came to stay here, late in the spring, and it came out in our conversation that I was a writer at Metro's, she said, Ha ha, I know you studio people! She says things like this with an air of genial complicity which a lingering reserve in my nature at first inclined me to pretend not to understand. But as the summer wore on, my reserve dropped off, and at present I don't suppose we have one secret between us. Sometimes while we are talking, she will go in my bathroom and continue the conversation with the door wide open and her seated figure in full view, looking out at me with the cloudlessly candid eyes of a child who has not yet learned that some things are meant to be private.

This is a house full of beds and I strongly suspect that big Olga has lain in them all. These big old-fashioned brass or white iron beds are like the keyboard of a concert grand piano on which she is running up and down in a sort of continual arpeggio of lighthearted intrigues, and I can't much blame her when I look at her husband. It is sentimental to think that all sick people deserve our sympathy. Ernie is sick but I can't feel sorry for him. He is a thin, sour man whose chronic intestinal trouble was diagnosed eight years ago as cancer, but whose condition today is neither much worse nor better than when the diagnosis was made, a fact that confirms the land lady's contempt for all opinions that don't come through "The Party."

Ernie does the woman's work around the apartment-hotel, while Olga soaks up the sun on the high front steps or from the mattress by the tomato patch out back. From those front steps her lively but unastonished look can comprehend the whole fantasy of Santa Monica Beach, as far north as the "Gone with the Wind" mansion of former film star Molly Delancey and as far south as the equally idiotic but somewhat gayer design of the roller coasters at Venice, California.

Somehow it seems to me, because I like to think so, that this is the summer hotel, magically transplanted from the Crimean seacoast, where Chekhov's melancholy writer, Trigorin, first made the acquaintance of Madame Arcadina, and where they spent their first weekend together, sadly and wisely within the quiet sound of the sea, a pair of middle-aged lovers who turn the lights off before they undress together, who read plays aloud to each other on heaps of cool pillows and sometimes find that the pressure of a hand before falling asleep is all that they really need to be sure they are resting together.

The Palisades is a big white wooden structure with galleries and gables and plenty of space around it. It stands directly over a municipal playground known as "Muscle Beach." It is here that the acrobats and tumblers workout in the afternoons, great powerful Narcissans who handle their weightless girls and daintier male partners with a sort of tender unconsciousness under the blare and activity of our wartime heavens.

While I am working at home, during my six-week lay-off-without-pay from the studio (a punishment for intransigence that presages a short term of employment and forces me to push my play anxiously forward), it is a comfort now and then to notice Big Olga dreaming on the front steps or sprawled on that old mattress in back of the building.

I like to imagine how the mattress got out there ...

This is how I see it.

On one of those diamond-bright mornings of early summer, Big Olga looms into an upstairs bedroom a soldier and his girlfriend have occupied for the week-end which has just passed. With nonchalant grunts, she looks at the cigarette stains and sniffs at the glasses on the bedside table. With only a token wrinkle or two of something, too mild to be defined as disgust, she picks up the used contraceptives tossed under the bed, counts them and murmurs "My God" as she drops them into the toilet and comes back out of the bathroom without having bothered to wash her hands at the sink. The boy and the girl have plainly enjoyed themselves and Olga is not the kind to resent their pleasure and she is philosophical about little damages to beds and tables incurred in a storm of lovemaking. Some day one of them will fall asleep or pass out in bed with a lighted cigarette and her summer hotel will burn down. She knows this will happen some day but till it happens, oh, well, why worry about it.

She goes back to the bed and jerks off the crumpled sheets to expose the mattress.

My God, she cries out, the condition this mattress is in!

Bad? says Ernie.

Completely mined, she tells him.

Pigs, says Ernie.

But Olga is not unhappy.

Pigs, pigs, pigs, says Ernie with almost squealing repugnance, but Olga says, Aw, shut up ! A bed is meant to make love on, so why blow your stack about it?

This shuts Ernie up, but inwardly he boils and becomes short-winded.

Ernie, says Olga, you take that end of the mattress. She picks up the other.

Where does it go? asks Ernie.

The little man backs toward the door but Olga thinks differently of it. She gives an emphatic tug toward the gallery entrance. This way, she says roughly, and Ernie, who rarely presumes anymore to ask her a question, tags along with his end of the mattress dragging the carpet. She kicks the screen door open and with a joyous gasp she steps out into the morning above the ocean and beach. The white clocktower of downtown Santa Monica is looking out of the mist, and everything glistens. She sniffs like a dog at the morning, grins connivingly at it, and shouts, Around this way!

The mattress is lugged to the inland side of the gallery and Ernie is still not aware of what she is up to.

Now let go, says Olga.

Ernie releases his end and staggers back to the scalloped white frame wall. He is broken and breathless, he sees pinwheels in the sky. But Olga is chuckling a little.

While the pinwheels blinded him, Olga has somehow managed to gather both ends of the mattress into her arms and has rolled them together to make a great cylinder. Hmmm, she says to herself. She likes the feel of the mattress, exults in the weight of it on her. She stands there embracing the big inert thing in her arms and with the grip of her thighs. It leans against her, a big exhausted lover, a lover that she has pressed upon his back and straddled and belabored and richly survived. She leans back with the exhausted weight of the mattress resting on her, and she is chuckling and breathing deeply now that she feels her power no longer contested. Fifteen, twenty, twenty-five years are in her of life still, not depleted more than enough to make her calm and easy. Time is no problem to her. Hugging the mattress, she thinks of a wrestler named "Tiger" who comes and goes all summer, remembers a sailor named Ed who has spent some liberties with her, thinks of a Marine Sergeant, brought up in a Kansas orphanage, who calls her Mama, feels all the weight of them resting lightly on her as the weight of one bird with various hurrying wings, staying just long enough to satisfy her and not a moment longer. And so she grips the big mattress and loves the weight of it on her. Ah, she says to herself, ah, hmmm ...

She sees royal palm trees and the white clocktower of downtown Santa Monica, and possibly says to herself, Well, I guess I'll have a hot barbecue and a cold beer for lunch at the Wop's stand on Muscle Beach and I'll see if Tiger is there, and if he isn't, I'll catch the five o'clock bus to L.A. and take in a good movie, and after that I'll walk over to Olivera Street and have some tamales with chili and two or three bottles of Carta Blanca and come back out to the beach on the nine o'clock bus. That will be after sundown, and three miles east of the beach, they turn the lights out in the bus (because of the wartime blackout), and Olga will have chosen a good seat companion near the back of the bus, a sailor who's done two hitches and knows the scoop, so when the lights go out, her knees will divide and his will follow suit and the traveling dusk will hum with the gossamer wings of Eros. She'll nudge him when the bus slows toward the corner of Wilshire and Ocean. They'll get off there and wander hand-in-hand into the booming shadows of Palisades Park, which Olga knows like a favorite book never tired of. All along that enormously tall cliff, under royal palms and over the Pacific, are little summer houses and trellised arbors with benches where sudden acquaintances burst into prodigal flower.

All of these things, these prospects, too vivid to need any thought, are in her nerves as she feels the weight of the mattress between her breasts and thighs, and now she is ready to show the extent of her power. She tightens the grip of her arms on the soft-hard bulk and raises the mattress to the height of her shoulders.

Watch out, my God, says Ernie, you'll rupture yourself!

Not I! says Olga, I'll not rupture myself!

Ha ha, look here! she orders.

Her black eyes flash as she coils up her muscles.

One for the money, two for the show, three to get ready, and four to GO!

Christ Almighty, says Ernie without much breath or conviction, as the mattress sails, yes, almost literally sails above the rail of the gallery and out into the glistening air of morning. Fountains of delicate cotton fiber spurt out of at least a thousand ruptures in its cover the moment the wornout mattress plops to the ground.

Hmmm, says Olga.

The act has been richly completed. She grips the rail of the gallery with her hands that have never yet been fastened on anything they could not overwhelm if they chose to. The big brass bangles she has attached to her ears are jingling with silly but rapturous applause, and Ernie is thinking again, as he has thought so often, since death so thoughtlessly planted a slow seed in his body: How is it possible that I ever lay with this woman, even so long ago as that now is!

With an animal's sense of what goes on behind it, Olga knows what her invalid husband feels when she exhibits her power, and her back to him is neither friendly nor hostile. And if to-

night he has a cramp in the bowels that doubles him up, she'll help him to the bathroom and sit yawning on the edge of the tub with a cigarette and a Hollywood fan-magazine, while he sweats and groans on the stool. She'll utter goodhumored "phews" and wave her cigarette at the stench of his anguish, sometimes extending a hand to cup his forehead. And if he bleeds and collapses, as he sometimes does, she'll pick him up and carry him back to bed and fall asleep with his hot fingers twitching in hers, doing it all as if God had told her to do it. There are two reasons: He is a mean and sick little beast that once mated with her and would have been left and forgotten a long time ago except for the now implausible circumstance that she bore two offspring by him – a daughter employed as "executive secretary to a big wheel at Warner's." (She has to stay at his place because he's a lush and needs her constant attention.) And this one, "My God, look at him." A blownup Kodachrome snapshot of a glistening wet golden youth on some unidentified beach that borders a jungle. He makes his nakedness decent by holding a mass of red flowers before his groin. Olga lifts the picture and gives it five kisses as fast as machine-gun fire, which leave rouge-stains on the glass, as bright as the blossoms the grinning boy covers his sex with.

So those are the circumstances she feels behind her in Ernie, and yet they cast no shadow over the present moment. What she is doing is what is usual with her, she's thinking in terms of comfort and satisfaction as she looks down at the prostrate bulk of the mattress. Her eyes are soaking up the possibilities of it. The past of the mattress was good. Olga would be the last to deny its goodness. It has lain beneath many summers of fornications in Olga's summer hotel. But the future of the mattress is going to be good, too. It is going to lie under Olga on afternoons of leisure and under the wonderful rocking-horse weather of Southern California.

That is what the veteran mattress has done for the last few

summers. The rain and the sun have had their influence on it. Unable to dissolve and absorb it into themselves, the elements have invested it with their own traits. It is now all softness and odors of ocean and earth, and it is still lying next to the prodigal patch of tomatoes that make me think of a deck of green-backed cards in which everything but diamonds and hearts have been thrown into discard.

(What do you bid? demands the queen of hearts. But that is Olga, and Olga is bidding *forever*!)

On afternoons of leisure she lies out there on this overblown mattress of hers and her slow-breathing body is steamed and relaxed in a one-piece sarong-type garment that a Hollywood pinup girl would hardly dare to appear in. The cocker spaniel named Freckles is resting his chin on her belly. He looks like a butterscotch pudding with whipped cream on it. And these two indolent creatures drift in and out of attention to what takes place in Olga's summer hotel. The quarrels, the music, the wailing receipt of bad news, the joyful shouting, everything that goes on is known and accepted. Without even feeling anything so strong as contempt, their glances take in the activities of the husband having words with a tenant about a torn window shade or sand in a bathtub or wet tracks on the stairs. Nobody pays much attention to poor little Ernie. The Ernies of the world are treated that way. They butt their heads against the walls of their indignation until their dry little brains are shaken to bits. There he goes now, I can see him out this window, trotting along the upstairs gallery of the projecting back wing of the building with some linen to air, some bedclothes on which young bodies have taken their pleasure, for which he hates them. Ernie treats everyone with the polite fury of the impotent cuckold, and they treat Ernie in such an offhand manner it turns him around like a top till he runs down and stops. Sometimes while he complains, they walk right past him dripping the brine of the ocean along the stairs, which Ernie must get down on his hands and knees

to wipe up. Pigs, pigs, is what he calls them, and of course he is right, but his fury is too indiscriminate to be useful. Olga is also capable of fury, but she reserves it for the true beast which she knows by sight, sound, and smell, and although she has no name for it, she knows it is the beast of mendacity in us, the beast that tells mean lies, and Olga is not to be confused and thrown off guard by smaller adversaries. Perhaps all adversaries are smaller than Olga, for she is almost as large as the afternoons she lies under.

And so it goes and no one resists the going.

The wonderful rocking-horse weather of California goes rocking over our heads and over the galleries of Olga's summer hotel. It goes rocking over the acrobats and their slim-bodied partners, over the young cadets at the school for flyers, over the ocean that catches the blaze of the moment, over the pier at Venice, over the roller coasters and over the vast beach-homes of the world's most successful kept women – not only over those persons and paraphernalia, but over all that is shared in the commonwealth of existence. It has rocked over me all summer, and over my afternoons at this green and white checkered table in the yellow gelatine flood of a burlesque show. It has gone rocking over accomplishments and defeats; it has covered it all and absorbed the wounds with the pleasures and made no discrimination. For nothing is quite so cavalier as this horse. The giant blue rocking-horse weather of Southern California is rocking and rocking with all the signs pointing forward. Its plumes are smoky blue ones the sky can't hold and so lets grandly go of ...

And now I am through with another of these afternoons so I push the chair back from the table, littered with paper, and stretch my cramped spine till it crackles and rub my fingers gently over a dull pain in my chest, and think what a cheap little package this is that we have been given to live in, some rubbery kind of machine not meant to wear long, but somewhere in it is a mysterious tenant who knows and describes its being. Who is

he and what is he up to? Shadow him, tap his wires, check his intimate associates, if he has any, for there is some occult purpose in his coming to stay here and all the time watching so anxiously out of the windows ...

Now I am looking out of a window at Olga who has been sunning herself on that smoking-car joke of a mattress the whole livelong afternoon, while she ages at leisure and laps up life with the tongue of a female bull. The wrestler Tiger has taken the room next to mine, that's why she keeps looking this way, placidly alert for the gleam of a purple silk robe through his window curtains, letting her know of his return from the beach, and before he has hung the robe on a hook on the door, the door will open and close as softly as an eyelid and Olga will have disappeared from her mattress by the tomato patch. Once the cocker spaniel had the impudence to sniff and bark outside Tiger's door and he was let in and tossed right out the back window, and another time I heard Tiger muttering, Jesus, you fat old cow, but only a few moments later the noises that came through the wall made me think of the dying confessions of a walrus.

And so it goes and no one resists the going.

The perishability of the package she comes in has cast on Olga no shadow she can't laugh off. I look at her now, before the return of Tiger from Muscle Beach and if no thought, no knowledge has yet taken form in the protean jelly-world of brain and nerves, if I am patient enough to wait a few moments longer, this landlady by Picasso may spring up from her mattress and come running into this room with a milky-blue china bowl full of reasons and explanations for all that exists.

Theodor W. Adorno: *Dialectic of Enlightenment* (with Max Horkheimer); *Philosophy of Modern Music;; Minima Moralia: Reflections from Damaged Life*

Terry Allen: *Lubbock (on everything)* [reissued on CD]

Bertolt Brecht: *Schweyk in the Second World War; The Caucasian Chalk Circle; The Private Life of the Master Race; The Duchess of Malfi; Galileo*

James M. Cain: *The Postman Always Rings Twice; Serenade; Mildred Pierce; Love's Lovely Counterfeit; Three of a Kind (Career in C Major, Double Indemnity* and *The Embezzler*); *Past All Dishonor; The Butterfly; Sinful Woman; The Moth*

Raymond Chandler: *The Big Sleep; Farewell, My Lovely; The High Window; The Lady in the Lake; The Little Sister*

Frank Chin: *Donald Duk, Gunga; Gunga Din Highway; Bulletproof Buddhists*

Robert Crosson: *Geographies, Abandoned Latitudes* (w. John Thomas & Paul Vangelisti), *Calliope, The Blue Soprano, In the Aethers of the Amazon*

Robert Craft: *Table Talk; Bravo Stravinsky; Stravinsky: The Chronicle of a Friendship, 1948–1971; Prejudices in Disguise: Articles, Essays, Reviews; Current Convictions: Views and Reviews;* (editor) *Stravinsky: Selected Correspondence*, vol.1; (w. Igor Stravinsky) *Conversations with Igor Stravinsky; Memories and Commentaries; Expositions and Developments; Dialogues and a Diary; Themes and Episodes; Retrospectives and Conclusions; Themes and Conclusions*

Edward Dahlberg: *Do These Bones Live; The Sorrows of Priapus; The Truth is More Sacred*

Joan Didion: *Slouching Towards Bethlehem; Play It As It Lays; A Book of Common Prayer; The White Album; Salvador; Democracy; Miami; The Last Thing He Wanted; After Henry; Robert Graham: The Duke Ellington Memorial in Progress*

John Fante: *Wait Until Spring, Bandini; Ask the Dust; Full of Life; Dreams From Bunker Hill; Dago Red; The Brotherhood of the Grape; 1933 Was a Bad Year; The Road to Los Angeles; The Wine of Youth; West of Rome*

William Faulkner: *Absalom! Absalom!*

F. Scott Fitzgerald: *The Last Tycoon*

Chester Himes: *If He Hollers Let Him Go*

Aldous Huxley: *After Many a Summer Dies the Swan; Grey Eminence; Time Must Have a Stop; The Art of Seeing; The Perennial Philosophy; Science, Liberty and Peace;Ape and Essence; Themes and Variations; The Devils of Loudun; The Doors of Perception; The Genius and the Goddess; Island; Tomorrow and Tomorrow and Tomorrow; Brave New World Revisited; Literature and Science; On Art and Artists; The Crows of Pearblossom; The Giconda Smile; Heaven and Hell*

Christopher Isherwood: *Prater Violet; The Condor and the Cows; The World in the Evening; Down There on a Visit; An Approach to Vendanta; Ramakrishna and His Disciples; Exhumations; A Single Man; A Meeting by the River; Kathleen and Frank; Christopher and His Kind; My Guru and His Disciple; October* (w. Don Bachardy)

Malcolm Lowry: *The Last Address* (early version of *Lunar Caustic*); *Under the Volcano*

Lewis MacAdams: *Africa and the Marriage of Walt Whitman and Marilyn Monroe; The River, Books 1–2*

Thomas Mann: *The Transposed Heads; Joseph the Provider; Doctor Faustus; The Holy Sinner; The Genesis of a Novel; The Confessions of Felix Krull, Confidence Man*

Thomas McGrath: *New and Selected Poems; Letter to an Imaginary Friend*

Carey McWilliams: *Ambrose Bierce: A Biography; Louis Adamic and Shadow America; Factories in the Field: The Story of Migratory Farm Labor in California; Ill Fares the Land: Migrants and Migratory Labor in the United States; Brothers Under the Skin; Prejudice: Japanese-Americans, Symbol of Racial Intolerance; Southern California Country: An Island on the Land; California: The Great Exception*

Henry Miller: *Insomnia; My Life and Times; On Turning Eighty; Henry Miller's Book of Friends: A Tribute to Friends of Long Ago; The World of Lawrence*

Anais Nin: *The Diary of Anais Nin: 1955–1966; The Novel of the Future; In Favor of the Sensitive Man and Other Essays; Little Birds Erotica; Delta of Venus Erotica*

Stuart Z. Perkoff: *The Sucide Room; Eat the Earth; Kowboy Pomes; Alphabet; Only Just Above the Ground; How It Is, doing What I Do; Visions for the Tribe; Love Is the Silence: Poems 1948–1974; Voices of the Lady: Collected Poems*

Thomas Pynchon: *V.; The Crying of Lot 49; Gravity's Rainbow*

Jean Renoir: *My Life and My Films*

SELECT BIBLIOGRAPHY

CHARLES BUKOWSKI, Neeli Cherkovski & Paul Vangelisti (editors) *Anthology of L.A. Poets* (Los Angeles/San Francisco: Laugh Literary/Red Hill Press, 1972)

MIKE DAVIS, *City of Quartz* (London/New York: Verso, 1990)

DAVID GEBHARD & ROBERT WINTER, *A Guide to Architecture in Southern California* (Los Angeles County Museum of Art, 1965)

———, *A Guide to Los Angeles and Southern California Architecture* (Salt Lake City: Peregrine Smith, 1977)

ROBERT GOTTLIEB & IRENE WOLT, *Thinking Big: the Story of the Los Angeles Times* (New York: Putnam, 1977)

ANTHONY HEILBUT, *Exiled in Paradise:German Refugee Artists and Intellectuals in America* (Boston: Beacon, 1984)

LAWRENCE LIPTON, *The Holy Barbarians* (New York: Grove, 1961)

JOHN ARTHUR MAYNARD, *Venice West: the Beat Generation in Southern California* (New Brunswick: Rutgers University Press, 1991)

CAREY MC WILLIAMS, *Southern California Country: An Island on the Land* (Salt Lake City: Peregrine Smith, 1973)

WILLIAM MOHR (editor), *The Streets Inside: Ten Los Angeles Poets* (Los Angeles: Momentum Press, 1978)

———, *Poetry Loves Poetry:Anthology of Los Angeles Poetry* (Los Angeles: Momentum, 1985)

LIONEL ROLFE, *In Search of Literary L.A.* (Los Angeles: California Classics Books, 1991)

KEVIN STARR, *Material Dreams: Southern California Through the 1920s* (London/New York: Oxford, 1990)

PAUL VANGELISTI (editor), *Specimen 73: a Catalog of Poetry* (Pasadena Museum of Modern Art, 1973)

Martha Ronk: *Desire in L.A.; Desert Geometries; State of Mind; Eyetrouble; Allegories*

Wiliam Saroyan: *Little Children; Love, Here Is My Hat; The Trouble With Tigers; My Name Is Aram; Razzle-Dazzle; The Human Comedy; The Bicycle Rider in Beverly Hills; The Laughing Matter; Mama, I Love You; Papa, You're Crazy*

Upton Sinclair: *King Coal; The Profits of Religion; The Book of Life; They Call Me Carpenter; The Goose-Step; Hell: A Verse Drama and Photoplay; Singing Jailbirds: A Drama in Four Acts; The Pot Boiler; Mammonart; Bill Porter: A Drama of O. Henry in Prison; Letters to Judd; Oil!; Money Writes! American Outpost; I, Governor of California—And How I Ended Poverty; The Epic Plan for California; I, Candidate for Governor—And How I Got Licked; Depression Island; Wally for Queen; No Parasan; Little Steel; Terror in Russia; Expect No Peace; Letters To a Millionaire; Peace or War in America; Dragon's Teeth; My Lifetime in Letters; Affectionately Eve; The Autobiography of Upton Sinclair*

John Steinbeck: *To a God Unknown*

John Thomas: *john thomas, john thomas; Il vecchio Strawinsky prova con orchestra; Epopoeia and the Decay of Satire*; *Abandoned Latitudes* (w. Crosson & Vangelisti)

Paul Vangelisti: *Alphabets, 1986–1995*; *A Life* (w. Don Suggs); *Luci e colori d'Italia* (w. William Xerra); *Nemo; Villa*; *Alephs Again*; *Domain: Works-in-Progress* (w. G.T. James & Joe Goode); *Rime* (w. Don Suggs); *Abandoned Latitudes* (w. Crosson & Thomas); *Another You*; *Un grammo d'oro* (w. Giuliano Della Casa); *Portfolio*; *Remembering the Movies*; *2 x 2*; *The Extravagant Room*; *Pearl Harbor*; *The Tender Continent*; *Air*; *Communion*

Gore Vidal: *Matters of Fact and of Fiction: Essays, 1973–1976*; *Kalki*; *Creation*; *The Second American Revolution and Other Essays*; *Duluth*; *Lincoln*; *Armageddon? Essays, 1983–1987*; *Empire*; *At Home: Essays*; *Hollywood: A Novel of America in the 1920s*; *A View from the Diner's Club: Essays, 1987–1991*; *Live from Golgotha: The Gospel According to Gore Vidal*; *Screening History*; *The Decline and Fall of the American Empire*; *United States: Essays, 1952–1992*; *Palimpsest: A Memoir*; *The Smithsonian Institution: A Novel*

Diane Ward: *Imaginary Movie; Human Feeling*; *Portraits and Maps* (with Michael C. McMillen)

Nathanael West: *Day of the Locust*

Tennessee Williams: *The Glass Menagerie*

ACKNOWLEDGMENTS

THEODOR W. ADORNO, from *Minima Moralia:*"Ego Is Id," "Folly of the Wise," "Wolf as grandmother." Copyright © 1993 by Verso Publishers.

TERRY ALLEN, "Truckload of Art." Copyright © 1977 by Terry Allen & Green Shoes Publishing BMI.

BERTOLT BRECHT, "Landscape of Exile," "On Thinking About Hell," "Hollywood Elegies," "Californian Autumn," "The Democratic Judge," "Letters About Things Read," "Letter to the Actor Charles Laughton," from *Poems 1913–1956*. Trans. copyright © 1998 by Routledge Publishers.

JAMES M. CAIN, from *Double Indemnity*. Copyright © 1964, 1971 by James M. Cain.

RAYMOND CHANDLER, from *The Little Sister*. Copyright © 1976 by Mrs. Helga Greene.

FRANK CHIN, from *Gunga-Din Highway*. Copyright © 1994 by Frank Chin.

ROBERT CRAFT, from *Stravinsky: Chronicle of a Friendship, 1948–1971*. Copyright © 1973 by Alfred A. Knopf Publisher.

ROBERT CROSSON, "The Day Sam Goldwyn Stepped Off the Train." Copyright © 1983 by Robert Crosson.

EDWARD DAHLBERG, from *Edward Dahlberg Reader*. Copyright © 1967 by New Directions Publishers.

JOAN DIDION, from *Play It As It Lays*. Copyright © 1970 by Farrar-Strauss & Giroux Publisher.

JOHN FANTE, from *Ask the Dust*. Copyright © 1984 by Black Sparrow Press.

WILLIAM FAULKNER, "Golden Land," from *Collected Stories*. Copyright © 1934 by Random House Publishers.

F. SCOTT FITZGERALD, from *The Last Tycoon*. Copyright © 1965 by Penguin Books.

CHESTER HIMES, from *If He Hollers Let Him Go* Copyright © 1986 by Thunder's Mouth Press.

ALDOUS HUXLEY, from *After Many a Summer Dies the Swan*. Copyright © 1939 by Harper & Row Publishers.

CHRISTOPHER ISHERWOOD, from *A Single Man*. Copyright © 1965 by Farrar-Straus & Giroux.

MALCOLM LOWRY, from *Under the Volcano*. Copyright © 1958 by Random House.

LEWIS MACADAMS, "L Fuckin' A," "Moguls and Monks," "The Meaning of the Universe at Night," "Malraux says..." "Two Lebanese boys..." Copyright © 1982 by Lewis MacAdams

THOMAS MANN, from *Dr. Faustus*. Trans. copyright © 1947 by Alfred A. Knopf.

THOMAS MCGRATH, from *Letter to an Imaginary Friend*. Copyright © 1997 by Copper Canyon Press.

CAREY MCWILLIAMS, from *Southern California: an Island on the Land*. Copyright © 1973 Carey McWilliams.

HENRY MILLER, from *Insomnia*. Copyright © 1974 by Doubleday Publishers.

ANAIS NIN, from *The Diary*, Copyright © 1981 by Harcourt Brace & Jovanovich Publishers.

DOROTHY PARKER, "Tombstones in the Starlight," "Midnight." Copyright © 1999 by Penguin.

P.M. PASINETTI, from *View from the Academy Bridge*. Copyright © 1970 by P.M. Pasinetti.

STUART Z. PERKOFF, "A Collage for Tristan Tzara," "In Memoriam Gary Cooper," "Letter to Jack Hirschman," Copyright © 1998 by Rachel Perkoff Di Paola.

THOMAS PYNCHON, from *The Crying of Lot 49*. Copyright © 1966 by J.P. Lippincott; from *Gravity's Rainbow*. Copyright © by 1973 by Viking-Penguin.

JEAN RENOIR, from *My Life and My Films*. Copyright © 1974 by Atheneum Publishers.

MARTHA RONK, from "Domestic Surrealism," "Pico Boulevard," "Neutra's Window," "Driving," "The Moon Over L.A." Copyright © 1994, 1996 by Martha Ronk.

WILLIAM SOROYAN, from *The Bicycle Rider in Beverly Hills*. Copyright © 1952 by Charles Scribners Publishers.

UPTON SINCLAIR, from *American Outpost*. Copyright © 1932 by Upton Sinclair.

JOHN STEINBECK, from *To a God Unknown*. Copyright © 1933 by John Steinbeck.

JOHN THOMAS, "Old Man Stravinsky Rehearsing with Orchestra." Copyright © 1975 by John Thomas.

GORE VIDAL, from *Screening History*. Copyright © 1992 by Gore Vidal.

DIANE WARD, "Re-Verse," copyright ©1992 by Diane Ward.

NATHANAEL WEST, from *The Day of the Locust*. Copyright ©1939 by the estate of Nathanael West.

TENNESSEE WILLIAMS, "The Mattress by the Tomato Patch," from *Collected Stories*. Copyright © 1986 Ballantine Books.